T1220 75¢  A Fawcett Crest Book

"RECOMMEN[...]

COM[...] MEALS IN ONE DISH

BY MYRA WALDO

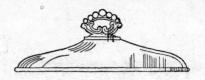

ONE-DISH RECIPES FROM AROUND THE WORLD

Myra Waldo is probably the world's most traveling cook. She has circled the globe several times, collecting recipes from every country, for every kind of culinary preparation. And from her enormous collection she has selected more than three hundred meal-in-a-dish recipes, including stews, casseroles, soups, and chafing-dish concoctions, with fishes, birds, and several kinds of meats as principal ingredients.

Meals in a single dish are a special boon to cooks whose time is limited, to hostesses who like to spend dinner with their guests instead of in the kitchen, and to those who have trouble getting everything ready at one time. Serving the one-dish dinner is as simple as walking into the dining room...and there'll be only one pot to wash!

The recipes in COMPLETE MEALS IN ONE DISH have been adapted by Miss Waldo to American taste and usage and carefully tested. You'll find easy-to-prepare recipes for exotic, unusual specialty dishes as well as quickly thrown together meals...all presented amidst the charming anecdotes and descriptions that make *every* Myra Waldo cook-book a delightful excursion for any cook.

COMPLETE MEALS

by Myra Waldo

Illustrated by Ruth Olsen Coleman

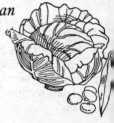

A FAWCETT CREST BOOK

Fawcett Publications, Inc., Greenwich, Conn.

IN ONE DISH

TABLE OF CONTENTS

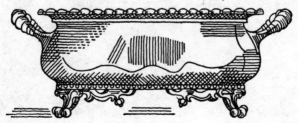

Introduction

IN THE BACK OF MY MIND, there is a particularly poignant memory of a scene which took place at twilight in the medieval village of Rocamadour in southwestern France. Rocamadour is precisely one street wide, the ancient houses perched precariously on the edge of a steep cliff, overlooking a flat, green plain. The countryside surrounding Rocamadour is agricultural, and the people of the region are peasants. As I walked slowly down the narrow street toward the country inn where I was staying, my eyes were attracted to a single lighted window at street level. Within the very simple frame house, an elderly couple were seated at a plain wooden table, the small room dimly illuminated by the flickering light of a single candle. The man and woman, both apparently in their seventies, appeared serene and contemplative, their eyes cast down upon the table. On it there was a large metal pot, the steam escaping in several thin white, irregular lines of vapor. There was also a straw basket containing bread, the crusty type favored in all of France, and also a bottle of red wine and wine glasses. Nothing else.

7

The entire scene, sketched like a Daumier drawing, has remained in my mind. The elderly couple, with the understanding and compatibility of perhaps a half century of married life, the obvious air of contentment, and the familiar food—some kind of peasant stew, a meal-in-one-dish, to be eaten with bread and drunk with wine—could be repeated in every country of Europe. It is a nostalgic scene that has never left my memory and, I hope, never will.

Before 1918, foreign food had but little acceptance and few enthusiasts in the United States. In the two decades or so that followed, Americans gradually began to be intrigued by the food of Europe, and during that period Italian and French restaurants opened in profusion throughout the nation. But since the end of World War II, an enormous interest in the food not only of Europe, but also of the entire world has been growing swiftly all over our country. Foreign food and foreign recipes are becoming increasingly popular, particularly with young married couples who enjoy entertaining frequently and informally.

Europeans, in particular, have always been fond of a meal-in-one-dish, and there isn't a country of Europe that does not feature that type of preparation. Although the dish may have originated for reasons of convenience or economy, meals-in-one-dish have subtle, unusual, and sophisticated combinations of tastes and flavors. As food consultant to Pan American World Airways, I have traveled extensively all over the world, usually in the company of my husband. We enjoyed these dishes abroad, and our guests at home have enjoyed them too.

When man first learned to control fire, he soon learned to cook his food, rather than eat it raw; this great step forward probably took place some ten to twenty thousand years ago, according to the estimates of many anthropologists. At first, all foods were cooked directly over an open fire, meat being roasted on a stick. Later, with the invention of the first containers which could be placed over direct heat, pots made of clay, man first began to boil foods in liquid. With this momentous step forward, cookery, as we understand it, began. Assyrian and Egyptian records, dating back to several thousand years B.C., make reference to cooking utensils made of clay, and commonly used by the general public in daily life. The Bible contains a well-remembered incident in which Esau sold his birthright for a mess of pottage.

. . . and Esau came from the field, and he was faint:

And Esau said to Jacob, Feed me, I pray thee, with that same red pottage; for I am faint: therefore was his name called Edom.

And Jacob said, Sell me this day thy birthright.

And Esau said, Behold, I am at the point to die: and what profit shall this birthright do to me?

And Jacob said, Swear to me this day; and he swore unto him: and he sold his birthright unto Jacob.

Then Jacob gave Esau bread and pottage of lentils; and he did eat and drink, and rose up, and went his way; thus Esau despised his birthright.

Genesis, 25:29–34

The classic "mess of pottage" requires a brief explanation, for the word mess originally had reference to any prepared dish, or a portion of food. The word pottage, now generally obsolete, was a dish of vegetables cooked with meat, a sort of thick soup or stew. The famous mess of pottage for which the unthinking Esau sold his birthright (the right to be head of his family and religious group), was actually a classic meal-in-one-dish.

During the Dark Ages in Europe, those slow-moving centuries, the people slowly learned to cook more skillfully, and culinary horizons were extended, but the popularity of the meal-in-one-dish continued unabated. All over the Continent, people continued to cook dishes which included vegetables, and sometimes a form of starchy food, so that a complete meal could be prepared in one cooking utensil, the whole bathed in a luscious sauce into which bread could be dipped.

The modern art of cuisine, as we now understand it, in the sense of a complete style of cooking, probably first came to fruition in Italy during the reign of the Médicis, during the sixteenth century.

In 1533 when Catherine de Médicis married the Duke of Orléans (who later became King Henry II of France), she brought with her several Italian cooks as part of her dowry, in order to teach the French how to cook. In sixteenth-century Italy, they had already standardized the preparation of various thick, rich, hearty vegetable soups, made with pieces of meat and strands of *pasta*, those satisfying bits of cooked dough which make up the world of Italian spaghetti, macaroni, etc. In the Middle Ages, a thick soup-stew was the standard dish for the vast majority of people, and constituted their daily diet.

The French may have been culinarily backward during the sixteenth century, but they subsequently acquired great skills and soon surpassed the Italians. The French developed the *pot-au-feu* (a soup with meats and vegetables); *boeuf Bourguignonne* (beef in red wine); *poulet au pot* (chicken in its own broth); the famous fish stew, *bouillabaisse*, and dozens of other meals-in-one-dish. From approximately 1600 to 1700, French chefs always cooked their stews and other slowly cooked preparations in a rather large container called a *casse*. About 1725, an inventive chef created a smaller version suitable for preparing only a few portions at a time; it was promptly called a *casserole*, a small *casse*. From that time on, the French people began to cook meals-in-one-dish in a casserole, and it still remains an ideal cooking utensil. To this day, in most houses in provincial France, at the back of the family stove there will be a pot cooking during the day, into which the thrifty housewife adds any leftover meat, scraps of vegetables, and remaining wine. The people of France, greatly respected in matters culinary, are devoted to the meal-in-one-dish. And not only in France does this hold true, for there is not a cuisine or culinary style in all of Europe where the meal-in-one-dish is not a prime favorite, probably for the following reasons.

Meals-in-one-dish are:

(1) *Convenient*. Much less effort is required to prepare a meal in which one dish contains the principal ingredient plus the vegetable and starchy food. In addition to the lessened preparation, when cleaning-up time comes, there are fewer pots to clean, and fewer plates to handle, wash, and dry.

(2) *Easily Prepared*. With separate courses for vegetables, time must be devoted to preparing them just before mealtime, and cooking time must be carefully watched so that the vegetables are not overcooked. The same effort and extra preparation must be extended to potatoes, rice, noodles or other starchy food. With the meal-in-one-dish, all of this trouble is avoided, and the three basic ingredients are cooked together.

(3) *Economical*. It is not necessary to use the very finest cuts of meat in making meals-in-one-dish, because the long, slow cooking process, by means of wet heat, softens and tenderizes the poorer cuts, which cannot be accomplished if meat is broiled or roasted. Even leftovers may be used; scraps of food from previous meals all add flavor and succulence to a slowly cooked preparation.

(4) *Ideal for Parties Because the Food Waits*. Inasmuch as meals-in-one-dish are cooked slowly with blended flavors and laden with delicious gravy and sauce, they may be held for almost any desired period, without fear that the food will dry out or become tasteless. The meal-in-one-dish can be prepared well in advance of the prospective serving time, even the day before,

if desired. In fact, preparing a meal-in-one-dish the day before can be recommended, because the taste will actually be improved when the dish is reheated the following day. In particular, this is a great help to the working woman, who can prepare the meal-in-one-dish the day before their guests are expected; this leaves her free to greet her guests and spend time with them, instead of being confined to the kitchen. However, if the dish is prepared the day before it is to be served, don't complete the cooking time in advance, but remove from the heat when about three-quarters finished, or the dish may be overcooked when reheated on the following day.

(5) *Simple to Serve.* One of the best things about a meal-in-one-dish, in these days of nonexistent or inexperienced domestic help is that no maid is required. The hostess can bring the cooking container directly to the table, place it on a trivet or other heat-resistant surface to protect the table top, and serve her guests directly. Inasmuch as there are no separate pots of vegetables cooking, the hostess need not leave her guests in order to bring them to the table. Bread and wine, previously placed upon the table, are all the accompaniments required.

(6) *Elaborate or Simple.* A meal-in-one-dish may be a gastronomical experience, representing a high point of culinary skill; in Europe, many outstanding examples of the finest of culinary art are actually meals-in-one-dish. This tremendous versatility offers great scope to the ambitious cook, because the wide range of meals-in-one-dish is so extensive. When guests are expected for dinner, it may contain the finest of ingredients, be prepared with wine, and be an exceptional conversation piece of a dish. At the other extreme, it might consist of a simple casserole dish prepared earlier during the day and ready for the family's dinner several hours later when everyone (including the person who prepared it) returns home.

(7) *Suitable for Variable Numbers of Guests.* Because of its nature, the meal-in-one-dish can serve many more people than planned, thus making it ideal when the precise number of guests is not known at the time of preparation. For example, suppose

that additional guests unexpectedly remain at your home after a cocktail party. A meal-in-one-dish prepared for eight persons can be readily extended to cover twelve or more by merely adding additional vegetables, potatoes, or other ingredients. The hostess who is in doubt as to the number of people she will ultimately be required to serve, would do well to prepare a meal-in-one-dish in preference to any other preparation.

(8) *Ideal for Freezing.* Any unused amount of food from the meal-in-one-dish can be frozen for future use. For best results, allow the food to cool, skim the fat (if any), place in a container, then wrap with foil or parchment paper, and freeze.

Meals-in-one-dish are truly the ideal smart way to serve food for your family or entertain friends at dinner, particularly if there is no domestic help. Bring the cooking utensil directly to the table and serve from it. It is advisable to have suitable large serving spoons and forks at the table.

There is also a marvelous opportunity offered for the ambitious host or hostess to prepare food before his guests in a chafing dish. A chafing dish may be inexpensive or elaborate, as you wish, but basically it consists of a metal pan resting over a water basin, and suspended over a source of heat (usually alcohol or electricity). Actually, it is a timesaver because there is no advance cooking and the dish itself is prepared in front of the guests; inasmuch as most people are interested in watching the

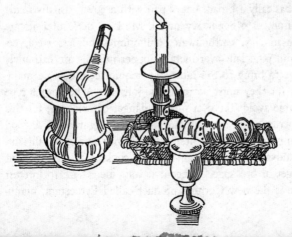

cooking process, they participate in the meal's preparation in a vicarious fashion. When you are cooking with a chafing dish, the uncooked ingredients should be carefully assembled and arranged attractively on a large plate or platter. The measuring or weighing of ingredients should be undertaken previously in the kitchen, not before your guests. This prevents delay and confusion, and lends a more professional, skilled air to the proceedings. Before cooking with a chafing dish, it is suggested that you attempt a practice run-through, to prevent embarrassing delay or inconvenience before your guests.

Never before has there been such an enormous selection of attractive and useful cooking utensils as are now available on the market. In addition to those manufactured domestically, an unbelievable choice is to be had of the imported products of France, Italy, Belgium, Spain, Denmark, and many more countries. Some of those are not only utilitarian but also extremely decorative.

Any cooking utensil, such as a saucepan with a cover, can be used for making meals-in-one-dish. However, whatever utensil is used, it should have a cover that fits fairly well, although a reasonable amount of looseness or play is not objectionable. The heavier the material used in the utensil the better, because this will protect foods that require long, slow cooking from burning or scorching. The classic utensils for meals-in-one-dish are "Dutch ovens," heavy saucepans or casseroles. A Dutch oven is basically a broad, heavy pan with a cover, usually made of cast iron, or other heavy metal. Most of these utensils are available in clay, earthenware, aluminum, stainless steel, ceramic, and porcelain over metal. Copper utensils are extremely attractive to bring to the table, but require considerable maintenance, for they must be regularly polished. A heatproof type of casserole avoids the ever present danger of breakage; for this reason perhaps glass or earthenware should be avoided. A good compromise is the metal utensil lined with porcelain; this offers the advantage of the non-metallic cooking surface without the danger of breakage. A recent development sure to interest everyone is the new Corning product called Pyroceram, manufactured as a "freezer-to-oven" type of cookware. The material used is almost indestructible, and may be taken from the freezer or refrigerator and placed over direct heat, or in the oven, without danger of breakage.

The correct size of the cooking utensil for the dish being prepared is always important, but especially so if it is to be brought to the table. A small quantity of food served from an extremely large utensil looks skimpy, and gives the guests a feeling that there is an insufficient amount of food; this inhibits people, and fearful of not leaving enough for everyone else, they inevitably take smaller quantities than they ordinarily would. Equally troublesome, although for another reason, is too large a quantity served in a utensil that is actually too small, with the food reaching the brim or leaking over. This leads to spills, stains, and a generally messy appearance. Ideally, the dish, when brought to the table, should be about three-quarters full. It will then be neither skimpy nor overflowing. If possible, one should have two different sizes of attractive cooking utensils, those that can be brought to the table. One should be somewhat shallow, and suitable for serving four to six people; a decorative skillet with ovenproof handle, or a Spanish *paella* dish are recommended. The larger one should be comparatively deep, and suitable for ten or more guests. An extremely useful and pleasant accessory is a Hotray, a device consisting of a flat, glasslike surface, kept hot electrically. With the Hotray, it is possible to keep meals-in-one-dish ready at the table for an indefinite period. Furthermore, second servings will be at the same temperature as the first serving—piping hot, steaming deliciously, and thus appealing to the eye.

As previously mentioned, the table should be set with French- or Italian-style bread; plain sliced white bread is not suitable. A dry (not sweet) wine is perfect with meals-in-one-dish, although there can be no objection to beer. Use white wine, chilled of course, for fish or shellfish preparations; red wine is best with meats. If you like, fill a pitcher with wine and place it on the table for guests to help themselves. Some people like to cut a fresh peach, pear, or apple (or all three) into the pitcher of wine for the fruity flavor it lends.

With meals-in-one-dish, nothing can match a crisp green salad for texture contrast, preferably one prepared with French or Roquefort dressing. Don't serve sweet or sticky salads, the kind made with fruits or nuts and mayonnaise. If the dish is comparatively bland, it is pleasant to put out some pickles or relishes, which offer a sharp, appetizing contrast in taste and texture. Another good idea is a bowl of cracked ice, filled with stalks of celery, carrot sticks, olives and the like, for your guests to nibble while waiting for dinner. If you do serve dessert, some fresh fruit or cheese is ideal and is particularly good with wine.

Meals-in-one-dish are perfect for your family, and equally good for entertaining guests. Simple or elaborate, meals-in-one-dish are the smart way to serve appetizing, appealing dishes.

MYRA WALDO

Fish

On ITALY'S EAST COAST, facing the Adriatic, there are a series of beach resorts, all very popular with the Italians. For some reason, American tourists rarely visit them, probably because there is little to see or do in the usual tourist sense. The beach is excellent, there are literally hundreds of hotels, and the atmosphere is very relaxing and pleasant. Stretching out into the sea are several very long piers; the restaurants on them all feature seafood. Of course, a day spent on the beach breathing fresh sea breezes, swimming in azure waters, and a late dinner hour all tend to develop a heroic appetite. Whatever the reason, I ordered *pesce alla pescatora* (that is, fish in fisherman's style) for dinner one evening. All I can say is that fishermen, at least around Rimini, eat very well indeed. But be sure to have some crusty Italian bread to dunk into the delicious sauce.

Pesce alla Pescatora

(MARINATED FISH STEW, ITALIAN STYLE)

1½ teaspoons salt	2 tablespoons chopped
½ teaspoon freshly	parsley
ground black pepper	3 cups dry red wine
3 tablespoons olive oil	6 slices mackerel, sea bass,
1½ cups chopped onions	or blue fish
1 clove garlic, minced	3 tablespoons butter
½ teaspoon basil	1 tablespoon flour
¾ cup grated carrot	

In a bowl mix together the salt, pepper, oil, onions, garlic, basil, carrot, parsley, and wine. Marinate the fish in the mixture 2 hours. Remove the fish. Cook the marinade in a deep skillet for 15 minutes over medium heat. Add the fish; cook over low heat 25 minutes, turning the fish once. Knead the butter and flour together and add to sauce in small pieces, stirring constantly until thickened. Serve with slices of French or Italian toasted bread.

Serves 6.

Cacciucco alla Florentina

(FISH STEW, FLORENTINE STYLE)

4 pounds sliced assorted
  fish (bass, whiting,
  snapper, eel)
Fish head and bones
1 lobster, cut up in
  the shell
¾ cup olive oil
3 cloves garlic, minced
3 sprigs parsley
½ cup celery leaves
½ teaspoon marjoram
1 tablespoon salt

½ teaspoon crushed dried
  red peppers
1 cup dry red wine
½ cup dry white wine
2 cups water
2 tablespoons tomato
  paste
¼ cup diced celery
2 cloves garlic, sliced
3 tablespoons minced
  parsley
¼ teaspoon thyme

Wash and dry the fish and lobster. Almost any combination can be used, but be sure to have a lobster. The fish head and bones should be used for making the stock, or, if they are unavailable, substitute 2 cups bottled clam juice for the 2 cups water.

Heat ½ cup oil in a saucepan; sauté the garlic, sprigs of parsley and celery leaves 5 minutes. Add the fish heads, marjoram, salt, red peppers, the wines, water, and tomato paste. Bring to a boil and cook over low heat 45 minutes. Strain, pressing through as much solids as possible.

Heat the remaining oil in the saucepan; sauté the diced celery, sliced garlic, minced parsley, and thyme 5 minutes. Arrange the fish over it and add the strained stock. Bring to a boil, cover, and cook over low heat 10 minutes. Add the lobster, recover, and cook 20 minutes longer. Taste for seasoning. Serve in deep bowls with toasted garlic bread.

Serves 6–8.

Caciucco

(LEGHORN FISH STEW)

12 clams
12 mussels (optional)
3 pounds sliced assorted
   salt-water fish (mackerel,
   whiting, halibut)
½ cup olive oil
¾ cup chopped onions
2 cloves garlic, minced

1½ cups dry red wine
1 20-ounce can Italian-
   style tomatoes, drained
1½ teaspoons salt
½ teaspoon crushed dried
   red peppers
2 tablespoons minced
   parsley

Scrub the clams and mussels under cold running water until water runs clear. Trim the beards of the mussels. Wash and dry the fish.

Heat the oil in a saucepan; sauté the onions and garlic 5 minutes. Add the wine; cook until reduced to half. Mix in the tomatoes, salt, and red peppers. Arrange the sliced fish in mixture. Bring to a boil and cook over low heat 25 minutes. Add the clams, mussels, and parsley; cover and cook 5 minutes longer, or until the shells open. Discard any clams or mussels that don't open. Serve in deep plates with toasted Italian or French bread lightly rubbed with garlic.

Serves 6–8.

Guisado de Pescado

(FISH SOUP-STEW)

½ cup olive oil
1½ cups chopped onions
2 cloves garlic, minced
3 cups water
3 cups bottled clam juice
3 pounds firm fleshed
   white-meat fish, cut into
   bite-sized pieces
1½ teaspoons salt
½ teaspoon white pepper

½ teaspoon thyme
2 cups diced potatoes
½ cup dry sherry
2 cups peeled diced
   tomatoes
1 package frozen green
   peas, thawed
2 egg yolks
3 tablespoons minced
   parsley

Heat the oil in a saucepan; sauté the onions and garlic until transparent and lightly browned. Add the water and clam juice; bring to a boil. Add the fish, salt, pepper, and thyme. Cover and cook over low heat for 20 minutes. Add the potatoes and sherry; recover and cook for 20 minutes. Mix in the tomatoes and peas; cook 10 minutes longer.

Beat the egg yolks in a bowl; gradually add about 2 cups of the fish stock, beating steadily to prevent curdling. Return to the saucepan with the parsley, mixing steadily. Heat, but do not let boil. Taste for seasoning.

Serves 6–8.

Baked Lobster and Rice

¼ pound (1 stick)
 butter
½ cup minced onion
1 clove garlic, minced
4 tablespoons flour
3 cups chicken broth
2 tablespoons tomato
 paste
½ cup dry sherry

1 pound cooked lobster
 meat, diced
1 8-ounce can green peas,
 drained
¼ cup chopped parsley
1 teaspoon salt
½ teaspoon freshly
 ground black pepper
3 cups cooked rice
½ cup grated Swiss cheese

Melt half the butter in a saucepan; sauté the onion and garlic 5 minutes, stirring frequently. Blend in the flour. Gradually add the broth, stirring constantly to the boiling point. Mix in the tomato paste. Cook over low heat for 15 minutes. Add the sherry, lobster, peas, parsley, salt, and pepper. Cook over low heat for 5 minutes. Mix in the rice and taste for seasoning.

Pour the mixture into a 2-quart buttered baking dish. Sprinkle with the cheese. Dot with the remaining butter. Bake in a 375° oven 20 minutes, or until lightly browned. *Serves 4–6.*

Crab Meat Stew

1 pound crab meat
½ cup dry sherry
2 tablespoons butter
¼ cup chopped green
 onion
3 tablespoons chopped
 green pepper
1 clove garlic, minced

¾ cup peeled tomatoes
2 cups bottled clam juice
1 teaspoon salt
¼ teaspoon freshly
 ground black pepper
1 cup raw rice
½ teaspoon rosemary
1 cup heavy cream

Pick over the crab meat, discarding any cartilage.

Combine the crab meat and sherry and marinate in the refrigerator 1 hour. Melt the butter in a saucepan or deep skillet; sauté the onion, green pepper, and garlic 5 minutes. Add the tomatoes, clam juice, salt, and pepper. Bring to a boil, add the rice and rosemary. Cover and cook over low heat 15 minutes. Stir in the cream and undrained crab meat. Cook 5 minutes longer and taste for seasoning. *Serves 6.*

Casserole de Poisson

(FISH CASSEROLE)

6 fillets sole	3 tablespoons minced
2½ teaspoons salt	parsley
¾ teaspoon freshly	2 cups peeled diced
ground black pepper	potatoes
4 slices crisp bacon,	1 cup peeled chopped
crumbled	tomatoes
1½ cups chopped onions	½ teaspoon thyme
1 cup grated carrots	½ cup diced cooked ham
½ pound mushrooms,	½ cup dry white wine
sliced	3 tablespoons butter

Cut the fish fillets in half. Season with 1½ teaspoons of the salt and ¼ teaspoon pepper. Spread the bacon on the bottom of a shallow greased casserole. Mix together the onions, carrots, mushrooms, parsley, potatoes, tomatoes, thyme, ham, and the remaining salt and pepper. Spread half the mixture over the bacon. Arrange the fish over the vegetables and cover with remaining vegetable mixture. Add the wine and dot with the butter. Cover and bake in a 375° oven 45 minutes, removing the cover for the last 15 minutes. *Serves 6–8.*

Shrimp and Vegetable Ragoût

3 tablespoons olive oil	¼ teaspoon saffron
¼ pound ham, diced	½ cup canned tomato
1 cup chopped onions	sauce
1 cup chopped green	1½ cups water
peppers	2 cups peeled cubed
1½ cups peeled chopped	potatoes
tomatoes	1 pound green peas,
2 teaspoons salt	shelled
⅛ teaspoon dried ground	2 pounds raw shrimp,
red peppers	shelled and deveined

Heat the oil in a deep heavy skillet or casserole; sauté the ham, onions, and green peppers for 10 minutes. Add the tomatoes, salt, red peppers, saffron, tomato sauce, and water. Cover and cook over low heat 30 minutes. Mix in the potatoes and peas; cover and cook over low heat 10 minutes. Add the shrimp; cook 10 minutes longer. Taste for seasoning. *Serves 6–8.*

Shrimp and Rice, Chinese Style

⅓ cup vegetable oil	¼ teaspoon freshly
1 cup raw rice	ground black pepper
2 cups boiling water	1 clove garlic, minced
1½ pounds raw shrimp,	½ cup hot chicken broth
shelled and deveined	3 tablespoons soy sauce
3 green peppers	1 egg, beaten
2 tomatoes	¼ cup thinly sliced green
1½ teaspoons salt	onions
½ teaspoon ground ginger	

Heat 2 tablespoons of the oil in a saucepan; stir in the rice until browned. Carefully add the boiling water to prevent splattering. Cover and cook over low heat 15 minutes. Drain.

Wash and dry the shrimp. Cut each pepper lengthwise in 8 pieces, discarding the seeds and fibers. Cut each tomato into 6 wedges.

Heat the remaining oil in a deep skillet; add the shrimp, salt, ginger, pepper, and garlic; cook over low heat 2 minutes, stirring constantly. Add the peppers; cook 1 minute, stirring. Add the broth and soy sauce; cover, bring to a boil and cook 3 minutes. Mix in the rice and tomatoes; cook 3 minutes. Stir in the egg and green onions; cook 1 minute. *Serves 6–8.*

Baked Almond Shrimp

4 tablespoons butter
¾ cup chopped green onions
2 pounds shrimp, cooked, cleaned, and diced
3 cups cooked rice
1½ teaspoons salt
⅛ teaspoon Tabasco
⅛ teaspoon nutmeg
¼ cup chopped pimiento-stuffed olives
1 cup peeled chopped tomatoes
1 8-ounce can green peas, drained
1 cup heavy cream
¼ cup dry sherry
½ cup blanched sliced almonds
¼ cup blanched ground almonds

Melt the butter in a skillet; sauté the green onions 5 minutes. Mix together the sautéed onions, shrimp, rice, salt, Tabasco, nutmeg, olives, tomatoes, peas, cream, sherry, and sliced almonds. Turn into a 2-quart buttered baking dish. Sprinkle with the ground almonds. Bake in a 350° oven 30 minutes or until delicately browned. *Serves 6–8.*

Shrimp Creole

¼ cup olive oil
1 cup sliced celery
1 cup sliced onions
¼ cup sliced green onions
1 cup chopped green
  peppers
1 teaspoon sugar
2 tablespoons flour
1 29-ounce can tomatoes,
  chopped

2 cups bottled clam juice
1 teaspoon salt
2 tablespoons chili
  powder
½ teaspoon celery seed
⅛ teaspoon Tabasco
1½ cups raw rice
2 pounds shrimp, cooked
  and cleaned

Heat the oil in a Dutch oven or saucepan; mix in the celery, onions, green onions, green peppers, sugar, and flour. Cook over low heat, stirring frequently, for 10 minutes. Add the tomatoes; cook 10 minutes, stirring frequently. Mix in the clam juice, salt, chili powder, celery seed, and Tabasco. Cover loosely and cook over very low heat 45 minutes. Add the rice; cook 20 minutes longer. Add the shrimp; heat, and taste for seasoning.
Serves 6–8.

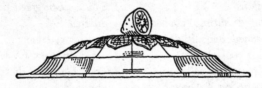

Baked Fried Fish and Vegetables

6 slices bacon
1 cup diced potatoes
1½ cups diced tomatoes
1 cup canned corn kernels
1½ cups chopped onions
¾ cup chopped green
  peppers
3 teaspoons salt

¾ teaspoon freshly
  ground black pepper
¼ cup flour
4 fillets of sole, cut in
  half
2 tablespoons olive oil
¼ cup dry sherry

Lightly brown the bacon; drain and cut in narrow strips.

Mix together the bacon, potatoes, tomatoes, corn, onions, green peppers, 1 teaspoon salt, and ½ teaspoon pepper.

Combine the flour with the remaining salt and pepper. Dip the fish in the mixture. Heat the oil in a deep skillet or casserole; lightly brown the fish in it. Spread the vegetable mixture over the fish, add the sherry, and bake in a 375° oven for 45 minutes.
Serves 4–6.

Sang Suhn Jim

(STEAMED FISH AND VEGETABLES)

1 pound ground beef
2 cloves garlic, minced
½ cup chopped green onions
2 teaspoons sugar
⅓ cup soy sauce
3 tablespoons peanut oil
6 fillets of white-meat fish, cut into 2-inch pieces
1½ cups sliced onions
1 cup sliced mushrooms
½ cup sliced celery
1½ cups sliced carrots
½ teaspoon powdered ginger
¼ teaspoon dried ground chili peppers
2 teaspoons salt
3 teaspoons freshly ground black pepper
2 cups water
1 egg, beaten

Mix together the beef, garlic, green onions, sugar, and 3 tablespoons soy sauce. Heat the oil in a Dutch oven or casserole and spread half the meat mixture on the bottom. Arrange half the fish over it. Mix the onions, mushrooms, celery, carrots, ginger, chili peppers, salt and pepper, and spread half the mixture over the fish. Cover with a layer of remaining meat mixture, a layer of remaining fish and the remaining vegetables. Add the remaining soy sauce and the water. Cover and cook over low heat 1 hour. Just before serving, fry the egg, shred, and sprinkle over the top.
Serves 6.

Poisson à la Portugaise

(FISH, PORTUGUESE STYLE)

2 pounds codfish steak
2 teaspoons salt
½ teaspoon freshly
  ground black pepper
4 tablespoons butter
½ cup olive oil
1 cup chopped onions
2 cloves garlic, minced
2 cups canned drained
  tomatoes

1 cup rice, half-cooked
  and drained
1 cup dry white wine
1 package frozen kale or
  spinach, cooked and
  drained
2 tablespoons minced
  parsley

Cut the fish into 4 serving-sized pieces. Season with the salt and pepper.

Heat the butter and oil in a large, deep skillet; sauté the onions 10 minutes. Stir in the garlic, tomatoes, rice, and wine. Arrange the fish in the pan; cover, bring to a boil, and cook over low heat 20 minutes. Add the kale and parsley; cook uncovered 5 minutes longer. Taste for seasoning.

Serves 4.

Mariscos y Legumbres en Salsa

(SEAFOOD AND VEGETABLES IN SAUCE, SPANISH STYLE)

1½ cups chopped onions
¼ cup olive oil
1 cup julienne-cut green
peppers
1½ cups peeled diced
potatoes
2 teaspoons salt
½ teaspoon freshly
ground black pepper
1 clove garlic, minced
2 teaspoons finely
chopped bay leaves
1 cup dry white wine

1 8-ounce can tomato
sauce
½ cup boiling water
1 pound fish fillets, cut
into bite-sized pieces
1 pound raw shrimp,
shelled and deveined
½ pound crab meat
2 tablespoons minced
parsley
Sautéed French or Italian
sliced bread

Sauté the onions in the hot oil 10 minutes. Add the green peppers and potatoes; cook 5 minutes. Mix in the salt, pepper, garlic, bay leaves, wine, tomato sauce, and boiling water. Cover and cook over low heat 20 minutes. Add the fillets; cook 10 minutes. Mix in the shrimp and crab meat; cook 10 minutes. Taste for seasoning. Sprinkle with the parsley and arrange the sautéed bread around the edge of the casserole.

Serves 6–8.

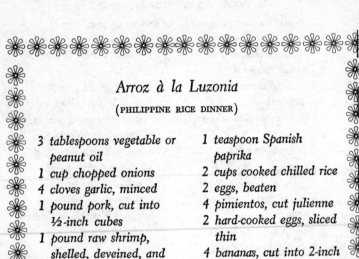

Arroz à la Luzonia

(PHILIPPINE RICE DINNER)

3 tablespoons vegetable or
  peanut oil
1 cup chopped onions
4 cloves garlic, minced
1 pound pork, cut into
  ½-inch cubes
1 pound raw shrimp,
  shelled, deveined, and
  cut in half
2 teaspoons salt
½ teaspoon freshly
  ground black pepper

1 teaspoon Spanish
  paprika
2 cups cooked chilled rice
2 eggs, beaten
4 pimientos, cut julienne
2 hard-cooked eggs, sliced
  thin
4 bananas, cut into 2-inch
  pieces
3 tablespoons butter

Heat the oil in a skillet; sauté the onions, garlic, pork, and shrimp until browned, stirring frequently. Mix in the salt, pepper, paprika, and rice. Cool 15 minutes. Add the beaten eggs; mix with 2 forks until blended. Taste for seasoning.

Arrange the pimientos and sliced eggs on the bottom of a well-oiled casserole or baking dish; turn the rice mixture into it. Cover with a piece of aluminum foil and place dish in a pan of water. Cook over low heat 30 minutes. While the mixture is cooking, sauté the bananas in the butter. Arrange around the rice mixture and serve directly from the dish. *Serves 6.*

DRIVING ALONG SPAIN'S SOUTHERN COAST, my husband and I headed for Gibraltar, the British stronghold on the Mediterranean. Because it was such a lovely day, we decided to spend a day or so (just before Gibraltar) at the Spanish port of Algeciras, which has a rather good hotel. Before turning up the road toward our hotel, we passed the ferry which crosses the Mediterranean to Tangier in North Africa. My husband looked at me; I looked at him. He stopped the car and walked over to the ferry landing in order to read the schedule. If we made an early morning ferry, we could return the same day in the late afternoon. He bought tickets, and we made the trip the following day, finding the boat ride and Tangier both extremely enjoyable.

But I am getting ahead of my story. After checking into the hotel, we had dinner and ordered *pez espada con arroz*, swordfish and rice, because that long-nosed fish is a great specialty of this region. It was delicious, and we enjoyed every last morsel of the fish and rice. The next morning, as previously related, we crossed on the ferry to Tangier. We returned in time for a late dinner, and I again ordered *pez espada con arroz*. Our waiter reminded me that I had ordered it the previous night, and even my husband looked at me somewhat speculatively. But I was determined and ordered the same dish again. I enjoyed every last morsel of the fish and rice.

Pez Espada con Arroz

(SWORDFISH WITH RICE, SPANISH FASHION)

3 pounds swordfish
5 cups water
6 peppercorns
3 cloves
3 teaspoons salt
½ cup olive oil
1 cup chopped onions
2 cups cooked rice

1½ cups chopped raw
    spinach
½ teaspoon freshly
    ground black pepper
¼ teaspoon thyme
2 tablespoons lime or
    lemon juice

Wash the fish and combine it in a skillet with the water, peppercorns, cloves, and 1½ teaspoons salt. Bring to a boil and cook over low heat 25 minutes. Drain, dry, and cut the fish into 2-inch squares.

Heat the oil in a skillet or casserole; sauté the onions 5 minutes, stirring frequently. Mix in the rice, spinach, pepper, thyme, lime juice, and remaining salt. Carefully stir in the fish. Bake in a 350° oven 20 minutes.

Serves 6.

Baked Tuna and Green Rice

2 7-ounce cans tuna fish,
    drained and flaked
1½ cups chopped cooked
    spinach
½ cup chopped parsley
3 cups cooked, drained
    rice
¼ cup minced green
    onions

1 8-ounce can green peas,
    drained
1 cup grated Parmesan
    cheese
¼ cup melted butter
½ teaspoon salt
¼ teaspoon white pepper
5 egg yolks, beaten
5 egg whites, stiffly beaten

Mix together the tuna, spinach, parsley, rice, onions, peas, cheese, butter, salt, pepper, and egg yolks. Fold in the egg whites. Turn into a greased 2-quart baking dish or casserole. Bake in a preheated 350° oven 35 minutes or until set and browned.

Serves 6–8.

Bahmi Goreng

(NOODLES, PORK, AND SHRIMP, INDONESIAN STYLE)

1½ pounds boneless
   pork
⅓ cup soy sauce
½ pound vermicelli or
   fine egg noodles
2 eggs, beaten
¾ cup oil
1½ cups thinly sliced
   onions
2 cloves garlic, minced
2 teaspoons minced ginger
   root

3 cups shredded Chinese
   or green cabbage
1 cup bean sprouts
1½ cups diced cooked
   shrimp
¼ cup chopped green
   onions
½ teaspoon freshly
   ground black pepper

Cut the pork into matchlike strips. Add all but 1 tablespoon soy sauce and refrigerate, tossing the meat occasionally while preparing the noodles.

Cook the noodles in boiling salted water until almost tender. Drain and spread on a flat surface to cool, then chill for 2 hours. Make an omelet of the eggs. Roll up and slice fine.

Heat 2 tablespoons oil in a skillet or chafing dish; sauté the pork for 10 minutes. Remove and keep warm. Heat 2 tablespoons oil in the same skillet; sauté the onions, garlic, and ginger root for 3 minutes. Remove and keep warm. Heat 2 tablespoons oil in the same skillet; sauté the cabbage and bean sprouts 3 minutes. Add the shrimp and sauté 2 minutes. Return all the sautéed ingredients, and add the green onions, pepper, and remaining soy sauce. Cook 2 minutes.

In a separate skillet, heat the remaining oil; turn the noodles into it and fry until browned. Drain. Add to the pork mixture and sprinkle with the sliced omelet. *Serves 4–6.*

Baked Rice, Shrimp, and Asparagus

2 cups cooked drained rice
2 packages frozen
  asparagus spears
4 tablespoons butter
3 tablespoons flour
1 teaspoon salt
⅛ teaspoon white pepper
1½ cups hot milk

½ cup grated Parmesan
  cheese
1 egg yolk
Dash cayenne pepper
½ cup heavy cream
1½ pounds shrimp,
  cooked and cleaned
Paprika

Spread the rice in a buttered 1½-quart casserole. Cook the asparagus 1 minute less than package directs. Drain well and arrange over the rice.

Melt the butter in a saucepan; blend in the flour, salt, and pepper. Gradually add the milk, stirring steadily to the boiling point, then cook over low heat 5 minutes. Stir in the cheese until melted. Beat together the egg yolk, cayenne pepper, and cream. Gradually add a little of the hot sauce, stirring steadily to prevent curdling. Return to the balance of the sauce and add the shrimp. Pour the mixture over the asparagus, sprinkle with paprika, and bake in a 450° oven 10 minutes. *Serves 4–6.*

Sayadiah

(FISH AND RICE, ARABIC STYLE)

4 fillets of sole
4 tablespoons olive oil
1½ cups raw rice
3 cups boiling water
3 teaspoons salt
4 tablespoons butter
1 cup chopped onions
1 clove garlic, minced

½ teaspoon freshly
  ground black pepper
¼ teaspoon orégano
¼ teaspoon ground
  allspice
3 tablespoons minced
  parsley
1 cup peeled chopped
  tomatoes

Wash and dry the fish. Cut into 2-inch pieces. Heat 2 tablespoons oil in a saucepan; add the rice and cook until yellow, stirring frequently. Add the boiling water and 2 teaspoons salt; bring to a boil, cover and cook over low heat 15 minutes. Drain, if any water remains.

Heat the butter and remaining oil in a large skillet or casserole; sauté the onions and garlic until browned. Add the fish, pepper, orégano, allspice, and remaining salt; sauté 5 minutes. Lightly mix in the rice, parsley, and tomatoes. Cook over low heat 15 minutes, stirring frequently. Taste for seasoning.

Serves 4–6.

Asopao

(PUERTO RICAN RICE DISH)

4 whole chicken breasts	1 teaspoon freshly ground
2 slices salt pork, finely	black pepper
chopped	2 cups raw rice
1½ cups finely chopped	1 pound lump crab meat,
onions	picked over
1 green pepper, finely	2 pimientos, sliced
chopped	½ cup capers, drained
1 8-ounce can tomato	½ cup sliced stuffed
sauce	olives
1 bay leaf	1 cup small canned peas,
¼ cup olive oil	heated
8 cups chicken broth	12 cooked or canned
1 teaspoon salt	asparagus tips, heated

Remove the bones of the chicken breasts and cut into 2-inch cubes. Cook the salt pork, onions, and green pepper in a saucepan over very low heat for 15 minutes, stirring frequently. Add the tomato sauce and bay leaf. Cook 15 minutes.

Heat the olive oil in a Dutch oven or large saucepan and

brown the chicken cubes lightly. Add the tomato mixture, broth, salt, and pepper. Cover and cook over low heat 10 minutes. Add the rice and cook over low heat 30 minutes, stirring frequently and adding more liquid if necessary. Mix in the crab meat, pimientos, capers, and olives and cook 5 minutes. The resulting dish will be liquidy. Serve in deep plates and garnish with the peas and asparagus. *Serves 8.*

Baked Salmon, Rice, and Spinach

2 7¾-ounce cans salmon	½ teaspoon dry mustard
2 tablespoons minced onion	2 cups milk
4 tablespoons butter	1½ cups grated cheddar cheese
4 tablespoons flour	3 cups cooked drained spinach
½ teaspoon salt	2 cups cooked drained rice
Dash cayenne pepper	

Drain the salmon, reserving the liquid. Flake the salmon and mix in the onion.

Melt the butter in a saucepan; blend in the flour, salt, cayenne, and mustard. Add the milk and salmon liquid, stirring steadily to the boiling point; then cook over low heat 5 minutes. Stir in 1 cup cheese until melted.

Spread the spinach in a 2-quart buttered casserole, then the rice and salmon over it; cover with the sauce and sprinkle with the remaining cheese. Bake in a 400° oven 20 minutes or until browned and bubbly hot. *Serves 4–6.*

Lohi Tulenkestava Vuoka

(BAKED SALMON AND POTATOES, FINNISH STYLE)

2 pounds salmon
3 tablespoons butter
1 cup chopped onions
1½ pounds potatoes,
    peeled and thinly sliced
2 teaspoons salt

½ teaspoon white pepper
3 tablespoons dry bread
    crumbs
2 eggs
2 cups milk

Cut the salmon into bite-sized pieces. Melt the butter in a skillet; sauté the onions 5 minutes. Grease a 2-quart baking dish. Arrange successive layers of potatoes, salmon, and onion, sprinkling each layer with salt and pepper. Start and end with the potatoes. Sprinkle with the bread crumbs. Beat the eggs and milk until frothy. Pour into the baking dish. Bake in a preheated 350° oven 1 hour. *Serves 4–6.*

Halibut with Cheese Sauce

2 pounds halibut
1¼ teaspoons salt
¼ teaspoon white pepper
¼ pound (1 stick) butter
2 tablespoons flour
1 cup milk
1 10½-ounce can
    condensed tomato soup
¾ cup grated cheddar
    cheese

½ pound mushrooms,
    sliced and sautéed
2 cups cooked potato
    balls or cubes
1 8-ounce can tiny green
    peas
⅛ teaspoon cayenne
    pepper

Season the halibut with the salt and pepper. Melt 2 tablespoons of the butter in a broiling pan; place the fish on it and broil 8 minutes on each side, or until fish flakes easily when tested with a fork. Discard skin and bones and cube the fish.

Melt 4 tablespoons of the remaining butter in a saucepan; blend in the flour, then the milk and soup, stirring steadily to the boiling point. Stir in ½ cup cheese until melted. Stir in the mushrooms, potatoes, peas, cayenne pepper, and then fold in the fish. Taste for seasoning. Turn into a buttered 1½-quart casserole; sprinkle with the remaining cheese and dot with the remaining butter. Bake in a 375° oven 20 minutes or until browned. *Serves 4–6.*

Baked Tuna Fish with Cheese Biscuits

2 7-ounce cans tuna fish
1¾ cups milk
1 cup finely chopped celery
¼ cup minced onions
¼ cup chopped green olives
1 tablespoon minced parsley
½ cup half-cooked drained rice

1 package frozen mixed vegetables, cooked and drained
¾ teaspoon salt
¼ teaspoon freshly ground black pepper
1 tablespoon melted butter
1 package ready-to-bake refrigerator biscuits
½ cup grated cheddar cheese

Drain and flake the tuna fish. Mix with the milk, celery, onions, olives, parsley, rice, vegetables, salt, pepper, and butter. Turn into a greased 1½-quart casserole. Bake in a preheated 425° oven 15 minutes, stirring once or twice. Arrange the biscuits over the tuna mixture, sprinkle with the cheese, and bake 15 minutes longer. *Serves 4.*

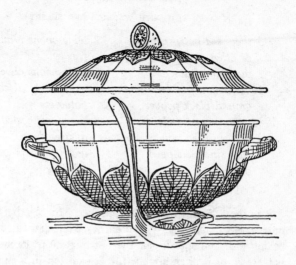

Spain usually has very good weather, but this particular year had been extraordinary. It rained for several days in Seville, and my husband and I decided to move southward to the Mediterranean in search of sunshine. We left Seville and drove toward Cadiz. While we were approaching the tiny town of Jerez de la Frontera, the sun came out, and stayed out. It seemed a good omen, and we decided to remain overnight at the old Hotel Cisnes, which everyone pronounces as if it were spelled This-Ness. We walked about the town and wandered into a very busy, dimly illuminated small restaurant. It was about 2:30 in the afternoon, the time for lunch in Spain, but pretty late for Americans. Everyone was eating small bowls of miniature eels, *anguillas*, fried in oil and garlic. I'm brave. I ordered some—they were absolutely marvelous. My husband ate most of mine, because he's bigger than I am.

For a main course, we had *pescado a la Jerez*, fish and vegetables prepared with sherry wine and walnuts. Superb, I thought. We stayed several days in Jerez and ate every meal at the same restaurant.

Pescado a la Jerez

(BAKED FISH WITH WALNUTS AND SHERRY)

6 slices sea bass, snapper,
or other firm fish

2 teaspoons salt

½ teaspoon freshly
ground black pepper

½ cup ground walnuts

2 cloves garlic, minced

2 cups finely chopped
onions

½ cup dry sherry

2 tablespoons minced
parsley

3 tablespoons olive oil

2 cups thinly sliced
potatoes

3 tomatoes, peeled and
quartered

2 green peppers, cut
julienne

Rub the fish with the salt and pepper. Mix together the walnuts, garlic, onions, sherry, and parsley. Pour half the oil into a baking dish and spread half the nut mixture in it. Spread the potatoes over it, then arrange the fish on top in a single layer and cover with the remaining nut mixture. Spread the tomatoes and green peppers over the nut mixture and sprinkle with the remaining oil. Cover the dish and bake in a 325° oven 50 minutes, removing the cover for the last 10 minutes.

Serves 6.

Pescado al Horno

(BAKED FISH, SPANISH STYLE)

3 tablespoons butter

3 cups peeled diced
tomatoes

¼ teaspoon saffron

3 teaspoons salt

¾ teaspoon freshly
ground black pepper

2 cups cooked white beans

4 fillets of mackerel, blue
fish, or sole

½ cup dry sherry

4 tablespoons olive oil

4 tablespoons dry bread
crumbs

2 tablespoons minced
parsley

¼ cup sliced stuffed
olives

4 slices lemon

Melt the butter in a saucepan; cook the tomatoes in it over low heat 10 minutes, stirring frequently. Mix in the saffron, 1½ teaspoons salt, and ¼ teaspoon pepper. Add the beans and spread on the bottom of a greased baking dish. Season the fish with the remaining salt and pepper; arrange over the tomatoes. Add the wine, and sprinkle with half the oil. Bake in a 375° oven 30 minutes. Sprinkle with a mixture of the bread crumbs, parsley, olives, then the remaining oil; bake 10 minutes longer. Garnish with the lemon slices. *Serves 4.*

Pesce al Forno alla Siciliana

(BAKED FISH, SICILIAN STYLE)

2 pounds swordfish or halibut steak	1 20-ounce can tomatoes
3 teaspoons salt	1 cup dry red wine
¾ teaspoon freshly ground black pepper	1 clove garlic, minced
1 cup chopped onions	½ cup sliced green olives
3 tablespoons olive oil	1 tablespoon chopped parsley
1 tablespoon flour	2 tablespoons capers
½ cup sliced celery	2 cups cooked elbow macaroni

Cut the fish into four serving-sized pieces; wash and dry. Season with half the salt and pepper. Sauté the onions in the olive oil 5 minutes. Blend in the flour. Add the celery, tomatoes, wine, garlic, and remaining salt and pepper; cover and cook over low heat 20 minutes. Add the olives, parsley, and capers.

Arrange the fish in a greased baking dish and pour half the tomato sauce over it. Bake in a 375° oven 30 minutes, basting occasionally. Add the macaroni and remaining sauce; bake 10 minutes longer.

Serves 4.

Many Americans find the food in Greece somewhat disappointing. They enjoy the country and the people and rave about the antiquities but do not have much enthusiasm for the local cuisine. Too much olive oil is the most frequently heard objection. I can understand this, and sympathize with it, but it is often possible to ask that a given dish be prepared without much oil.

This complaint does not usually apply to the Greek style of preparing fish and vegetables; in fact, it often does not contain any oil. An Athenian family wanted me to spend the day driving out to Cape Sunion, a beautiful spot just a short drive from Athens. When we reached Sunion, my host suggested lunch at the very large, elaborate hotel which stands near the point. It is very difficult, when one is a guest, to change the plans, but I gently suggested a more local place for lunch. My host's eyes lit up with pleasure. Encouraged, I went on to say that I wanted Greek food, not the sort of international food that could be expected at the fancy hotel—I had had enough of broiled chicken with green peas and mashed potatoes. Amid expressions of pleasure, we went to a tiny seaside restaurant, ramshackle and unpainted but nonetheless attractive, with small tables arranged outdoors. We ordered a marvelous baked-fish dish, prepared with artichoke hearts, potatoes, and white wine. That, crusty white bread, and a pitcher of *retsina*, the resin-flavored wine of Greece, made up the meal, and I don't know when I've enjoyed myself more. Or eaten so much.

Psari Plaki

(BAKED FISH, GREEK STYLE)

8 small potatoes
4-pound whole sea bass, pike, or whitefish
2 teaspoons salt
½ teaspoon freshly ground black pepper
⅓ cup lemon juice

1 package frozen artichoke hearts, thawed
1 tablespoon dry mustard
½ cup cognac
1¼ cups dry white wine
¼ cup capers

Cook the potatoes in boiling salted water for 15 minutes. Drain and peel. Wash and dry the fish; season with the salt and pepper. Place in a greased baking dish and sprinkle with the lemon juice. Arrange the potatoes and artichoke hearts around it. Mix the mustard with a little cognac until smooth, then combine with all the cognac and the wine. Add to the fish; bake in a 425° oven 45 minutes, or until the fish flakes easily when tested with a fork. Stir the capers into the sauce. *Serves 4.*

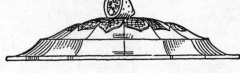

Plaki

(BAKED FISH AND VEGETABLES, GREEK STYLE)

⅓ cup olive oil
1½ cups chopped onions
2 cloves garlic, minced
3 cups boiling water
1½ cups sliced celery
1½ cups sliced carrots
3 potatoes (1½ pounds), peeled and sliced 1 inch thick
3 tomatoes, sliced

2½ teaspoons salt
¾ teaspoon freshly ground pepper
6 slices pike, sea bass, or salmon
3 tablespoons lemon juice
½ cup sliced black olives
3 tablespoons minced parsley

Heat the oil in a casserole; sauté the onions until browned. Mix in the garlic and water; bring to a boil. Add the celery, carrots, potatoes, tomatoes, 1½ teaspoons salt, and ¼ teaspoon pepper. Cook over low heat 15 minutes. Season the fish with the remaining salt and pepper; arrange over the vegetables. Sprinkle with the lemon juice. Cover and bake in a 350° oven 30 minutes. Remove cover, sprinkle with the olives and parsley; bake uncovered 15 minutes longer. Serve directly from the casserole.

Serves 6.

Bᴇғᴏʀᴇ ɪ ʟᴇғᴛ on a trip to South America, I anticipated having an authentic *vatapa*, the classic shrimp and coconut stew of Brazil. Once in Rio, I checked into the Copacabana Hotel. At dinnertime, I searched the menu for *vatapa*, but couldn't find it. The captain shook his head; the Copa (as everyone called it) specialized in French food. The next day, I determinedly set out for a restaurant famous for its Brazilian dishes. Of course, *vatapa* was not on the menu, and I was informed that it was only made on Tuesday. This being Thursday, it was a long wait. On Wednesday, the owner of another important restaurant informed me that they featured international cuisine, and I should look for *vatapa* in a restaurant of the "second class," as he put it. Finally, in Belo Horizonte, a booming young town, I ate *vatapa*. It was worth the trouble, and I ate a great deal of it. You will too.

Vatapa

(SHRIMP-COCONUT STEW, BRAZILIAN STYLE)

2 tablespoons olive oil
1½ cups finely chopped
    onions
2 cloves garlic, minced
4 cups water
2 teaspoons salt
⅛ teaspoon cayenne
    pepper
2 bay leaves

2 pounds white-meat fish,
    cut into 2-inch pieces
1½ pounds raw shrimp,
    shelled and deveined
½ cup flaked coconut
2 cups milk
2 cups ground peanuts
½ cup yellow corn meal
3 tablespoons butter

Heat the oil in a saucepan; sauté the onions and garlic 10 minutes. Add the water, salt, cayenne pepper, and bay leaves. Bring to a boil; add the fish and shrimp. Cook over low heat 10 minutes. Remove the fish and shrimp; strain the stock. Combine the coconut, milk, and peanuts. Bring to a boil and cook over low heat 15 minutes. Strain.

Combine the reserved stock with the peanut mixture; bring to a boil, and stir in the corn meal. Cook over low heat 25 minutes, stirring frequently. Stir in the butter and return the fish and shrimp. Taste for seasoning. Serve in deep bowls.
Serves 6–8.

Seafood Stew

¼ cup olive oil
1½ cups chopped onions
2 green peppers, cut julienne
2 potatoes, peeled and sliced
2 teaspoons salt
¼ teaspoon freshly ground black pepper
1 clove garlic, minced
1 bay leaf
3 tablespoons tomato paste

1 cup bottled clam juice
3 cups boiling water
1 pound fillet of sole, cut into 2-inch strips
1 pound raw shrimp, shelled and deveined
½ pound lump crab meat
3 tablespoons chopped parsley

Heat the oil in a Dutch oven or saucepan; sauté the onions 5 minutes. Add the green peppers and potatoes and cook 5 minutes. Mix in the salt, pepper, garlic, bay leaf, tomato paste, clam juice, and boiling water. Cover and cook over low heat 20 minutes. Add the fish fillets and cook 10 minutes. Mix in the shrimp and crab meat and cook 15 minutes longer. Sprinkle with chopped parsley. Serve in deep plates, with toasted Italian or French bread. *Serves 6.*

Quick Seafood Chowder

4 tablespoons butter
1 cup minced onions
2 cups bottled clam juice
2 cups chicken broth
½ cups diced potatoes
package frozen mixed
vegetables, thawed

1 cup dry white wine
⅛ teaspoon marjoram
1 6-ounce can lobster
meat
1 5-ounce can shrimp
1 6-ounce can crab meat

Melt the butter in a saucepan; sauté the onions for 5 minutes.
Add the clam juice, broth, and potatoes; bring to a boil and
cook over low heat 5 minutes. Add the vegetables, wine, and
marjoram; cook 10 minutes. Mix in the seafood; cook 3 minutes. Serve in deep dishes with slices of French bread.
Serves 4–6.

Matelote à la Canotière

(FISH STEW IN WHITE WINE)

3 pounds assorted
fresh-water fish
(whitefish, pike, carp,
eel)
1 slice salt pork
6 tablespoons butter
4 tablespoons flour
1 bottle dry white wine
12 small white onions
1 clove garlic, minced
2 teaspoons salt

¼ teaspoon freshly
ground black pepper
1 bay leaf, finely crushed
¼ teaspoon marjoram
⅛ teaspoon nutmeg
2 tablespoons minced
parsley
¼ cup cognac
12 mushroom caps,
sautéed
Sautéed French or Italian
bread slices

Cut the fish into serving-sized pieces. Cover the salt pork with water; bring to a boil then drain and chop coarsely.

Melt the butter in a casserole. Stir in the flour until browned. Gradually add the wine, stirring constantly to the boiling point. Mix in the onions, garlic, salt, pepper, bay leaf, marjoram, nutmeg, and parsley. Cover and cook over low heat 15 minutes. Add the fish and cook 20 minutes. Heat the cognac, set it aflame, and pour into the casserole; shake the casserole until flames die. Add the mushrooms. Garnish with the toast. Serve in deep plates, *Serves 6–8.*

Guisado de Pescado
(FISH STEW, MAJORCA STYLE)

1 cup raw long-grain rice	1½ teaspoons salt
½ cup olive oil	¾ teaspoon freshly
2 cups thinly sliced onions	ground black pepper
2 cups thinly sliced potatoes	1½ cups diced tomatoes
	1½ cups dry white wine
2 pounds fillet of fish, cut into 2-inch pieces	2 cups bottled clam juice

Wash the rice under cold running water until water runs clear. Rub a casserole with 2 tablespoons of the oil. Spread half the onions on the bottom with half the potatoes over them. Spread the fish over the potatoes; sprinkle with half the salt and pepper and half the remaining oil. Cover the fish with the remaining onions, then the remaining potatoes, the rice, tomatoes, and remaining oil. Sprinkle with the remaining salt and pepper. Add the wine and clam juice. Cover and bake in a 350° oven 1 hour, removing the cover for the last 10 minutes.

Serves 6–8.

Fish Stew, Niçoise Style

3 pounds red snapper,
   whitefish, or halibut
4 tablespoons olive oil
1½ cups chopped onions
1 clove garlic, minced
3 tablespoons flour
2 cups bottled clam juice
3 cups water

½ cup dry white wine
1½ cups peeled, diced
   tomatoes
½ teaspoon salt
⅛ teaspoon Tabasco
¼ teaspoon thyme
2 tablespoons minced
   parsley

Cut the fish into serving-sized pieces. Wash and dry.

Heat the oil in a saucepan; sauté the onions and garlic for 5 minutes. Blend in the flour; gradually add the clam juice, stirring steadily, to the boiling point. Add the water, wine, tomatoes, salt, Tabasco, and thyme. Cook over medium heat for 30 minutes. Add the fish and parsley; cover and cook over low heat for 30 minutes. Taste for seasoning. Serve in deep bowls with garlic toast. *Serves 6–8.*

Zuppa de Pesce alla Veneziana

(FISH STEW, VENETIAN STYLE)

3 pounds sliced assorted
   fish
2 cups bottled clam juice
2 cups water
1 cup canned Italian-style
   tomatoes
1 teaspoon salt
½ teaspoon freshly
   ground black pepper
1 cup sliced onions

1 bay leaf
½ teaspoon marjoram
½ cup olive oil
½ cup finely chopped
   onions
2 cloves garlic, minced
1 cup dry white wine
¼ teaspoon saffron
2 tablespoons minced
   parsley

Buy at least three varieties of firm-fleshed fish—red snapper, sea bass, pike, or whitefish are good. Have the fish cut into 1-inch-thick slices and then in half through the bone. Wash and dry the fish.

In a saucepan, combine the heads, clam juice, water, tomatoes, salt, pepper, sliced onions, bay leaf, and marjoram. Bring to a boil and cook over low heat 45 minutes. Strain.

Heat the oil in a deep, large skillet; sauté the chopped onions and garlic 5 minutes. Add the fish; brown on both sides. Add the wine; cook over medium heat 5 minutes. Add the saffron, parsley, and reserved stock. Cook over low heat 15 minutes. Taste for seasoning. Serve in deep plates, with sautéed sliced Italian or French bread. *Serves 6–8.*

Fish Ragoût, Creole Style

4 tablespoons vegetable oil	2 teaspoons Worcestershire sauce
1½ cups chopped onions	3 teaspoons salt
2 cloves garlic, minced	⅛ teaspoon cayenne pepper
½ cup flour	
3 tablespoons minced parsley	6 fillets of sole or red snapper
½ teaspoon basil	½ cup dry white wine
1 bay leaf, chopped fine	½ teaspoon freshly ground black pepper
1 20-ounce can tomatoes	
2 cups water	1 cup raw rice

Heat 1 tablespoon of the oil in a saucepan; sauté the onions and garlic 10 minutes. Stir in 2 tablespoons of the flour until browned. Add the parsley, basil, bay leaf, tomatoes, water, Worcestershire sauce, 1½ teaspoons salt, and the cayenne pepper. Bring to a boil and cook over low heat 30 minutes. Prepare the fish meanwhile.

Wash and dry the fillets. Cut each in half crosswise. Dip in the wine, sprinkle with the remaining salt and the black pepper, then dip in the remaining flour. Heat the remaining oil in a skillet; lightly brown the fish in it. Drain. Add the rice to the sauce and arrange the fish over it. Cover and cook over low heat 20 minutes. *Serves 6.*

Bouillabaisse, Louisiana Style

3 pounds red snapper, pike, or sole
3 teaspoons salt
½ teaspoon freshly ground black pepper
⅛ teaspoon ground cloves
⅛ teaspoon ground allspice
1 clove garlic, minced
Fish heads
1 quart water
1 cup sliced onions
1 stalk celery
1 bay leaf
2 tablespoons olive oil
2 tablespoons butter
¾ cup thinly sliced carrots
1 cup chopped onions
1 cup chopped tomatoes
¼ teaspoon saffron
¼ teaspoon thyme
3 slices lemon
12 shucked oysters
½ pound raw shrimp, shelled and deveined
⅛ teaspoon cayenne pepper
¼ cup dry sherry
2 tablespoons minced parsley
Toasted French bread slices

Cut the fish into serving-sized pieces and rub with 1½ teaspoons salt, the pepper, cloves, allspice, and garlic. Cover and refrigerate while preparing the stock.

Wash the fish heads and combine with the water, sliced onions, celery, and bay leaf. Bring to a boil and cook over low heat 1 hour. Strain, pressing through as much solids as possible.

Heat the oil and butter in a Dutch oven or heavy saucepan. Sauté the carrots and chopped onions 10 minutes. Arrange the fish over it, cover, and cook 10 minutes. Remove the fish and add the strained stock, tomatoes, saffron, thyme, lemon, and remaining salt. Bring to a boil and cook over low heat 20 minutes. Return the fish and add the oysters, shrimp, cayenne pepper, sherry, and parsley. Cook over low heat 20 minutes. Taste for seasoning. Serve in deep plates, with a slice of toast in each.

Serves 6–8.

Bacalao a la Vizcaina

(CODFISH, SPANISH STYLE)

2½ pounds dried codfish
½ cup flour
3 pounds tomatoes, peeled
3 large onions
¾ cup olive oil
2 cloves garlic, minced
½ teaspoon crushed dried red peppers

1 teaspoon salt
¼ cup boiling water
¾ cup dry bread crumbs
1 pound potatoes, cooked and cut into matchlike strips
4 pimientos, cut julienne

Wash the codfish, cover with water, and let soak overnight. Drain, add fresh water to cover, and bring to a boil; cook 5 minutes. Drain, and remove the skin and bones. Cut into cubes; toss with the flour and reserve.

Chop one pound of the tomatoes and cut the remaining two pounds in quarters. Chop one onion and slice the other two.

Heat ¼ cup oil in a saucepan; sauté the chopped onions 10 minutes. Mix in the garlic, chopped tomatoes, red peppers, salt, and water. Bring to a boil and cook over low heat 45 minutes, stirring frequently and adding a little more water if too thick. Purée the mixture in an electric blender or force through a sieve. Stir in the bread crumbs.

Heat the remaining ½ cup oil in a skillet; brown the fish in it. Drain. In the oil remaining in the skillet, sauté the sliced onions 5 minutes. Add the quartered tomatoes; cook over low heat 10 minutes. Add to the sauce.

In a casserole, arrange successive layers of the sauce, fish, and potatoes, starting and ending with the sauce. Arrange the pimientos on top. Bake in a 375° oven 15 minutes.

Serves 6–8.

Moru à l'Auvergnate

(CODFISH, AUVERGNE STYLE)

1½ pounds dried codfish
2 tablespoons olive oil
2 pounds potatoes, peeled and sliced
¼ pound butter
2 cloves garlic, minced
1 16-ounce can green peas, drained

2 egg yolks
1 cup light cream
1 cup milk
¼ teaspoon salt
¼ teaspoon freshly ground black pepper
2 tablespoons minced parsley

Wash the codfish, cover with water and let soak 24 hours, changing the water a few times. Drain, cover with fresh water, bring to a boil and cook over low heat 10 minutes. Drain, remove the skin and bones and flake the fish.

Heat the oil in a large skillet; sauté the potatoes until yellow. Add the butter, garlic, and fish; cook over low heat 10 minutes. Add the peas. Beat together the egg yolks, cream, milk, salt, pepper, and parsley. Add to the fish mixture and cook, stirring steadily with a fork, until egg mixture sets.

Serves 4–6.

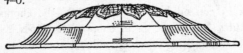

Poultry

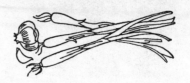

ONE OF THE FAVORITE DISHES all over Spain is *paella*, a unique creation of rice and assorted ingredients (meat, sausage, poultry, seafood, and the like). It is almost always well prepared, but everyone in Spain agrees that the town of Valencia, along the Mediterranean, does the most interesting variation. This is because the shellfish found near Valencia are fresh and flavorsome and apparently inspire the local cooks to greater inspiration.

My husband and I, together with another American couple, were invited (while we were in Valencia) to the beach home of a Spanish family we all knew. (He had once been a commercial attaché with the Spanish consul's office in New York.) The house, just fifteen minutes outside of town, was a delightful-looking place at the water's edge, surrounded by roses and so romantic you felt like singing something. Anything. In the moonlit night, it was almost unbearably beautiful. Knowing the Spanish habit of inviting people for 9 P.M., but really meaning 10 P.M. (yes, for dinner!), we arrived at about 10:15. At that, only our host was dressed and the hostess made her first appearance some twenty minutes later, looking surprised at our early arrival, but gracious nonetheless. We had sherry and biscuits for about an hour, while we grew steadily hungrier. Then a maid brought in a large platter of shrimp, clams, and that delicious clawless lobster found in the Mediterranean. I was so hungry that I ate a very large quantity of shellfish, as did everyone else. Another interminable hour later, we finally sat down to our long-anticipated dinner which featured the famed *paella a la Valenciana*, that is, as prepared in Valencia. It was a beautiful presentation, served in a rather flat metal dish, measuring more than three and a half feet in diameter. It was filled with rice, colored a most attractive yellow shade with saffron. Scattered about the rice were shrimp, clams, lobster, bits of fish, scarlet strips of pimientos, and green peas. Because of the late hour, and having stuffed myself with the shellfish appetizers, I simply could not eat the *paella*. However, I did manage to mess up my plate, swallow a mouthful or two, compliment our hostess several times, and, all in all convinced myself that no one had noticed.

I was wrong. On the way back to our hotel in Valencia, my husband asked why I hadn't eaten the *paella*. I admitted the truth, because even a white lie should only be used where there is a likelihood that it will be believed. The following day I ordered *paella a la Valenciana* in the hotel restaurant. It was fairly good, but my husband said that it was better the night before. If this story has a moral (and I doubt it), all I can say is don't eat too much before the main course.

Paella

(SPANISH NATIONAL RICE DISH)

12 clams or mussels

3½-pound frying chicken, disjointed

1½ teaspoons salt

½ teaspoon freshly ground black pepper

1 clove garlic, minced

6 tablespoons olive oil

⅛ pound smoked ham, cut julienne

1 Spanish or other spicy sausage, sliced

1 cup chopped onions

½ cup chopped green pepper

2 cups raw rice

2 tablespoons canned tomato sauce

1 pound raw shrimp, shelled and deveined

3½ cups boiling water

½ teaspoon saffron

1 8-ounce can tiny peas

½ pound cooked lobster meat, cut into bite-sized pieces

3 pimientos, cut julienne

Wash the clams or mussels; scrub with a brush, rinse, and dry. Place in a skillet with a little water, cover and cook over high heat until shells open. Discard any that do not open.

Wash and dry the chicken pieces; rub with a mixture of the salt, pepper, garlic, and 2 tablespoons oil. Heat the remaining oil in a *paella* pan or Dutch oven; brown the chicken in it over low heat. Add the ham, sausage, onions, and green pepper. Cook over low heat 15 minutes, stirring frequently. Add the rice; cook 5 minutes, stirring frequently.

Mix in the tomato sauce, shrimp, water, and saffron. Cover and cook over medium low heat 18 minutes. Turn the mixture over from the top to the bottom with two forks. Add the peas and lobster; recover and cook 3 minutes. Garnish with the pimientos and clams or mussels. Recover and cook 3 minutes longer.

Serves 4–6.

Chicken and Egg Barley Stew

4 tablespoons olive oil	2 green peppers, chopped
4-pound pullet, disjointed	1½ cups egg barley
2 quarts boiling water	1 cup sliced black olives
2 teaspoons salt	2 pimientos, chopped
¼ teaspoon freshly	1 cup grated Parmesan
ground pepper	cheese
2 cups chopped onions	

Heat the oil in a skillet. Add the chicken pieces and brown well on all sides. Reserve the oil in the skillet and transfer the chicken to a saucepan; add the water, salt, and pepper. Bring to a boil, and cook over low heat 1½ hours or until chicken is tender. Remove the chicken and cut meat off the bones. Reserve the stock.

Sauté the onions and green peppers in the reserved oil until browned. Add to the boiling stock with the egg barley. Cook over medium heat 8 minutes. Mix in the olives, pimientos, grated cheese, and chicken. Cook 3 minutes. Serve in deep plates.

Serves 4–6.

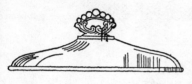

Nasi Goreng
(INDONESIAN FRIED RICE)

2 cups rice
3½ cups chicken broth
½ cup oil
2 cups chopped onions
3 cloves garlic, minced
2 cups julienne-cut cooked chicken
1½ cups diced cooked ham
1½ cups diced cooked shrimp

½ teaspoon ground cumin
½ teaspoon dried ground chili peppers
1 teaspoon ground coriander
2 tablespoons ground cashew nuts
4 tablespoons peanut butter

Wash the rice under cold running water for several minutes; drain. Combine the rice and broth in a saucepan; cover, bring to a boil and cook over low heat 20 minutes. Spread on a flat surface to cool, then chill for 2 hours.

Heat the oil in a deep skillet or chafing dish; sauté the onions 10 minutes. Add the garlic and rice; sauté until browned, stirring frequently. Mix in the chicken, ham, shrimp, cumin, chile peppers, coriander, cashew nuts, and peanut butter. Cook over low heat 10 minutes, stirring occasionally.

Serves 4–6.

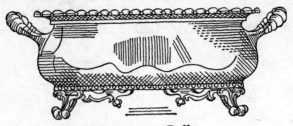

Arroz con Pollo

(CHICKEN WITH RICE)

3½-pound fryer,
   disjointed
2 teaspoons salt
¼ teaspoon freshly
   ground black pepper
½ cup olive oil
¾ cup chopped onions
2 cloves garlic, minced
1 green pepper, chopped
1 cup canned tomatoes,
   drained

1 bay leaf
3 cups chicken broth
¼ teaspoon saffron
1 cup rice
1 8-ounce can
   French-style peas
8 canned asparagus tips
2 pimientos, cut julienne

Rub the chicken with the salt and pepper. Heat the oil in a skillet; brown the chicken in it and transfer to a *paella* dish or large, deep skillet with heatproof handle. Add the onions, garlic, and green pepper to the oil remaining in the skillet. Sauté 10 minutes, add the tomatoes; cook 5 minutes. Add to the chicken with the bay leaf, chicken broth, and saffron. Bring to a boil and add the rice. Cover and bake in a 350° oven 25 minutes or until chicken and rice are tender. Watch carefully, and add a little more broth if necessary. Discard bay leaf. Taste for seasoning. Sprinkle the peas over the top and arrange the asparagus and pimientos over them. Bake 10 minutes longer, uncovered.
   Serves 4–5.

Baked Chicken and Rice

5-pound roasting chicken,
  disjointed
3 tablespoons olive oil
1 cup minced onions
¾ cup chopped green
  peppers
2 cloves garlic, minced
1 tablespoon minced
  parsley
1 8-ounce can tomato
  sauce
2 cups dry white wine

1 cup boiling water
2½ teaspoons salt
¼ teaspoon dried ground
  red peppers
½ cup seedless raisins
4 cups cooked, drained
  rice
½ cup grated cheddar
  cheese
1 cup sliced toasted
  almonds

Wash and dry the chicken pieces.

Heat the oil in a Dutch oven or heavy saucepan; sauté the onions and green peppers 5 minutes. Add the garlic, parsley, and chicken; sauté 15 minutes, turning the chicken to brown all sides. Mix in the tomato sauce, wine, water, salt, and red peppers. Cover and cook over low heat for 1 hour or until tender. Cut the chicken from the bones and return to the sauce. Add the raisins; cook over low heat 15 minutes. Taste for seasoning.

Mix together the rice and chicken mixture. Turn into a greased 2-quart baking dish or casserole; sprinkle with the cheese and almonds. Bake in a 350° oven 10 minutes.

Serves 6–8.

Jolov

(RICE AND CHICKEN, LIBERIAN STYLE)

4-pound pullet, disjointed
3 teaspoons salt
½ teaspoon freshly
   ground black pepper
¼ pound butter
3 tablespoons vegetable
   oil

1½ cups chopped green
   peppers
2½ cups onions
2 6-ounce cans tomato
   paste
2½ cups water
1½ cups raw rice

Sprinkle the chicken pieces with 1½ teaspoons salt and the pepper. Melt the butter in a Dutch oven or saucepan and brown the chicken well on all sides. Cover and cook over low heat 35 minutes, turning the pieces frequently. Heat the oil in a saucepan and sauté the green peppers and onions 10 minutes. Mix in the tomato paste, water, and remaining salt; bring to a boil. Add the rice, cover, and cook over low heat 15 minutes. Add to the chicken, taste for seasoning, and cook 10 minutes longer. *Serves 4.*

Oriental Chicken with Rice

3-pound frying chicken,
   disjointed
3 cups boiling water
1 onion
3 tablespoons soy sauce
½ teaspoon white pepper
2 tablespoons cornstarch
2 tablespoons vegetable
   oil

1 cup raw rice
1½ cups cold water
1½ teaspoons salt
½ cup seedless raisins
½ cup sliced toasted
   almonds
¼ cup flaked coconut

Combine the chicken, water, onion, soy sauce, and pepper in a saucepan. Bring to a boil and cook over low heat 45 minutes or until chicken is tender. Remove chicken and strain the broth. Return 1¼ cups to the saucepan and reserve the balance. Mix the cornstarch with 2 tablespoons cold water; stir into the 1¼ cups broth in the saucepan and cook over low heat until thickened.

Heat the oil in a saucepan; stir in the rice until coated. Add the water, salt, and remaining broth. Cover and cook over low heat 20 minutes or until tender and dry. Lightly mix in the raisins and almonds; return the chicken, cut off the bone if you like. Add thickened broth. Sprinkle with the coconut and cook 5 minutes.

Serves 4.

Chicken-Rice Curry

4 tablespoons butter
1½ teaspoons salt
¼ teaspoon white pepper
1 tablespoon curry
    powder
3½-pound frying
    chicken, disjointed

1 cup sliced, blanched
    almonds
1 cup heavy cream
1 cup raw rice
2 cups hot chicken broth

Melt the butter in a deep skillet or casserole; stir in the salt, pepper, and curry powder. Add the chicken pieces and turn them to coat with the seasoned butter; cook 5 minutes. Stir in the almonds and cream. Cover and bake in a 350° oven 30 minutes. Add the rice and broth. Recover and bake 30 minutes longer, removing the cover for the last 10 minutes.

Serves 4.

Poulet aux Choux

(CHICKEN AND CABBAGE STEW)

2 4-pound pullets,
  disjointed
3 tablespoons butter
2 tablespoons olive oil
1½ cups chopped onions
3 cloves garlic, minced
3 tablespoons chopped
  parsley
1 cup grated carrots

4 cups shredded cabbage
2 teaspoons salt
½ teaspoon freshly
  ground black pepper
¾ cup dry white wine
3 potatoes, peeled and
  quartered
½ cup pitted green
  olives

Wash and dry the chicken pieces. Heat the butter and oil in a Dutch oven or casserole; brown the chicken in it. Remove. In the fat remaining in the pan, sauté the onions, garlic, and parsley 10 minutes. Return the chicken, and add the carrots, cabbage, salt, and pepper. Cook over low heat 15 minutes. Add the wine, potatoes, and olives. Cover and cook over low heat 45 minutes, or until the chicken is tender.

Serves 6–8.

Browned Chicken and Vegetables

5-pound roasting chicken,
  disjointed
2½ teaspoons salt
½ teaspoon freshly
  ground black pepper
1 clove garlic, minced
1 teaspoon paprika
4 tablespoons butter

12 small white onions
3 potatoes, peeled and
  quartered
12 mushroom caps
3 carrots, quartered
½ cup chicken broth
2 tablespoons chopped
  parsley

Season the chicken pieces with a mixture of the salt, pepper, garlic, and paprika. Melt the butter in a deep, large skillet or casserole; brown the chicken in it. Add the onions and potatoes and brown lightly. Mix in the mushrooms, carrots, and broth. Cover and cook over low heat 45 minutes or until chicken is tender. Sprinkle with the parsley.

Serves 4–5.

Brunswick Stew

3-pound fryer, disjointed	1 16-ounce can
1½ pounds boneless	cream-style corn
beef, cut into 1-inch	2 cups diced potatoes
cubes	1½ cups diced onions
6 cups water	¾ cup raw rice
3 teaspoons salt	1 package frozen okra
½ teaspoon freshly	½ teaspoon celery seed
ground black pepper	Dash cayenne pepper
1 20-ounce can tomatoes	

Combine the chicken, beef, and water in a Dutch oven or large casserole. Bring to a boil, skim the top, and add 2 teaspoons salt and the pepper. Cover and cook over low heat 1 hour. Drain the meat and chicken. Cut the chicken into bite-sized pieces, discarding the bones. Pour off all but 2 cups broth. Return the meat and chicken, and add the tomatoes, corn, potatoes, onions, rice, okra, celery seed, cayenne pepper, and remaining salt. Cover and cook over low heat 45 minutes.

Serves 6–8.

Braised Chicken with Vegetables

4-pound roasting
chicken
2 teaspoons salt
1 slice salt pork, diced
½ cup diced carrots
8 small white onions

¼ cup boiling water
¼ teaspoon freshly
ground black pepper
2 cups green peas
2 cups diced potatoes

Rub the cleaned, trussed chicken with the salt.

Brown the diced salt pork in a Dutch oven or casserole. Remove the browned pieces and reserve. Place the chicken in the pan and brown it on all sides. Add the carrots and onions; cook 10 minutes. Add the water and pepper; cover and cook over low heat 40 minutes, turning the chicken every 10 minutes. Add the peas, potatoes, pork bits, and a little more boiling water if necessary. Cook 20 minutes longer or until chicken is tender. Remove and carve the chicken. Serve the vegetables around it, and the pan juices. *Serves 4.*

Poularde aux Tomates

(CHICKEN AND TOMATOES, FRENCH STYLE)

3½-pound frying
chicken, disjointed
¼ pound butter
2 tablespoons olive oil
2 teaspoons salt
½ teaspoon freshly
ground black pepper
2 cups firm-cooked rice
1 cup chopped onions
1 clove garlic, minced

2 green peppers, cut
julienne
4 tomatoes, quartered
12 small mushroom caps
16 pitted green olives
2 tablespoons minced
parsley
½ cup dry white wine
½ cup heavy cream

Wash and dry the chicken pieces. Heat the butter and oil in a Dutch oven or casserole; brown the chicken in it on all sides.

Season with the salt and pepper. Cover and bake in a 375° oven for 30 minutes. Add the rice, onions, garlic, peppers, tomatoes, mushrooms, olives, parsley, and wine. Bake uncovered 15 minutes longer. With a fork, stir in the cream and taste for seasoning.

Serves 4.

Coq au Vin

(CHICKEN IN RED WINE, FRENCH PROVINCIAL STYLE)

5-pound roasting chicken, disjointed	2 teaspoons tomato paste
8 slices bacon	1 teaspoon finely chopped bay leaf
6 tablespoons butter	¼ teaspoon thyme
1½ teaspoons salt	12 small white onions
¼ teaspoon freshly ground black pepper	12 mushroom caps
¼ cup warm cognac	2 teaspoons arrowroot or cornstarch
3 cups dry red wine	3 tablespoons port wine
1 clove garlic, minced	

Wash and dry the chicken pieces. Cook the bacon in boiling water 10 minutes. Drain and dry. In a casserole or Dutch oven, brown the bacon. Remove the bacon, crumble, and set aside; pour off all but 1 tablespoon fat. Add 2 tablespoons butter to the fat; brown the chicken in it. Season with the salt and pepper. Set the cognac aflame and pour it over the chicken. When flames die, add the wine, garlic, tomato paste, bay leaf, thyme, and bacon bits. Cover and cook over low heat 20 minutes.

Melt 2 tablespoons butter in a skillet; sauté the onions until browned, shaking the pan frequently. Add to the chicken; cook 15 minutes. Sauté the mushrooms in the remaining butter 5 minutes. Add to the chicken; cook 15 minutes longer.

Mix the arrowroot or cornstarch with the port; stir into the gravy until thickened. Taste for seasoning.

Serves 4–5.

Gallo en Chicha

(CHICKEN IN APPLE BRANDY SAUCE)

¼ pound butter
2 cups finely chopped onions
2 4-pound pullets, disjointed
2 teaspoons salt
1 teaspoon freshly ground black pepper
2 cloves garlic, minced
2 green peppers, cut julienne
¼ teaspoon dried ground chili peppers
3 tablespoons wine vinegar

1 cup apple brandy
1 cup cider
12 stuffed olives
12 prunes, presoaked
12 small white onions, peeled
3 tablespoons capers
4 potatoes, peeled and cut into 1-inch cubes
6 chorizos (Spanish-style sausages), cut into small pieces and browned

Melt the butter in a Dutch oven or casserole; sauté the chopped onions until browned. Remove and reserve onions. Rub the chicken pieces with the salt and pepper and brown all over in the butter remaining in the pan. Add the sautéed onions, the garlic, green peppers, chili peppers, vinegar, brandy, and cider. Cover and cook over low heat 1 hour, or until chicken is almost tender. Add the olives, prunes, white onions, capers, and potatoes, and cook 10 minutes. Add the sausages and cook 10 minutes longer, or until chicken is tender. *Serves 8.*

Hühner mit Pflaumen

(CHICKEN WITH PRUNES, GERMAN STYLE)

2 2½-pound broilers,
  quartered
2½ teaspoons salt
½ teaspoon freshly
  ground black pepper
4 tablespoons butter
1 cup diced carrots

½ cup chopped onions
1 pound pitted prunes
4 potatoes, peeled and
  quartered
1 tablespoon lemon juice
1½ cups boiling water

Wash and dry the chickens; rub with 2 teaspoons of the salt and the pepper. Melt the butter in a Dutch oven or deep skillet; brown the chicken in it. Add the carrots and onions. Cover and bake in a 375° oven 20 minutes, basting frequently. Add the prunes, potatoes, lemon juice, water, and remaining salt. Re-cover and bake 35 minutes longer, or until the chicken and potatoes are tender.

Serves 8.

✳✳✳✳✳✳✳✳✳✳✳✳✳✳✳

Poulet Valle d'Auge

(CHICKEN AND APPLES IN CIDER)

2 2½-pound fryers,
  disjointed
4 tablespoons butter
2 tablespoons vegetable
  oil
¼ cup warm apple
  brandy or cognac
¼ cup minced onions
1¼ teaspoons salt

¼ teaspoon freshly
  ground black pepper
⅛ teaspoon marjoram
2 tablespoons minced
  parsley
3 apples, peeled, cored
  and quartered
½ cup cider
½ cup heavy cream

Wash and dry the chicken pieces. Heat the butter and oil in a Dutch oven or casserole; brown the chicken in it over low heat. Set the warm apple brandy aflame and pour over the chicken. When flames die, mix in the onions, salt, pepper, marjoram, parsley, apples, and cider. Cover and cook over low heat 25 minutes, or until chicken is tender. Stir the cream into the pan juices. Heat, but do not let boil, and taste for seasoning.

Serves 6–8.

Pollo con Crema

(CHICKEN IN CREAM)

4-pound roasting chicken, disjointed	½ teaspoon white pepper
3 tablespoons butter	½ teaspoon saffron
12 small white onions	1 bay leaf
1½ cups sliced carrots	2 cups potato balls or cubes
½ cup dry sherry	1 egg yolk
1¼ cups chicken broth	1 cup heavy cream
1½ teaspoons salt	

Wash and dry the chicken pieces. Melt the butter in a deep skillet or casserole; lightly brown the chicken in it. Remove. In the butter remaining in the pan, sauté the onions and carrots 5 minutes. Return the chicken, and add the sherry, broth, salt, pepper, saffron, and bay leaf. Cover and bake in a 350° oven 30 minutes. Add the potatoes; recover and bake 30 minutes longer or until the chicken is tender.

Beat the egg yolk, then stir in the cream. Gradually add a little of the pan juices, stirring steadily. Pour over the chicken, leave in the oven for 2 minutes, and serve.

Serves 4.

Braised Chicken with Peas in Cream

4-pound pullet, disjointed
2 teaspoons salt
½ teaspoon freshly
   ground black pepper
3 tablespoons butter
1 cup chopped onions
1 clove garlic, minced
¼ cup julienne-cut ham
¼ teaspoon thyme
1 bay leaf, finely chopped

2 tablespoons minced
   parsley
1½ cups boiling water
1 tablespoon cornstarch
1 cup light cream
1 16-ounce can green
   peas, drained
2 cups peeled diced
   potatoes

Wash and dry the chicken pieces. Season with the salt and pepper. Melt the butter in a Dutch oven or heavy saucepan. Sauté the chicken 10 minutes, turning the pieces several times. Mix in the onions; cook until browned. Add the garlic, ham, thyme, bay leaf, and parsley; cook 5 minutes, stirring frequently. Add the water; cover and cook over low heat 1 hour.

Mix the cornstarch with the cream; stir into the gravy until mixture boils. Add the peas and potatoes; cook 10 minutes longer. Taste for seasoning. *Serves 4.*

Chicken in Sour Cream Sauce

1 3½-pound fryer,
   disjointed
½ cup flour
1½ teaspoons salt
¼ teaspoon white pepper
4 tablespoons butter
1 cup sour cream

1 cup chicken broth
½ pound mushrooms,
   sliced
2 teaspoons paprika
2 cups cooked egg
   barley

Wash and dry the chicken pieces; roll in a mixture of the flour, salt, and pepper. Melt the butter in a Dutch oven or casserole; brown the chicken in it on all sides.

Mix in the sour cream, broth, mushrooms, and paprika. Cover the casserole loosely and bake in a 350° oven 45 minutes or until chicken is tender. Mix in the egg barley; bake 10 minutes longer.

Serves 4.

Chicken in Bourbon Sauce

4-pound roasting
   chicken, disjointed
2 teaspoons salt
½ teaspoon white pepper
6 tablespoons butter
½ cup bourbon

1 cup sliced onions
1 cup grated carrots
2 cups chopped
   tomatoes
1½ cups heavy cream
4 canned pears, sliced

Wash and dry the chicken pieces; season with the salt and pepper. Melt the butter in a deep skillet; brown the chicken in it. Add the bourbon; cook over high heat 2 minutes. Add the onions, carrots, tomatoes, and cream. Bring to a boil, cover and cook over low heat 30 minutes, or until the chicken is tender. Add the pears; cook 3 minutes.

Serves 4.

70

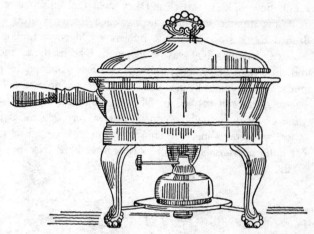

AMERICANS LOVE TO VISIT ITALY, and who can blame them? However, the vast majority head northward toward Florence and Venice. Of course, a fair proportion do go south to see Sorrento, Naples, and Capri. The percentage of those touring further southward into Sicily is far too small, because Sicily is a fascinating place, with rugged mountains, an ever present seashore, perfumed air, delightful climate, and rather good food.

We drove from Rome to Naples, put our car upon the overnight steamer, and the next morning found ourselves in noisy, bustling Palermo. After a day's sightseeing, we drove westward through Monreale and over the mountains until we reached the ruins of Segesta, an archaeological treat. Wandering about at Segesta uplifted our spirits, but it was noon and we were starved and also quite thirsty. We drove toward Trapani, on Sicily's west coast, and searched for a restaurant, but they all looked rather depressing, which is difficult to imagine in our hungry state. My husband parked the car on a side street in order to make inquiries. His look of helplessness apparently attracted the eye of several men who were conversing on the street, one of whom spoke fairly good English. After he asked for a good restaurant, my husband became the center of a group of gesticulating, emphatic people. It was clear (they said) that only one restaurant was suitable for these distinguished foreign visitors (us). It was the Ristorante Russo, but we could never find it unassisted. A young boy was delegated to take us there, and he did in a walk of several minutes. The Russo proved to be a pleasant place, friendly and busy, and there we ordered *pollo al Marsala*, chicken cooked in Marsala wine, the famous sweet wine of Sicily, actually produced only a very few miles from where we were eating. We enjoyed it immensely, and we often eat *pollo al Marsala* at home, because we liked it so much in Sicily.

Pollo al Marsala

(CHICKEN IN MARSALA)

4-pound roasting chicken, disjointed	1 clove garlic, minced
2 teaspoons salt	1 bay leaf
½ teaspoon freshly ground black pepper	½ teaspoon thyme
4 tablespoons butter	2½ cups chicken broth
½ cup minced onions	1¼ cups raw rice
1 cup Marsala wine	2 tablespoons minced parsley
1 cup sliced mushrooms	2 tablespoons capers

Rub the chicken pieces with the salt and pepper. Melt the butter in a Dutch oven or casserole; add the chicken and onions. Cover and cook over low heat 20 minutes; turn the chicken pieces once. Add the wine, mushrooms, garlic, bay leaf, thyme, and ½ cup of the broth. Cover and cook over low heat 25 minutes. Discard bay leaf. Add the rice and remaining broth; recover and cook 20 minutes longer. Sprinkle with the parsley and capers. Cook over medium heat 5 minutes.

Serves 4.

Quick Creole Gumbo

3 tablespoons vegetable oil
2 cups chopped onions
2 cloves garlic, minced
¼ cup flour
6 cups chicken broth
1 29-ounce can tomatoes
1 cup chopped celery
½ cup chopped green peppers

1 package frozen okra, thawed and sliced
2 teaspoons salt
½ teaspoon freshly ground black pepper
1 bay leaf
4 cups diced cooked chicken or turkey
2 cups cooked rice

Heat the oil in a saucepan; sauté the onions and garlic 5 minutes. Blend in the flour until browned, then add the broth, stirring steadily to the boiling point. Add the tomatoes, celery, green peppers, okra, salt, pepper, and bay leaf. Bring to a boil and cook over low heat 30 minutes. Mix in the chicken and rice; cook 5 minutes longer. *Serves 8–10.*

Chicken-Okra Gumbo

3 tablespoons olive oil
4-pound pullet, disjointed
½ pound ham, diced
1½ cups chopped onions
1½ pounds okra, or 2 packages frozen, cut into ½-inch pieces
1½ pounds tomatoes, peeled and chopped
2 teaspoons salt

½ teaspoon freshly ground black pepper
¼ teaspoon cayenne pepper
½ teaspoon thyme
2 tablespoons minced parsley
1 bay leaf, finely chopped
8 cups boiling water
1 cup raw rice

Heat the oil in a Dutch oven or heavy, deep saucepan; add the chicken and ham. Cover and cook over low heat 15 minutes, turning the chicken to brown all sides. Add the onions and okra;

cook until lightly browned, stirring frequently. Mix in the tomatoes, salt, pepper, cayenne pepper, thyme, parsley, and bay leaf. Cook 10 minutes, then add the water. Cover loosely and cook over low heat 30 minutes. Add the rice; cook 25 minutes longer, or until chicken and rice are tender. Taste for seasoning. *Serves 4–6.*

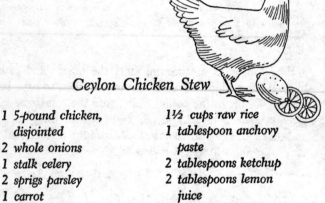

Ceylon Chicken Stew

1 5-pound chicken, disjointed
2 whole onions
1 stalk celery
2 sprigs parsley
1 carrot
1 clove garlic
2 teaspoons salt
4 cups water
2 tablespoons butter

1½ cups raw rice
1 tablespoon anchovy paste
2 tablespoons ketchup
2 tablespoons lemon juice
¾ teaspoon paprika
¾ teaspoon freshly ground black pepper
4 tablespoons dry sherry

Wash the chicken pieces and combine in a deep saucepan with the onions, celery, parsley, carrot, garlic, salt, and water. Bring to a boil, cover, and cook over low heat for 1 hour, or until chicken is tender. Remove the chicken and onions. Mash the onions. Strain the stock.

Melt the butter in a saucepan; stir in the rice until translucent. Add the reserved stock, mashed onions, the anchovy paste, ketchup, lemon juice, paprika, pepper, and sherry. Cook over low heat 20 minutes. Return the chicken to the pan and heat thoroughly. Serve hot. *Serves 4–5.*

74

Ajam Boomboo Roldjak

(INDIAN SPICED CHICKEN)

1 cup flaked coconut

1 cup light cream

6 tablespoons peanut or vegetable oil

2 3-pound fryers, disjointed

1½ cups finely chopped onions

1 clove garlic, minced

⅓ cup ground blanched almonds

¼ teaspoon dried ground red peppers

1 tablespoon dark corn syrup

2 tablespoons lemon juice

2 teaspoons grated lemon rind

1 bay leaf

1½ teaspoons salt

1½ cups raw rice

3 cups boiling water

Rinse the coconut under cold running water and drain. Combine the coconut and cream in a saucepan. Bring to a boil and let stand 30 minutes.

Heat the oil in a Dutch oven or heavy casserole; brown the chicken in it. Add the onions and garlic; sauté 10 minutes. Mix in the almonds, red peppers, corn syrup, lemon juice and rind, bay leaf, salt, rice, water, and undrained coconut. Cover and cook over low heat 30 minutes or until chicken is tender. Shake the pan frequently.

Serves 6–8.

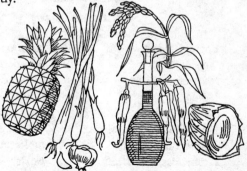

Palm Oil Chop

(AFRICAN CHICKEN-PEANUT STEW)

2 4-pound chickens,
  disjointed
6 cups water
2 cups ground peanuts
1 cup chopped onions

1½ pounds sweet
  potatoes, peeled and
  quartered
8 hard-cooked eggs,
  shelled
4 cups hot cooked rice

Wash the chicken pieces and combine in a saucepan with the the water. Bring to a boil and cook over medium heat 45 minutes. Add the peanuts, onions, and potatoes. Cover loosely and cook over low heat 45 minutes longer, or until the chicken is tender.

The stew is served in deep plates. Place an egg in each, cover the egg with some rice, and put some chicken and gravy over the top. Serve with side dishes of diced cucumber, chutney, and sliced bananas. *Serves 8.*

Sopa de Gallina

(CHICKEN SOUP-STEW)

4-pound pullet,
  disjointed
1½ quarts water
1 onion
2 stalks celery
1½ pounds potatoes,
  peeled and sliced
2 tomatoes, sliced thin

6 green onions, sliced
2 teaspoons salt
¼ teaspoon white pepper
2 packages frozen green
  beans, thawed
¼ cup drained capers
2 tablespoons minced
  parsley

Wash the chicken; combine in a heavy saucepan with the water, onion, and celery. Bring to a boil and cook over low heat 1 hour. Discard the onion and celery; add the potatoes, tomatoes, green onions, salt, and pepper. Cook over low heat 30 minutes. Remove about half the potatoes and mash them. Return to the pan. Add the beans; cook 5 minutes longer. Taste for seasoning. Just before serving, add the capers and parsley. Serve in deep plates.

Serves 4–6.

Poulet à la Niçoise

(CHICKEN, NIÇOISE STYLE)

1 cup dried white beans	3 cloves garlic, minced
3 teaspoons salt	2 bay leaves
5-pound roasting chicken, disjointed	¼ teaspoon thyme
	¼ teaspoon tarragon
½ teaspoon freshly ground black pepper	2 cups diced tomatoes
	1 cup dry white wine
3 tablespoons olive oil	1 cup chicken broth
2 tablespoons butter	½ cup pitted green olives
½ teaspoon saffron	½ cup pitted black olives

Wash the beans, cover with water, bring to a boil, remove from heat and let soak 1 hour. Drain, add fresh water to cover, bring to a boil, and cook over low heat 1½ hours, adding 1½ teaspoons salt after 1 hour. Drain.

Rub the chicken pieces with the pepper and remaining salt. Heat the olive oil and butter in a Dutch oven or casserole; brown the chicken in it. Mix in the saffron, garlic, bay leaves, thyme, tarragon, tomatoes, wine, and broth. Cover and cook over low heat 45 minutes. Add the beans; cook 15 minutes. Mix in the olives; taste for seasoning and cook 10 minutes longer. Discard bay leaves.

Serves 4–5.

Risotto de Pollo e Peperoni

(CHICKEN, RICE, AND PEPPERS, ITALIAN STYLE)

4 tablespoons butter
¾ cup minced onions
1 clove garlic, minced
4-pound roasting chicken, disjointed
2 teaspoons salt
½ teaspoon freshly ground black pepper
2 cups chopped tomatoes
3½ cups chicken broth

3 green or red sweet peppers, cut into narrow strips
3 tablespoons olive oil
1½ cups raw rice
¼ cup grated Romano or Parmesan cheese
2 tablespoons minced parsley

Melt the butter in a Dutch oven or heavy skillet; sauté the onions and garlic 10 minutes. Add the chicken; cook until browned. Add the salt, pepper, tomatoes, and 1 cup broth. Cover and cook over low heat 20 minutes.

While the chicken is cooking, sauté the peppers in the olive oil. Add to the chicken with the rice and remaining broth; cook 20 minutes longer. Fold in the cheese, taste for seasoning, and sprinkle with the parsley.

Serves 4.

Morg Polou

(CHICKEN PILAFF, PAKISTAN STYLE)

1½ cups raw rice
3½-pound fryer, disjointed
4 tablespoons vegetable oil
1 cup thinly sliced onions
1½ cups light cream
1 tablespoon lemon juice

2 teaspoons salt
¼ teaspoon white pepper
½ teaspoon powdered ginger
2 cups hot chicken broth
1 green pepper, sliced thin

Wash the rice, cover with water and bring to a boil; let stand 15 minutes, then drain well. Wash and dry the chicken pieces.

Heat the oil in a Dutch oven or casserole; brown the chicken and onions in it. Add the cream, lemon juice, salt, pepper, and ginger; bring to a boil and cook over low heat 20 minutes. Add the rice and broth and arrange the green pepper on top. Cover and cook over low heat 35 minutes. The pilaff should be fairly dry, but watch carefully while cooking, and add a little boiling water if necessary. *Serves 4.*

Mayaguay Chicken Stew

4-pound roasting chicken, disjointed
2½ teaspoons salt
½ teaspoon freshly ground black pepper
3 tablespoons olive oil
1½ cups thinly sliced onions
1 cup chopped green peppers

2 cloves garlic, minced
1 cup peeled chopped tomatoes
¾ cup boiling water
2 cups canned or frozen corn kernels
1 8-ounce can peas
½ cup sliced pimiento-stuffed olives

Wash and dry the chicken pieces; rub with the salt and pepper. Heat the oil in a Dutch oven or casserole; brown the chicken in it. Add the onions and green peppers; cook 10 minutes. Mix in the garlic, tomatoes, and water. Cover and cook over low heat 40 minutes, or until the chicken is tender. Add the corn kernels, peas, and olives; recover and cook 10 minutes longer. Taste for seasoning.

Serves 4–5.

Pollo a la Mallorcian

(CHICKEN, MAJORCA STYLE)

5-pound roasting chicken, disjointed	1¼ cups peeled chopped tomatoes
⅓ cup olive oil	3½ cups boiling water
¾ cup diced raw ham	2 cups raw rice
¾ cup chopped green peppers	1 small bay leaf
1 cup sliced onions	¼ teaspoon saffron
2 cloves garlic, minced	½ cup sliced pimiento-stuffed olives
2½ teaspoons salt	
½ teaspoon freshly ground black pepper	

Wash and dry the chicken pieces. Heat the oil in a Dutch oven or heavy casserole. Add the chicken, ham, green peppers, onions, and garlic, and cook until the chicken is browned on all sides. Add the salt, pepper, and tomatoes; cover and cook over low heat 30 minutes.

Add the water; bring to a boil. Add the rice, bay leaf, and saffron. Cover and cook over low heat 20 minutes or until the rice and chicken are tender. Watch carefully and add more liquid if necessary.

Discard the bay leaf and garnish with the olives.

Serves 4–5.

Pollo alla Siracusa

(SAUTÉED CHICKEN AND EGGPLANT, SYRACUSE STYLE)

16 small white onions,
    peeled
4-pound roasting chicken,
    disjointed
½ cup olive oil
2½ teaspoons salt
½ teaspoon freshly
    ground black pepper
1 clove garlic, minced

¾ cup Marsala or sweet
    sherry
1 cup peeled diced
    tomatoes
3 tablespoons minced
    parsley
1 small eggplant, peeled
    and sliced
⅓ cup flour

Cook the onions in boiling water 5 minutes; drain and dry. Wash and dry the chicken. Heat 4 tablespoons of the oil in a skillet; brown the chicken and onions in it. Add 1½ teaspoons of the salt, the pepper, garlic, and wine; cook over medium heat until almost all the wine is evaporated. Mix in the tomatoes and parsley. Cover and cook over low heat 30 minutes or until chicken is tender. Taste for seasoning.

Dip the eggplant slices in the flour, then sauté in the remaining oil until browned on both sides. Sprinkle with the remaining salt. Arrange the eggplant slices over the chicken; cook 10 minutes longer.

Serves 4.

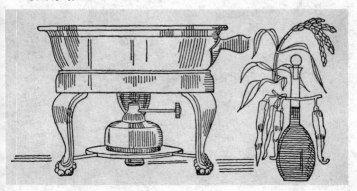

African Peanut Stew

4-pound roasting chicken, disjointed
5 cups water
1½ cups chopped onions
1½ cups ground peanuts

2 sweet potatoes, peeled and quartered
2 cups rice
2 teaspoons salt
4 hard-cooked eggs, shelled

Bring the chicken and water to a boil in a deep saucepan. Cook over medium heat 30 minutes. Stir in the onions and peanuts. Cook over low heat 30 minutes. Add the sweet potatoes, rice, and salt. Cook 30 minutes longer. Taste for seasoning. Put an egg in each serving. Serve with side dishes of chutney, sliced bananas, and sliced cucumbers. *Serves 4.*

Por Ajam

(ASIATIC CHICKEN AND PINEAPPLE)

3 whole chicken breasts
½ teaspoon dried ground chili peppers
1½ teaspoons salt
3 cloves garlic, minced
½ cup minced shallots or onions
½ teaspoon shrimp or anchovy paste
3 tablespoons vegetable oil
1½ cups diced fresh or canned pineapple

2 tablespoons lime or lemon juice
2 teaspoons grated lime or lemon rind
2 cups light cream
½ cup flaked coconut
2 teaspoons soy sauce
2 cups cooked rice
1 cup sautéed sliced scallions

Cut the chicken from the bones and into cubes. Pound or chop to a paste the chili peppers, salt, garlic, shallots, and shrimp paste. Toss with the chicken and let stand 1 hour.

Heat the oil in a deep skillet or saucepan; sauté the chicken and pineapple until lightly browned. Add the lime juice, rind, cream, coconut, and soy sauce. Cook over low heat 20 minutes. Mix in the rice; cook 5 minutes. Sprinkle the sautéed scallions on top.

Serves 4–6.

Chicken with Dumplings in Saffron Sauce

4-pound roasting chicken,
  disjointed
2¾ teaspoons salt
¼ teaspoon freshly
  ground black pepper
4 tablespoons butter
2 cloves
8 small white onions
¼ pound mushrooms,
  sliced
1 clove garlic, minced
¼ teaspoon thyme

¾ cup dry white wine
¼ teaspoon saffron
¾ cup sour cream,
  scalded
¾ cup sifted flour
1 teaspoon baking
  powder
1 egg, beaten
3 tablespoons milk
2 teaspoons minced
  chives or parsley

Wash and dry the chicken pieces; rub with 2 teaspoons of the salt and the pepper. Melt the butter in a Dutch oven or casserole; brown the chicken in it. Stick the cloves in an onion and add to the chicken with all the onions and the mushrooms; cook 5 minutes. Add the garlic, thyme, and wine. Cover and bake in a 375° oven 1 hour or until chicken is almost tender. Remove pan from the oven and place over direct low heat. Dissolve the saffron in the sour cream and mix into the chicken. Prepare the dumpling batter while the chicken is cooking.

Sift the flour, baking powder, and remaining salt into a bowl. Stir in the egg and milk until smooth. Mix in the chives or parsley. Drop the batter by the teaspoon around the edge of the casserole. Cover and cook over low heat 15 minutes without lifting the cover.

Serves 4.

Chicken Sukh

(CHICKEN-CHICK-PEA STEW, INDIAN STYLE)

4-pound pullet,
  disjointed
1½ teaspoons salt
¼ teaspoon powdered
  ginger
6 tablespoons butter
2 cups chopped onions
2 cups cooked or canned
  chick-peas

1 teaspoon ground cumin
1 tablespoon ground
  coriander
¾ teaspoon freshly
  ground black pepper
3 cups hot chicken broth
¾ cup raw rice

Wash and dry the chicken; rub with the salt and ginger. Melt the butter in a deep skillet or casserole; brown the chicken and onions in it. Add the chick-peas, cumin, coriander, and pepper; cover and cook over low heat 10 minutes, shaking the pan frequently. Stir in the broth and rice; cover and cook 30 minutes, removing the cover for the last 10 minutes. The dish should have very little gravy. Taste for seasoning.

Serves 4.

Colombo Creole
(CHICKEN AND PORK, GUADELOUPE STYLE)

½ cup vegetable oil
1½ cups chopped onions
3-pound chicken,
  disjointed
1½ pounds boneless
  pork, cubed
2 cloves garlic, minced
2 cups sliced carrots
3 cups cubed potatoes

3 cups diced eggplant
1 tablespoon curry powder
2 teaspoons salt
½ teaspoon freshly
  ground black pepper
½ teaspoon thyme
¼ teaspoon dried ground
  red peppers
2 cups water

Heat the oil in a heavy saucepan and sauté the onions 10
minutes. Remove and reserve. Add the chicken and pork to the
pan and brown all over. Return onions to pan, cover, and cook
over low heat 25 minutes, stirring frequently.

Mix in the garlic, carrots, potatoes, eggplant, curry powder,
salt, pepper, thyme, red peppers, and water. Cover and cook
45 minutes or until chicken is tender. Taste for seasoning.

Serves 6–8.

Adobong Manok at Baboy
(PHILIPPINE CHICKEN AND PORK DISH)

1 5-pound roasting
  chicken
1½ pounds boneless
  pork, cut into 1½-inch
  cubes
2 teaspoons salt
½ teaspoon freshly
  ground black pepper
4 cloves garlic, minced

¼ cup dry vermouth
¼ cup cider vinegar
1 bay leaf
3 tablespoons oil
1 cup water
1 cup light cream
½ cup packaged flaked
  coconut
2 cups cooked rice

Have the chicken cut up into 2-inch pieces, bone and all.

Marinate the pork in a mixture of the salt, pepper, garlic, vermouth, vinegar, and bay leaf for 30 minutes. Drain, reserving the marinade.

Heat the oil in a Dutch oven or heavy saucepan; brown the chicken and pork in it. Add the marinade and water. Cover and cook over medium heat 30 minutes, or until tender. Stir in the cream, coconut, and rice. Cook 5 minutes. Taste for seasoning. *Serves 6–8.*

❋❋❋❋❋❋❋❋❋❋❋❋❋❋❋❋❋

Chapon Sauté à la Bordelaise

(CAPON WITH ARTICHOKES)

3 tablespoons olive oil	1 package frozen
¼ pound (1 stick) butter	artichokes, thawed
5-pound capon,	3 potatoes, peeled and
disjointed	very thinly sliced
2 cups thinly sliced	1 clove garlic, minced
onions	¾ cup dry white wine
3 teaspoons salt	2 teaspoons tomato paste
½ teaspoon freshly	
ground black pepper	

Heat the oil and 2 tablespoons butter in a Dutch oven or heavy saucepan; sauté the capon in it until browned on all sides. Add the onions, 2 teaspoons salt, and pepper. Cover and cook over very low heat 35 minutes; watch carefully to prevent burning.

While capon is cooking, sauté the artichokes in 3 tablespoons butter for 3 minutes, turning them frequently. Sprinkle with ½ teaspoon salt. Dry potatoes thoroughly and sauté in the remaining butter until golden brown on both sides. Sprinkle with ½ teaspoon salt. To the capon add the artichokes, potatoes, and a mixture of the garlic, wine, and tomato paste. Cook 10 minutes longer or until the capon is tender.

Serves 4–6.

Pavo Español

(TURKEY, SPANISH STYLE)

8-pound turkey,
  disjointed
4 cups medium sherry
1 tablespoon salt
½ teaspoon freshly
  ground black pepper
¼ pound (1 stick)
  butter

18 small white onions
1 29-ounce can tomatoes
2 bay leaves
⅛ teaspoon basil
18 mushroom caps,
  sautéed
1 cup sliced
  pimiento-stuffed olives

Wash and dry the turkey pieces. Combine the sherry, salt, and pepper in a glass or pottery bowl. Marinate the turkey in the mixture in the refrigerator for 24 hours, turning the pieces occasionally. Drain the turkey, reserving the marinade.

Heat the butter in a Dutch oven or heavy casserole; brown the turkey in it. Add the onions and cook until browned. Mix in the tomatoes, bay leaves, basil, and reserved marinade. Cover and bake in a 350° oven 1½ hours. Add the mushrooms and olives; bake uncovered for 30 minutes or until the turkey is tender. Discard bay leaves. Taste for seasoning.

Serves 6–8.

Turkey and Wild Rice Casserole

1 cup wild rice	3 cups diced cooked
6 tablespoons butter	turkey
1 cup chopped onions	1 package frozen green
1 pound mushrooms,	peas, thawed
sliced	3 cups chicken broth
2 teaspoons salt	1½ cups heavy cream
¼ teaspoon freshly	½ cup blanched sliced
ground black pepper	almonds

Wash the rice very thoroughly until water runs clear. Cover with water, bring to a boil, cook 2 minutes, remove from heat, and let soak 1 hour. Drain.

Melt half the butter in a skillet; sauté the onions 5 minutes. Add the mushrooms; sauté 5 minutes. Mix the sautéed vegetables with the drained wild rice, the salt, pepper, turkey, peas, broth, and cream. Turn into a buttered casserole. Cover and bake in a 350° oven 1 hour. Mix in the almonds, dot with the remaining butter, and bake, uncovered, 20 minutes longer. *Serves 6–8.*

Turkey Fricassee

8-pound turkey, cut into	2 tablespoons minced
serving-sized pieces	parsley
½ cup flour	1 bay leaf
2½ teaspoons salt	2 slices lemon
¾ teaspoon freshly	1½ cup dry white wine
ground black pepper	2½ cups boiling water
4 tablespoons olive oil	½ cup egg barley
12 small white onions	1 pound mushrooms,
½ teaspoon thyme	sliced and sautéed

Wash and dry the turkey pieces; roll in a mixture of the flour, salt, and pepper.

Heat the oil in a Dutch oven or heavy casserole; sauté the onions 10 minutes. Add the turkey pieces and brown well. Add the thyme, parsley, bay leaf, lemon, and wine. Bring to a boil and cook 10 minutes. Add the water. Cover and cook over low heat 1¼ hours or until tender. Mix in the egg barley; cook 10 minutes. Add the mushrooms; cook over low heat 5 minutes.

Serves 6–8.

Marinated Turkey Casserole

8-pound turkey, disjointed	2 cloves garlic, minced
3 cups dry white wine	3 tablespoons olive oil
1 cup sliced onions	2 cups chopped onions
3 bay leaves	1½ cups chopped
3 teaspoons salt	tomatoes
1 teaspoon freshly ground	½ teaspoon cinnamon
black pepper	1½ cups raw rice

Wash and dry the turkey pieces. Combine the wine, sliced onions, bay leaves, and half of the salt, pepper, and garlic in a bowl. Marinate the turkey in the mixture 4 hours at room temperature, turning and basting frequently. Drain and dry. Strain the marinade.

Heat the oil in a Dutch oven or casserole; add the turkey, chopped onions, tomatoes, cinnamon, and the remaining salt, pepper, and garlic. Cover and cook over low heat 1¾ hours, turning the turkey pieces occasionally.

Heat the marinade, add to the turkey, bring to a boil, and add the rice. Recover and cook 25 minutes longer.

Serves 8–10.

Baked Curried Rice and Turkey

2 tablespoons butter
½ cup chopped onions
1 8-ounce can green peas,
    drained
3 cups cooked rice
1 tablespoon curry powder
3 cups diced cooked
    turkey

½ cup sliced stuffed
    olives
1 10-ounce can cream of
    mushroom soup
½ cup chicken broth
¼ cup grated Parmesan
    cheese
4 tablespoons ground
    almonds

Melt the butter in a skillet; sauté the onions 5 minutes. Mix
with the peas, rice, and curry powder. Spread in a greased baking dish. Mix together the turkey, olives, soup, and broth.
Pour over the rice. Sprinkle with the cheese and almonds. Bake
in a 350° oven 25 minutes. *Serves 6–8.*

Peru al Jerez
(MARINATED TURKEY)

8-pound turkey,
    disjointed
3 cloves garlic, minced
1 tablespoon salt
½ teaspoon freshly
    ground black pepper
¾ cup wine vinegar
¾ cup dry sherry
2 cups cubed tomatoes

2 cups julienne-cut green
    peppers
½ cup chopped parsley
¾ cup olive oil
½ cup water
3 cups potato balls or
    cubes
¼ pound prosciutto or
    cooked ham, cut
    julienne

Rub the turkey pieces with a mixture of the garlic, salt, and pepper. Let it stand for 1 hour. In a glass or pottery bowl, mix the vinegar, sherry, tomatoes, green peppers, parsley, and ½ cup of the oil. Marinate the turkey in the mixture in the refrigerator overnight. Baste and turn turkey frequently.

Remove the turkey from refrigerator 2 hours before cooking time and baste a number of times. Drain turkey, reserving the marinade. Heat the remaining oil in a Dutch oven or casserole, brown the turkey pieces in it. Add the marinade and water. Bring to a boil, cover, and cook over low heat 1 hour, or until turkey is almost tender. Add the potatoes and ham; cook uncovered 20 minutes longer. Taste for seasoning.

Serves 8–12.

New Orleans Squab Pie

1½ cups flour	1 pound small mushrooms
3½ teaspoons salt	1 teaspoon Worcestershire
¾ pound (3 sticks) butter	sauce
⅓ cup ice water	12 small white onions
1 egg white	3 tablespoons flour
3 squabs, split	1½ cups chicken broth
¾ teaspoon freshly	¼ teaspoon marjoram
ground black pepper	Dash cayenne pepper
1 clove garlic, minced	¼ cup Madeira or sweet
1 bay leaf	sherry
½ teaspoon thyme	½ cup dry bread crumbs
½ cup boiling water	

Sift the flour and ½ teaspoon salt into a bowl; cut in half the butter. Add just enough of the ice water to make the particles adhere. Form into a ball and chill 30 minutes. Roll out and line a 3-quart casserole with it. Brush with the egg white. Chill while preparing the squabs.

Wash and dry the squabs. Rub with the pepper and remaining salt. Melt 3 tablespoons of the remaining butter in a large skillet; brown the squabs in it. Add the garlic, bay leaf, thyme, and boiling water. Cover and cook over low heat 20 minutes. Drain and cool.

Chop enough of the mushroom stems to make ¾ cup. Sauté in 1 tablespoon of the remaining butter. Mix in the Worcestershire sauce. Put some in the cavity of each half squab, then reform the squabs and arrange in the lined casserole. Lightly brown the onions and the mushroom caps in 3 tablespoons butter. Add to the squabs.

Melt 3 tablespoons butter in a saucepan; blend in the flour. Gradually add the broth, stirring steadily to the boiling point. Mix in the marjoram and cayenne pepper; cook 5 minutes and mix in the wine. Cool slightly and pour over the squabs. Sprinkle with the bread crumbs and dot with the remaining butter. Bake in a preheated 400° oven 30 minutes. Serve directly from the casserole. *Serves 6.*

Braised Squabs

4 tablespoons butter
4 1¼-pound squabs, quartered
2 slices salt pork, diced
3 tablespoons flour
2½ cups chicken broth
2 teaspoons salt
½ teaspoon freshly ground black pepper
½ teaspoon thyme

1 bay leaf
16 small white onions
3 cups potato balls or cubes
16 mushroom caps
3 cups sliced pimiento-stuffed green olives
3 tablespoons minced parsley

Heat the butter in a Dutch oven or heavy casserole. Brown the squabs in it, then remove. Add the salt pork; cook until browned. Pour off all but 2 tablespoons fat. Stir in the flour until browned; add the broth, stirring to the boiling point. Replace squabs and add the salt, pepper, thyme, bay leaf, and onions. Cook over medium heat 30 minutes. Add the potatoes, mushroom caps, and olives. Cover and cook 15 minutes longer. Discard the bay leaf and sprinkle with the parsley.

Serves 4.

Stuffed Squabs

1 cup raw wild rice	6 squabs or Rock Cornish
6 cups chicken broth	hens
1 cup chopped onions	1 tablespoon salt
1 cup chopped mushrooms	1 teaspoon paprika
⅜ pound (1½ sticks)	1 cup sliced onions
butter	1 cup sliced carrots
¾ teaspoon freshly	½ cup warm cognac
ground black pepper	2 cups cooked or canned
1 teaspoon Worcestershire	peas
sauce	

Wash the wild rice under cold running water very well. Combine in a saucepan with 4 cups of the chicken broth; bring to a boil and cook over low heat 25 minutes, or until tender but still firm. Drain if any liquid remains. Sauté the chopped onions and the mushrooms in 6 tablespoons butter for 10 minutes. Add to the rice with ¼ teaspoon of the pepper and the Worcestershire sauce. Toss lightly and taste for seasoning.

Season the birds with the salt, paprika, and the remaining pepper; stuff with the wild rice mixture. Close the openings with skewers or foil.

Melt the remaining butter in a casserole; sauté the sliced

onions and carrots for 10 minutes. Add the birds and brown on all sides. Stir in remaining broth. Cover and roast in a 350° oven 45 minutes or until tender. Remove from oven and place over direct heat. Pour the warmed cognac over the birds and set aflame. When flames die, add the peas.

Serves 6.

Peking Ja

(DUCK WITH VEGETABLES, PEKING STYLE)

5-pound duck, quartered	1 teaspoon powdered
1½ teaspoons salt	ginger
¼ teaspoon freshly	2 packages frozen spinach,
ground black pepper	thawed
½ cup chopped onions	¼ pound mushrooms,
1 cup chicken broth	sliced
¼ cup dry sherry	1 cup sliced water
3 tablespoons soy sauce	chestnuts
2 tablespoons honey	8 preserved kumquats

Wash and dry the duck; remove as much fat as possible and season with the salt and pepper. Place in a deep skillet or Dutch oven, skin side down. Sprinkle with the onions, and add a mixture of the broth, sherry, soy sauce, honey, and ginger. Bring to a boil, cover, and cook over medium heat 25 minutes. Skim off all the fat, turn duck skin side up, and roast in a 400° oven uncovered 20 minutes, or until duck is tender.

Return the pan to direct low heat and push the duck to one side. Add the spinach, mushrooms, and water chestnuts. Cook 10 minutes, stirring the vegetables once or twice. Add the kumquats. Cook 1 minute.

Serves 4.

Duck with Sauerkraut

...d duck, disjointed
...poons salt
...spoon freshly
...nd black pepper
...espoons butter
...p chopped apples
...p chopped onions

1 pound sauerkraut,
   drained
2 cups grated potatoes
1 teaspoon caraway seeds
¼ teaspoon marjoram
1 cup dry white wine

...d dry the duck pieces, removing as much fat as pos-
...n with 1½ teaspoons salt and ½ teaspoon pepper.
...duck in a skillet. Remove the duck and pour off the

...butter in the skillet; sauté the apples and onions
... Mix in the sauerkraut, potatoes, caraway seeds,
...and remaining salt and pepper. Arrange the duck
...ixture and add ½ cup wine. Roast in a 375° oven
...adding the remaining wine after 30 minutes.

Duck with Sweet Potatoes

...d duck, disjointed
...spoon vegetable oil
...ll white onions
...t, sliced
... garlic, minced
...oons salt
...poon freshly
...d black pepper

1 cup dry white wine
1½ cups chicken broth
½ pound mushrooms,
   sliced
3 cups peeled, cubed sweet
   potatoes

Braised Duck and Rice

5-pound duck, disjointed
2 teaspoons salt
¼ teaspoon freshly
   ground black pepper
3½ cups chicken broth
1 cup raw rice

8 small white onions,
   halved
2 carrots, sliced
1 cup cooked or canned
   green peas
2 tablespoons minced
   parsley

Wash and dry the duck pieces, removing as much fat as possible. Lightly rub a heated deep skillet or casserole with a piece
of duck fat, then brown the duck in it. Pour off the fat. Add the
salt, pepper, and ½ cup of the broth. Cover and cook over low
heat 35 minutes. Pour off the fat. Add the remaining broth;
bring to a boil. Add the rice, onions, and carrots. Cover and
bake in a 350° oven 25 minutes, or until the duck and rice are
tender. Add the peas and parsley; bake uncovered 5 minutes
longer. *Serves 4.*

Canard Braisé à la Limousine

(BRAISED DUCK WITH RED CABBAGE AND CHESTNUTS)

6 tablespoons butter
1 cup sliced onions
½ cup grated carrots
2 pounds red cabbage
3 apples, peeled and sliced
2 cloves garlic, minced
2 cups beef broth
2 cups dry red wine
⅛ teaspoon ground cloves

¼ teaspoon finely crushed
   bay leaf
⅛ teaspoon nutmeg
4 teaspoons salt
1 teaspoon freshly ground
   black pepper
1 duck, disjointed
1 pound chestnuts, peeled

Melt the butter in a Dutch oven or heavy casserole. Mix in the onions, carrots, and cabbage; cover and cook over low heat 15 minutes, stirring frequently. Add the apples, garlic, broth, wine, cloves, bay leaf, nutmeg, 2 teaspoons salt, and ½ teaspoon pepper. Mix well, bring to a boil and bake in a 325° oven 2½ hours.

While the cabbage is cooking, wash and dry the duck pieces. Rub with the remaining salt and pepper. Heat a skillet and brown the duck in it on all sides over medium heat. Drain the duck pieces well. Add to the cabbage with the chestnuts. Recover and bake 1¼ hours longer.

Serves 4.

Caneton à la Campagne

(DUCK, FRENCH COUNTRY STYLE)

5-pound duck, disjointed	1 carrot, sliced
2 teaspoons salt	1 clove garlic, minced
½ teaspoon freshly ground black pepper	1½ cups dry white wine
1 tablespoon butter	1 cup chicken broth
4 slices cooked ham, cut julienne	2 cups shelled peas
6 small white onions	½ pound green beans, cut
2 leeks, sliced	½ pound mushrooms, sliced
	1½ cups cubed potatoes

Wash and dry the duck pieces. Rub with the salt and pepper. Melt the butter in a Dutch oven or casserole. Brown the duck in it on all sides. Pour off the fat. Add the ham, onions, leeks, carrot, and garlic; cook 5 minutes. Add the wine and broth. Cover and cook over low heat 40 minutes. Skim the fat, then add the peas, beans, mushrooms, and potatoes. Cook 25 minutes longer. Taste for seasoning.

Serves 4.

Bhae-Tha-Woon Bai

(SPICED DUCK, BURMESE ST

1½ cups raw rice	2 te
5-pound duck, disjointed	gi
3 tablespoons soy sauce	¾ t
2 teaspoons salt	ch
1 teaspoon saffron	2 b
2 tablespoons oil	4 cu
2 cups finely chopped onions	4 o
3 tablespoons minced garlic	

Wash the rice, cover with boiling w
preparing the duck. Wash and dry the
as possible. Rub with a mixture of the
fron; let stand ½ hour.

Heat the oil in a deep skillet, sauté
garlic 10 minutes. Add the ginger, chi
duck. Cook 15 minutes, turning the
the fat and add 1 cup of the water.
heat 45 minutes, basting occasionally
to the duck with the remaining water
over the top; cover and cook 15 minu
and duck are tender. Discard the

Serves 4–5.

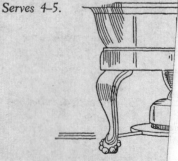

Wash a
sible. Seas
Brown the
fat.

Melt th
10 minute
marjoram,
over the m
1¼ hours,

Serves 4

5-pou
3 tea
¾ cu gro
3 tab
¾ cu
¾ cu

5-poun
1 tabl
12 sm
1 carr
1 clov
2 teas
½ tea grou

Wash and dry the duck pieces. Heat the oil in a Dutch oven or casserole; brown the duck in it on all sides. Pour off the fat. Add the onions, carrot, garlic, salt, and pepper; cook 10 minutes. Pour off the fat again. Add the wine and broth. Cover and cook over low heat 35 minutes. Skim the fat, then add the mushrooms and potatoes. Cook 25 minutes longer or until duck and potatoes are tender. Taste for seasoning.

Serves 4.

Caneton Nantais

(ROAST DUCK WITH PEAS AND ONIONS, FRENCH STYLE)

5-pound duck	1 tablespoon butter
2 teaspoons salt	2 pounds green peas,
½ teaspoon freshly	shelled, or 2 packages
ground black pepper	frozen, thawed
2 tablespoons diced lean	4 small potatoes, peeled
bacon	¼ teaspoon thyme
12 small white onions	½ cup chicken broth

Rub the duck with the salt and pepper. Place on a rack in a roasting pan. Roast in a 375° oven 1½ hours, draining the fat frequently.

Lightly brown the bacon; pour off the fat and add the onions and butter; sauté the onions until golden, shaking the pan frequently.

To the duck add the peas, onions, potatoes, thyme, and broth; roast 1 hour longer or until duck is tender, basting occasionally.

Serves 4.

Risotto con Anitra

(DUCK WITH RICE, ITALIAN STYLE)

2 tablespoons butter
5-pound duck, disjointed
2½ cups chopped
  tomatoes
½ cup dry red wine
2 teaspoons salt
½ teaspoon pepper

½ teaspoon basil
⅛ teaspoon marjoram
2 tablespoons chopped
  parsley
1¼ cups raw rice
2½ cups hot chicken
  broth

Melt the butter in a skillet. Add the duck pieces and brown lightly. Pour off the fat. Mix in the tomatoes. Cook over low heat 15 minutes. Add the wine, salt, pepper, basil, marjoram, and parsley. Cover and cook over low heat 1 hour. Add the rice and broth; cook 20 minutes longer, or until duck and rice are tender. Taste for seasoning.

Serves 4.

Pato al Jerez

(DUCK IN SHERRY, SPANISH STYLE)

5-pound duck, disjointed
1½ teaspoons salt
½ teaspoon freshly
  ground black pepper
2 tablespoons vegetable oil
¾ cup chopped onions
1 cup chopped green
  pepper
1 clove garlic, minced
½ cup canned tomato
  sauce

1 cup dry sherry
1 bay leaf
2 cups cooked or canned
  green peas
½ pound mushrooms,
  sliced and sautéed
½ cup sliced pimiento-
  stuffed olives

Wash and dry the duck pieces. Rub the pieces with the salt and pepper.

Heat the oil in a Dutch oven or deep skillet; brown the duck pieces in it. Remove the duck. Pour off half the fat. In the fat remaining, sauté the onions, green pepper, and garlic 10 minutes. Drain the fat, return the duck, and add the tomato sauce, sherry, and bay leaf. Cover and bake in a 350° oven 1 hour, or until duck is tender. Skim the fat, discard the bay leaf, and add the peas, mushrooms, and olives. Bake 5 minutes longer.

Serves 4.

Braised Duck in Bread Sauce

5-pound duck, disjointed	2 teaspoons salt
1 cup thinly sliced onions	½ teaspoon freshly
2 cups boiling water	ground black pepper
1 cup sliced carrots	4 potatoes, peeled and
½ cup sliced celery	halved
2 green peppers, cut	½ cup fresh bread crumbs
julienne	3 hard-cooked eggs,
2 cloves garlic, minced	sliced

Brown the duck pieces in a Dutch oven or saucepan; pour off the fat. Add the onions and brown lightly. Add the water, carrots, celery, green peppers, garlic, salt, and pepper. Bring to a boil, cover, and cook over low heat for 35 minutes. Add the potatoes, recover, and cook for 25 minutes. Mix in the bread crumbs; cook 5 minutes longer. Arrange eggs on top.

Serves 4.

Chicken Liver Ragout

1½ pounds chicken livers
4 tablespoons butter
1¼ teaspoons salt
¼ teaspoon freshly
    ground black pepper
¼ cup chopped parsley
¼ pound mushrooms,
    sliced and sautéed

1 cup cooked or canned
    green peas
1½ cups cooked egg
    barley
¼ cup dry sherry

Wash the livers, removing any discolored areas. Melt the butter in a skillet; sauté the livers 5 minutes or to desired degree of rareness. Season with the salt and pepper, then add the parsley, mushrooms, peas, egg barley, and sherry. Cook 3 minutes.

Serves 4–6.

Soup-Stews

SOUTHERN SPAIN can become oppressively hot during the summer months. Knowing this, I planned a trip through Andalusia during the month of May, so as to avoid the heat; but the hot weather came very early that year. My husband was driving our small car from Algeciras east toward Torremolinos, the road running attractively along the Mediterranean. The usually refreshing sea breezes were insufficient to cool the car, and, consulting our road map, we decided to head northward into the mountains toward Ronda, a fascinating old town built along the edge of a ravine. We bumped along a mediocre mountain road for two hours, always climbing toward the mountains, but it was much cooler than along the coast. Ronda's old-fashioned hotel was full of atmosphere, the rooms right out of another century, and when the sun set, it actually became chilly. Our languid appetites were stimulated, and we headed for the dining room with considerable anticipation. The waiters were courtly, and the dining room spoke of a long-past elegance. All in all, it was like Spain as it must have been a century or more ago. We ordered *olla podrida*, the classic dish of Spain which so much resembles a boiled dinner in New England, except that it's much better. We didn't order anything as an appetizer, and we couldn't eat a thing afterward—it was the perfect meal-in-one-dish.

Olla Podrida

(BOILED DINNER, SPANISH STYLE)

4 quarts water
4-pound fowl, disjointed
2 pounds short ribs of beef
1 pound fatty pork, cut
 into strips
6 whole carrots, peeled
2 teaspoons salt
½ teaspoon freshly
 ground black pepper
6 cloves garlic, minced
4 sliced and browned
 sausages

6 whole onions, peeled
6 tomatoes
1 2-pound yellow squash,
 peeled and sliced
1 green pepper, thinly
 sliced
6 potatoes, peeled
6 leeks
1 can chick-peas, drained
1 cabbage, cut in eighths
2 tablespoons chopped
 parsley

Bring the water to a boil. Add the chicken, beef, and pork. Cover and cook over medium heat 1½ hours. Add the carrots and cook 30 minutes. Add the salt, pepper, garlic, sausages, onions, tomatoes, squash, green pepper, potatoes, leeks, chick-peas, cabbage, and parsley. Cook 30 minutes longer. Skim the fat and taste for seasoning. Serve the soup in deep plates with the meat and vegetables arranged on a platter at the same time.

Serves 8–10

Cocido

(SPANISH NATIONAL SOUP-STEW)

1½ cups dried chick-peas
    or 2 cans, drained
1 4-pound fowl, quartered
2 pounds short ribs of beef
1 pound smoked ham
5 quarts water
1 pound kale or spinach,
    washed
2 leeks
2 carrots, sliced

1 tomato, diced
1 tablespoon salt
2 chorizos (Spanish
    sausages)
2 tablespoons olive oil
1 cup chopped onions
2 cups raw rice
2 teaspoons Spanish
    paprika
2 teaspoons tomato paste

If dried chick-peas are used, wash them, cover with water, and bring to a boil; cook 2 minutes, remove from the heat, and let soak 1 hour. Drain.

Combine the dried chick-peas (if canned chick-peas are used, add with the sausages) chicken, beef, ham, and water in a deep, large pan. Bring to a boil, skim the top, and cook over low heat 1½ hours. Tie the kale or spinach and leeks with white thread. Add to the pot with the carrots, tomato, and salt. Cook 30 minutes, then add the sausages. Cook 30 minutes longer. Transfer the meats to a heated platter, cover, and keep hot. Strain the broth, reserving all the vegetables and chick-peas; put on the platter with the meat.

Heat the oil in a saucepan; sauté the onions 5 minutes. Mix in the rice until translucent. Add the paprika, tomato paste, and 4 cups of the broth; cover and cook over low heat 20 minutes or until rice is tender and dry.

To serve the *cocido*, pour the remaining hot broth into a tureen. Arrange the meats on a platter surrounded with portions of chick-peas and kale. Heap the rice in a deep serving dish. The soup is eaten first, then the meats and rice. *Serves 6–10.*

Poulet Henri IV

(CHICKEN IN THE POT, FRENCH STYLE)

2 pounds stewing beef, cut
into 2-inch cubes
Marrow bones
4-pound fowl
2½ quarts water
1½ cups sliced carrots
1 cup sliced leeks, white
part only
1 cup sliced celery
6 small white onions

3 sprigs parsley
½ teaspoon thyme
2 cloves
1 bay leaf
2½ teaspoons salt
½ teaspoon white pepper
Toasted French bread
slices
Grated Gruyère or Swiss
cheese

Pour boiling water over the beef; let stand 5 minutes; then drain. Wash the bones and wrap in cheesecloth to keep the marrow in. Combine the meat, bones, chicken, and water in a large kettle. Bring to a boil and skim the top. Add the vegetables, herbs, and seasoning. Cover and cook over low heat 3 hours. Remove the meat, chicken, and vegetables. Cut up the chicken into serving-sized pieces. Strain the broth into the pot or a tureen. Return the meat, chicken, and vegetables. Remove the marrow from the bones and add to the pot. Serve very hot, in deep plates, with the toasted bread and grated cheese.

Serves 6–8.

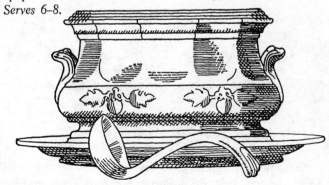

Waterzooï de Poulet

(BELGIAN CHICKEN IN THE POT)

3 whole chicken breasts	4 sprigs parsley
2 veal knuckles	1 tablespoon salt
7 cups water	½ teaspoon white pepper
1 cup sliced celery	3 slices lemon
1 parsnip	2 egg yolks
2 carrots	1 cup light cream

Cut the breasts in half through the breastbone; wash and dry. Combine the veal knuckles, water, celery, parsnip, carrots, parsley, salt, pepper, and lemon in a saucepan. Bring to a boil; cover and cook over low heat 2 hours. Strain into an attractive pot or casserole. Add the chicken; bring to a boil and cook over low heat 25 minutes, or until the chicken is tender.

Beat the egg yolks and cream in a bowl. Gradually add a little of the hot stock, stirring steadily to prevent curdling. Return to balance of soup. Heat, stirring until thickened, but do not let boil. Serve with French bread. *Serves 4–8.*

New England Boiled Dinner

4 pounds corned brisket of beef	8 small potatoes, peeled
	8 small white onions
1 yellow onion, peeled	8 small carrots, scraped
1 clove garlic, sliced	3-pound head cabbage cut
1 bay leaf	into 8 wedges
4 peppercorns	

Wash the corned beef, cover with water, and bring to a boil. Skim the top. Add the yellow onion, garlic, bay leaf, and

108

peppercorns. Cover and cook over low heat 3 hours, or until the meat is tender. Transfer the meat to a heated platter and keep warm.

Cook the potatoes, whole onions, carrots, and cabbage in the corned beef liquid 30 minutes. Drain and arrange around the beef.

Serves 8.

Rinderbrust

(BOILED BEEF, GERMAN STYLE)

3 pounds brisket of beef	4 parsnips, cut in quarters
2 quarts water	1 turnip, sliced
Beef bone	12 small white onions
4 peppercorns	1 tablespoon salt
½ teaspoon thyme	1 bay leaf
4 carrots, cut in quarters	4 sprigs parsley

Rinse and dry the meat. Bring the water to a boil; add the meat, bone, peppercorns, and thyme. Bring to a boil again, cover, and cook over low heat 1½ hours. Add the carrots, parsnips, turnip, onions, salt, bay leaf, and parsley. Recover and cook 1 hour longer or until meat is tender. Slice the meat, and serve in deep plates with the broth and vegetables.

Serves 6–8.

IRELAND is one of the most peaceful, pleasant, and soothing countries in Europe. Life seems to flow by in a freshet of charmingly enunciated words and good food, the entire mixture bound together with the very gentle rain that seems to fall every other day. All of which makes Ireland a very green country, with many excellent conversationalists.

Driving across Ireland should be compulsory for tourists. To visit Dublin only, and not see the countryside is a sad state of affairs indeed. (Almost said Begorrah!) The roads are almost deserted, and except for the local traffic near a town, the mood is sheer pleasure. My husband and I were driving dreamily northwest from Limerick one lovely July day. Without warning, it began to rain gently, just barely enough to require the use of the windshield wipers. At the small town of Ennis, we decided to stop for the night, since it was about four o'clock in the afternoon. The Old Ground Hotel looked like a real Irish inn, and it was. That evening in the dining room, my husband tried to order an Irish Lamb Stew for his third unsuccessful try, and finally settled for Irish Boiled Beef, which he enjoyed immensely.

Irish Boiled Beef

3 pounds brisket of beef	12 small white onions
½ cup barley	6 carrots, sliced
2½ teaspoons salt	3 turnips, cubed
½ teaspoon freshly	6 potatoes, peeled and
ground black pepper	halved

Put the beef in a Dutch oven. Add the barley and boiling water to cover the beef. Bring to a boil. Cover loosely, and cook over low heat 1¾ hours. Add the salt, pepper, and vegetables; cook 1 hour longer, or until the meat and vegetables are tender. Serves 6.

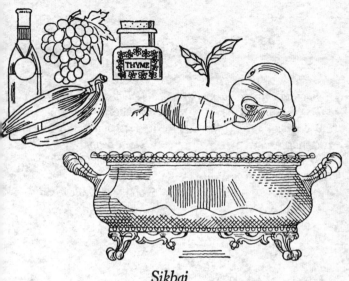

Sikbaj

(MEAT-FRUIT STEW, PERSIAN STYLE)

2 tablespoons vegetable oil
3 pounds eye round or
   cross rib of beef, cut
   into 1½-inch cubes
2½ cups boiling water
¾ teaspoon crushed
   coriander
1 teaspoon cinnamon
1½ cups sliced onions
1 cup sliced carrots

12 green onions, quartered
   lengthwise
2 teaspoons salt
½ teaspoon freshly
   ground black pepper
¼ cup wine vinegar
½ cup honey
1 cup sliced almonds
1 17-ounce can figs,
   drained

Heat the oil in a Dutch oven or heavy casserole; lightly brown the meat in it. Add half the water, the coriander, cinnamon, sliced onions, carrots, and green onions. Cook over low heat 1½ hours. Mix in the salt, pepper, vinegar, honey, and remaining water. Cook 45 minutes. Add the almonds and figs. Cover the pan, remove from the heat, and let stand 1 hour. Reheat just before serving. *Serves 6–8.*

Bollito Misto

(BOILED MIXED MEATS)

4-pound smoked tongue
2 whole onions
2 carrots
2 stalks celery
4 sprigs parsley
2 pounds eye round of
   beef
4-pound fowl

8 Italian-style pork
   sausages
½ teaspoon freshly ground
   black pepper
3-pound head of cabbage,
   cut in eights
6 potatoes, peeled and
   halved

Cover the tongue with water in a very large kettle, bring to a boil, and drain. Add fresh boiling water to cover, and add the onions, carrots, celery, and parsley. Bring to a boil and cook over low heat 1 hour. Skim the top. Add the beef; cook 1 hour. Skim the top. Add the chicken, sausages, and pepper. Cook 45 minutes. Add the cabbage and potatoes; cook 30 minutes longer. Slice the meats and chicken and arrange on a serving dish with the vegetables and serve a mustard or vinaigrette sauce. Serve the strained broth in deep plates at the same time.

Serves 8–10.

Polévka s Knedlíčky

(BEEF SOUP-STEW WITH LIVER DUMPLINGS)

3 pounds short ribs of beef
1 pound onions, peeled
and sliced
4 stalks celery and leaves,
sliced
2 quarts water
2 tomatoes, peeled and
chopped
3 carrots, sliced

½ cup minced parsley
4 teaspoons salt
¾ teaspoon freshly
ground black pepper
½ pound calf's liver
2 eggs, beaten
3 tablespoons flour
Dash nutmeg
¾ cup fresh bread crumbs

Wash the meat and combine in a large kettle with the onions, celery, and water. Bring to a boil and skim the top. Cook over low heat 1½ hours. Add the tomatoes, carrots, ¼ cup parsley, 3½ teaspoons salt, and ½ teaspoon pepper. Cover loosely and cook 1 hour. Prepare the liver dumplings meanwhile.

Grind or chop the liver very fine. Mix in the eggs, flour, nutmeg, and remaining salt, pepper, and parsley. Add just enough of the bread crumbs to make a stiff batter. Chill 1 hour. If mixture isn't firm enough to shape at this point, add a little more bread crumbs. Shape into walnut-sized balls.

Cut the short ribs into bite-sized pieces, discarding the bones. Return the meat to the soup, add dumplings, cover, and cook over medium heat 20 minutes. Serve in bowls. *Serves 4–6.*

In many respects, Buenos Aires, Argentina, has the mood and superficial appearance of Paris. There are old buildings full of character, imposing boulevards, and many small parks. The atmosphere of B.A. (as everyone calls it) is almost Gallic, and there are smart shops, fine hotels, and thousands of restaurants.

The country is famous for its fine beef, and almost every restaurant features enormous steaks, actually too big for any one person, at very reasonable prices. Delicious as a steak may be, it can soon grow tiresome as a daily item, and even my husband asked if we couldn't have something different. One day, we flew to Mendoza, a good-sized city in the western part of the country; it is here that many of the country's best wines are produced.

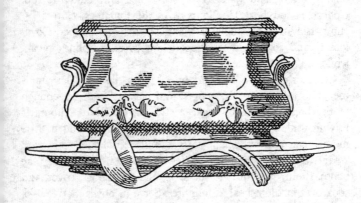

At the airport, we were met by some local residents of Mendoza, friends of friends of ours, who hospitably offered to show us around. We didn't wish to stay at their house, which we felt would be an imposition, but would be delighted to sight-see with them the following day. Early the next morning, we received a telephone call from our hosts, and were told to dress "country-style." An hour later, they picked us up and we drove through absolutely magnificent countryside, almost completely unspoiled, to their "ranch." The "ranch" turned out to be a large, rather elaborate country estate, but there were several hundred head of cattle, and many Argentine-style cowboys, here called *gauchos*. We wandered about the grounds and were fascinated by what we saw, and then came the big surprise. The cowboys prepared lunch for us, and we all sat down at a very long table, our hosts, ourselves, and the cowboys, under the shade of a tree that must have been well over a hundred feet in height. One of the two cooks brought to the table what may only be described as a cauldron, an immense pot, filled with a steaming mixture. We were served by our hostess, who, with a giant ladle, dished out tremendous portions of the Argentine national stew, *carbonada Criollo*, into triple-size soup plates. There was a bottle of dry red Argentine wine before every two persons, lots of crusty bread, and nothing else. And who needed anything else? Later, there was singing, and then some impromptu folk dancing.

By now it was five o'clock, the sun was low on the horizon, and we began to think of heading back to Mendoza. It was three and a half hours since we originally had sat down, and frankly, I was tired of sitting. To be brief, our host told us, it was now time to have tea; apparently lunchtime and teatime had run together into one continuous session, some four and a half hours long. There was a selection of pastries worthy of Vienna, plus strong, dark tea. Most of the gauchos, however, preferred to drink *maté*, a drink which resembles tea but has a more astringent taste. Much, much later we finally reached our hotel in Mendoza, went to our room, and promptly dozed off. No, we did not eat dinner that night.

Carbonada Criollo

(MEAT AND FRUIT STEW, ARGENTINA STYLE)

3 pounds chuck or rump
    of beef
2 tablespoons olive oil
4 tablespoons butter
1½ cups diced onions
1½ cups dry white wine
1 tablespoon tomato paste
1 bay leaf
2 teaspoons salt
½ teaspoon freshly
    ground black pepper

½ teaspoon thyme
1 cup beef broth
3 cups peeled, cubed
    sweet potatoes
3 pears, peeled and cubed
3 peaches or apples, peeled
    and sliced
3 tablespoons currants or
    seedless raisins
½ cup diced bananas

Cut the meat into 1-inch cubes. Heat the oil and butter in a Dutch oven or heavy casserole; brown the beef in it. Remove the meat. Brown the onions in the fat remaining in the pan. Stir in the wine, tomato paste, bay leaf, salt, pepper, thyme, and broth; return the meat. Bring to a boil, cover, and cook over low heat 1 hour. Add the sweet potatoes; recover and cook 30 minutes. Carefully mix in the pears, peaches or apples, and raisins. Cook uncovered 10 minutes longer. Taste for seasoning and sprinkle with the bananas.

Serves 6–8.

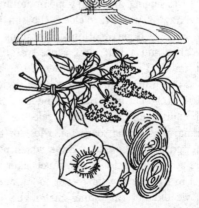

Beef

LATE ONE AUTUMN, I was visiting the Moselle Valley, which winds attractively through western Germany. From here come many of the country's finest wines, and the life, work, and conversation of the people is bound up with the production of grapes and the making of the light, flowery wines that have made Germany famous. All of my thoughts were of the dedication required for people to work all year long, so that ultimately the world could have the pleasure of holding a glass filled with the precious amber-yellow fluid and breathing in its delicate aroma.

The very air seemed filled with the perfume of wine. We stopped for lunch at a tiny inn on the banks of the Moselle River in the village of Trabach; it might have been a scene preserved intact from medieval times. The inn itself was a wooden building, fancifully decorated with scrolls and carvings, obviously many centuries old. Inside, the decor matched the old-world atmosphere of the village. There was no menu, and the cheerful waiter, gnarled and flatfooted, acted as if we were members of his family, commenting on each dish as it was served. First, we were given thick slices of dark bread and rich, dark yellow butter. Then came a plate of herring with onions, salty and appetizing. This was followed by a large casserole containing sliced meat in a dark brown sauce. As the waiter lifted the cover, a heavy cloud of white steam arose. We were served with enormous portions of the meat, which proved to be beef. But the sauce, delicious and tantalizing, seemed difficult to analyze. In this wine region, wouldn't the chef naturally cook with wine? But it wasn't wine; in fact, to me it tasted like beer. Had the herring played havoc with my taste buds? Finally, I asked the waiter. It was made with *bier*, he told us. No, absolutely no *wein* in the *rindfleisch gedämpft in bier*, he assured us. Why did they cook in beer in the heart of the Moselle Valley, famous the world over for its wine? The chef, he told us, came from Munich where he had trained as an apprentice cook, and although now settled in the wine regions, still loved to prepare the old dishes of his beloved city to the south, where beer is the favorite.

Rindfleisch Gedämpft in Bier

(BRAISED BEEF IN BEER, GERMAN STYLE)

1 slice salt pork, minced
2 cups sliced onions
1 cup sliced celery
2 cups sliced carrots
1 pound mushrooms, sliced
3 pounds eye round or rump of beef

2 teaspoons salt
½ teaspoon freshly ground black pepper
1 teaspoon grated lemon rind
2 cups beer
1 tablespoon flour
2 tablespoons water

Spread the salt pork on the bottom of a Dutch oven or heavy saucepan. Spread the onions, celery, carrots, and mushrooms over it. Add the meat; sprinkle with the salt, pepper, and lemon rind. Cover and cook over low heat 30 minutes, turning the meat several times. Add the beer; recover and cook 2½ hours longer. Skim the fat from the gravy. Mix the flour with the water and stir into the gravy until thickened, then cook 5 minutes longer. Taste for seasoning. Slice the meat and serve with the gravy.
Serves 6–8.

Pot Roast with Prunes and Sweet Potatoes

1 pound prunes
2 cups water
1¼ cups chopped onions
3 pounds brisket, chuck, or rump of beef
2 tablespoons butter
1½ teaspoons salt

1 bay leaf
2 tablespoons lemon juice
3 tablespoons brown sugar
1 teaspoon cinnamon
¾ cup orange juice
8 small sweet potatoes, peeled

Wash the prunes and soak in the water for 1 hour. Drain; reserve water.

Brown the onions and meat in the butter. Add the salt, bay leaf, lemon juice, sugar, cinnamon, and the prune water. Cover and cook over low heat 2 hours. Add the prunes, orange juice, and sweet potatoes; cook 45 minutes longer, or until the meat is tender. Discard bay leaf.

Serves 8.

Boeuf à la Mode

(MARINATED POT ROAST, FRENCH STYLE)

4 pounds cross rib, brisket, or eye round of beef, larded	1 bottle dry red wine
	¼ cup cognac
	¼ cup olive oil
2½ teaspoons salt	2 tablespoons vegetable oil
½ teaspoon freshly ground black pepper	
1 cup thinly sliced onions	1½ cups beef broth
1 cup sliced carrots	1 veal knuckle, cracked
2 cloves garlic, sliced	16 small white onions
2 teaspoons thyme	4 carrots, quartered
¼ cup minced parsley	1 tablespoon cornstarch
2 bay leaves	2 tablespoons port wine

Rub the meat with the salt and pepper. Spread half the sliced onions, carrots, garlic, thyme, parsley, and bay leaves in a large bowl. Put the meat in the bowl and cover with the remaining vegetables and herbs. Mix together the wine, cognac, and olive oil; pour over the meat. Cover and marinate in the refrigerator 24 hours, or 4 hours at room temperature. Turn and baste meat frequently. Drain the meat thoroughly, and dry with paper towels. Heat the marinade.

Heat the vegetable oil in a Dutch oven or heavy casserole; brown the meat on all sides. Pour off the fat. Add the heated marinade. Cook over high heat until reduced to half. Add the broth and knuckle. Bring to a boil, skim the top, cover, and bake in a 325° oven 3 hours, turning the meat several times. Add the white onions and carrots; recover and bake 30 minutes longer. Discard veal knuckle and bay leaves. Mix the cornstarch and port until smooth; stir into the gravy until thickened. Serve in a sauceboat. *Serves 8.*

Pot Roast, Virgin Islands Style

2 cloves garlic, minced
2 teaspoons salt
1 teaspoon freshly ground black pepper
½ teaspoon thyme
½ teaspoon mace
½ teaspoon nutmeg
4 pounds top round of beef, cut 1½ inches thick
2 cups sliced onions
2 tomatoes, peeled and chopped
2 tablespoons chopped parsley
¼ cup cider vinegar
2 tablespoons butter
1 cup boiling water
3 cups cooked dried white beans
3 green peppers, cut in strips

Mix together the garlic, salt, pepper, thyme, mace, and nutmeg. Rub into the meat. Put the meat in a bowl; add the onions, tomatoes, parsley, and vinegar. Mix well, cover, and marinate 2 hours. Remove meat, reserving marinade. Melt the butter in a saucepan and brown the meat over high heat. Add half the boiling water and reserved marinade, cover, and cook over low heat 45 minutes. Add the beans, peppers, and remaining boiling water; cook 30 minutes longer.
Serves 8–10.

Gewürztes Rindfleisch

(SPICED POT ROAST, GERMAN STYLE)

1 cup fine barley

3 pounds eye round or
rump of beef

2 teaspoons salt

½ teaspoon freshly
ground black pepper

2 tablespoons vegetable
oil

1 cup thinly sliced onions

3 tablespoons gingersnap
crumbs

⅛ teaspoon ground cloves

¼ teaspoon marjoram

1 bay leaf

2½ cups boiling water

1 cup sour cream

Wash the barley, cover with boiling water, and let stand while
preparing the meat. Rub the meat with the salt and pepper.
Heat the oil in a Dutch oven or heavy saucepan; brown the meat
in it on all sides. Pour off the fat. Add the onions; cook 5 minutes. Add the gingersnap crumbs, cloves, marjoram, bay leaf, and
1 cup of the boiling water. Cover and cook over low heat 1¼
hours. Add the drained barley and remaining boiling water. Recover and cook 1 hour longer, or until barley and meat are
tender. (Add boiling water from time to time if necessary.) Add
the sour cream, mixing steadily. Strain the gravy and skim the
fat. Taste for seasoning, heat, and serve.

Serves 6–8.

STOCKHOLM is a rather formal city, handsome and attractive, but somewhat austere. The old part of the town is built upon a series of islands, all connected by bridges. There are many atmospheric restaurants, some candlelit, others with gentle background music, featuring Swedish cuisine. One evening, in a basement restaurant with less than ten tables, lit only by flickering candles, my husband and I enjoyed a superb Swedish-style pot roast (*slöttstek*), made with onions, anchovies and cream—unusual and distinctively flavored.

Slöttstek

(POT ROAST, SWEDISH STYLE)

1 tablespoon salt	2 tablespoons vinegar
1 teaspoon freshly ground pepper	1 tablespoon sugar
4 pounds round steak	6 potatoes, peeled and quartered
2 tablespoons butter	1 package frozen green peas, thawed
2 cups beef broth	½ cup heavy cream
1 cup chopped onions	2 tablespoons cognac
4 anchovies, minced	
2 bay leaves	

Rub the salt and pepper into the meat. Melt the butter in a Dutch oven; brown the meat in it. Remove the meat. Stir the broth into the pan and bring to a boil. Mix in the onions, anchovies, bay leaves, vinegar, and sugar; return the meat. Cover and cook over low heat 2 hours. Add the potatoes and peas; cook 20 minutes. Stir the cream and cognac into the gravy. Taste for seasoning. *Serves 8.*

123

Boeuf à la Flamande
(BEEFSTEAK, FLEMISH STYLE)

4 pounds eye round of beef
4 tablespoons butter
2 pounds onions, sliced
2 tablespoons flour
2½ cups beer
2 tablespoons vinegar
1 teaspoon sugar
2 teaspoons salt
½ teaspoon freshly ground black pepper
½ teaspoon thyme
2 bay leaves
3 tablespoons chopped parsley
4 potatoes, peeled and halved
2 cups sliced carrots

Cut the meat into slices 1 inch thick. Melt the butter in a Dutch oven or saucepan; sauté the onions until browned, stirring frequently. Remove onions. Add the beef to the fat remaining in the pan and brown on all sides. Remove. Mix the flour into pan juices until smooth and browned. Gradually add the beer, stirring steadily to the boiling point. Replace onions and beef. Stir in the vinegar, sugar, salt, pepper, thyme, bay leaves, and parsley. Cover and cook over low heat 1½ hours. Add the potatoes and carrots; cook 30 minutes longer, or until the meat is tender. *Serves 8.*

Beef in Sesame Seed Sauce

2 pounds fillet of beef
½ cup sesame seeds
2 cups finely chopped green onions
½ cup soy sauce
2 tablespoons sugar
1 clove garlic, minced
¼ cup sesame seed or vegetable oil
12 small canned white onions
1 16-ounce can green peas, drained

Cut the beef into 1-inch cubes. Brown the sesame seeds in a skillet. Mix together the sesame seeds, green onions, soy sauce, sugar, garlic, and half the oil. Marinate the beef in the mixture for 1 hour at room temperature. Remove the meat, reserving the sauce.

Heat the remaining oil in a deep skillet; brown the meat in it over high heat. Add the marinade, white onions, and peas. Bring to a boil and cook over medium heat 10 minutes.

Serves 4–6.

Manzo al Vino Bianco

(BEEF IN WHITE WINE, ITALIAN STYLE)

2½ teaspoons salt	¼ cup wine vinegar
½ teaspoon freshly ground black pepper	1½ pounds tomatoes, peeled and chopped
1 clove garlic, minced	2 bay leaves
4 pounds chuck or rump of beef	¼ teaspoon sugar
3 tablespoons butter	3½ cups dry white wine
1 cup thinly sliced onions	1½ cups raw rice
½ cup sliced carrots	¼ cup heavy cream

Mix together the salt, pepper, and garlic; rub into the meat. Melt the butter in a Dutch oven or heavy saucepan; add the meat, onions, and carrots. Cook over medium heat until meat browns on all sides. Add the vinegar, tomatoes, bay leaves, sugar, and half the wine. Cover and cook over low heat 2½ hours. Add the rice and remaining wine. Recover and cook 30 minutes longer. Taste for seasoning. Using a fork, stir in the cream.

Serves 6–8.

Beef in Lemon Sauce

1 cup fine egg noodles	½ teaspoon freshly
4 tablespoons butter	ground black pepper
¾ cup chopped onions	¼ teaspoon nutmeg
1½ pounds ground beef	¾ cup water
1 pound mushrooms,	2 egg yolks
sliced	3 tablespoons lemon juice
1¾ teaspoons salt	2 tablespoons dry sherry

Cover the noodles with boiling water and let stand 20 minutes. Drain.

Melt the butter in a skillet; sauté the onions 5 minutes. Add the beef, mushrooms, and noodles; cook over high heat 5 minutes, stirring almost constantly. Mix in the salt, pepper, nutmeg, and water; cook over low heat 10 minutes.

Beat the egg yolks, lemon juice, and sherry in a bowl. Add a little meat mixture, stirring steadily to prevent curdling. Return to skillet; heat, but do not let boil. *Serves 6–8.*

Beef in Horseradish Sauce

3 pounds chuck or rump	1 bay leaf
of beef, cut into 1½-	½ teaspoon thyme
inch cubes	3 cups potato balls or
¼ cup flour	cubes
2 teaspoons salt	1 package frozen green
¾ teaspoon freshly	peas, thawed
ground black pepper	3 tablespoons prepared
¼ cup vegetable oil	horseradish
¾ cup minced onions	1 cup sour cream
1½ cups tomato juice	

Toss the meat in a mixture of the flour, salt, and pepper. Heat the oil in a Dutch oven; brown the meat in it. Add the onions; cook 5 minutes. Add the tomato juice, bay leaf, and thyme. Bring to a boil, cover, and cook over low heat 2 hours. Add the potatoes and peas; cook 15 minutes. Stir in the horseradish and sour cream. Heat, but do not let boil. Discard the bay leaf.

Serves 6–8.

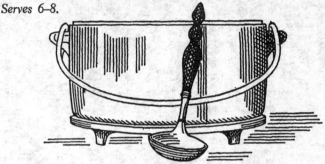

Beef and Rice in Sour Cream Sauce

¼ cup vegetable oil
3 pounds chuck or eye round of beef, cut into 1-inch cubes
2 teaspoons salt
½ teaspoon freshly ground black pepper
½ cup minced onions
1 cup tomato juice
1 bay leaf
½ teaspoon marjoram
1½ cups raw rice
2½ cups boiling beef broth
1 package frozen peas, thawed
1 tablespoon prepared horseradish
1 cup sour cream

Heat the oil in a casserole; brown the meat in it. Season with the salt and pepper. Stir in the onions until lightly browned. Add the tomato juice, bay leaf, and marjoram; cover and cook over low heat 1½ hours. Add the rice, broth, and peas; cook 20 minutes longer. Blend in the horseradish and sour cream. Reheat, but do not let boil.

Serves 6–8.

Carne en Salsa Negra

(SPANISH BEEF IN BLACK SAUCE)

3 pounds eye round or
  chuck of beef
¼ cup olive oil
1½ cups sliced onions
2½ teaspoons salt
¼ teaspoon freshly
  ground black pepper
¼ cup lemon juice

½ cup currants or seedless
  raisins
3 cups water
4 potatoes, peeled and
  sliced
4 carrots, quartered
½ cup sliced black olives
2 teaspoons capers

Cut the meat into serving sized pieces.

Heat the oil in a casserole; brown the meat and onions in it very well. Add the salt, pepper, lemon juice, currants, and water. Cover and cook over low heat 1½ hours. Add the potatoes, carrots, olives, and capers; cook 45 minutes longer. Taste for seasoning. *Serves 6–8.*

Sztufada

(POLISH BEEF AND NOODLES)

4 pounds short ribs of
  beef
2 strips bacon, diced
1½ cups chopped onions
1 teaspoon salt
2 tablespoons caraway
  seeds

⅓ cup wine vinegar
1 cup boiling water
1 package frozen
  cauliflower, thawed
3 cups cooked fine noodles

Cut the short ribs into serving-sized pieces. In a Dutch oven or casserole, cook the bacon until it begins to brown. Add the onions and short ribs; cook over medium heat 10 minutes, stirring frequently. Mix in the salt, caraway seeds, vinegar, and water. Cover and bake in a 350° oven 2 hours. Baste frequently, and add a little more boiling water if pan becomes dry. Skim the fat, and add the cauliflower and noodles; bake 10 minutes longer.

Serves 4–6.

Meat-Potato Layers

2 pounds potatoes
¼ pound (1 stick) butter
½ cup light cream
1 egg, beaten
¼ teaspoon nutmeg
3 teaspoons salt
1½ cups chopped onions
1½ pounds boneless beef,
   cut into ½-inch cubes

½ cup beef broth
½ teaspoon freshly
   ground black pepper
Dash of ground cloves
1 bay leaf
1 package frozen mixed
   vegetables, cooked and
   drained
¼ cup dry bread crumbs

Cook the unpeeled potatoes until tender. Drain, peel, and mash. Beat in 3 tablespoons of the butter, the cream, egg, nutmeg, and 1½ teaspoons salt until very light and fluffy. Taste for seasoning.

Melt 3 tablespoons butter in a skillet; sauté the onions 5 minutes. Add the meat; cook over high heat, stirring almost constantly, until browned. Mix in the broth, pepper, cloves, bay leaf, and remaining salt. Cook over low heat 20 minutes. Discard the bay leaf, stir in the mixed vegetables, and taste for seasoning.

In a greased 2-quart casserole, arrange as many layers as possible of the potatoes and meat mixture, starting and ending with the potatoes. Sprinkle with the bread crumbs and dot with the remaining butter. Bake in a 400° oven 25 minutes, or until browned.

Serves 6–8.

Beef and Egg Barley Casserole

¼ cup olive oil
1½ cups chopped onions
1 clove garlic, minced
1½ pounds ground beef
1 cup peeled chopped
   tomatoes
¾ cup beef broth
2½ teaspoons salt
¼ teaspoon freshly
   ground black pepper

¼ teaspoon thyme
1 cup sliced almonds
3 whole eggs
½ cup grated Parmesan
   cheese
1 package egg barley,
   cooked and drained
2 egg yolks
½ cup heavy cream

Heat the olive oil in a skillet; sauté the onions and garlic 10 minutes. Add beef; sauté 10 minutes, stirring almost constantly. Mix in the tomatoes, broth, 1½ teaspoons salt, the pepper, and thyme. Cook over medium heat 15 minutes. Stir in the almonds.

Beat the whole eggs; stir in the cheese and egg barley. Spread half the mixture in a buttered 2-quart casserole. Spread the meat mixture over it. Cover with the remaining egg-barley mixture. Beat together the egg yolks, cream, and remaining salt and pour over top. Bake in a 350° oven 25 minutes, or until custard is set and lightly browned.

Serves 6–8.

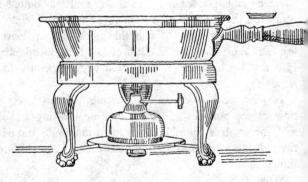

Beef with Rice in White Wine Sauce

3 pounds eye round or
  rump of beef
4 tablespoons butter
3 cups thinly sliced onions
1½ cups peeled diced
  tomatoes
1 cup sliced carrots
½ cup sliced celery

2 teaspoons salt
½ teaspoon freshly
  ground black pepper
½ teaspoon basil
1½ cups dry white wine
1½ cups raw rice
2 cups boiling beef broth

Rinse the meat and pat dry. Melt the butter in a Dutch oven or heavy saucepan; sauté the onions until soft and yellow. Add the meat and brown it on all sides. Mix in the tomatoes, carrots, celery, salt, pepper, basil, and wine. Bring to a boil, cover, and cook over low heat 1¾ hours. Add the rice and broth; cook 30 minutes longer. Slice the meat and serve with the rice and gravy.

Serves 6–8.

Peasant Casserole

4 tablespoons butter
2 pounds top sirloin of
  beef, cut into 1-inch
  cubes
1½ cups thinly sliced
  onions
1¼ teaspoons salt
½ teaspoon freshly
  ground black pepper

¼ teaspoon nutmeg
4 cups seasoned mashed
  potatoes
2 cups thinly sliced apples
2 tablespoons bread
  crumbs

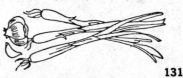

Melt 2 tablespoons of the butter in a skillet; brown the meat in it and remove. In the fat remaining, sauté the onions 10 minutes. Mix in the salt, pepper, and nutmeg.

In a greased 2-quart casserole, arrange as many layers as possible of the potatoes, meat mixture, and apples, sprinkling each layer with seasoned onions and starting and ending with the potatoes. Sprinkle with the bread crumbs and dot with the remaining butter. Bake in a 375° oven 25 minutes.

Serves 4–6.

Texas Chili Casserole

6 cups water
3½ teaspoons salt
2½ tablespoons chili
  powder
2 cups yellow corn meal
2 eggs
¼ cup vegetable oil
1½ pounds boneless beef,
  cut into ½-inch cubes

1½ cups thinly sliced
  onions
2 cloves garlic, minced
1 20-ounce can tomatoes,
  chopped
1 cup seedless raisins
1 cup sliced black olives
½ cup grated cheddar
  cheese

Bring the 6 cups water to a boil in a saucepan. Add half the salt and 2 teaspoons chili powder; gradually add the corn meal, stirring steadily until thickened, then cook over medium heat 15 minutes, stirring occasionally. Cool a few minutes, then beat in the eggs.

While the corn meal is cooking, heat the oil in a deep skillet; brown the meat in it. Add the onions; sauté 5 minutes. Mix in the garlic, tomatoes, raisins, olives, and the remaining salt and chili powder. Bring to a boil and cook over low heat 1 hour.

Spread one third of the corn-meal mixture on the bottom of a greased 2½-quart casserole. Slowly pour in the meat mixture, then spread the remaining corn meal over the meat. Bake in a 350° oven 1 hour. Sprinkle with the cheese and bake 15 minutes longer.

Serves 6–8.

Beef and Liver Ragoût

1½ cups fine egg noodles
2 pounds beef tenderloin,
    cut ½ inch thick
1 pound calf's liver, sliced
    ½ inch thick
¼ cup flour
2 teaspoons salt
½ teaspoon freshly
    ground black pepper

6 tablespoons butter
1½ cups thinly sliced
    onions
1 cup beef broth
½ cup dry red wine
1 package frozen green
    beans, half cooked and
    drained

Cover the noodles with boiling water and let stand while preparing the meat.

Cut the beef and liver into strips 1 inch wide and 2 inches long. Toss in mixture of the flour, salt, and pepper. Melt half the butter in a large skillet; sauté the onions until golden. Remove. Melt the remaining butter in the skillet; brown the meat and liver in it. Return the onions and add the broth and wine. Bring to a boil and cook over low heat 10 minutes. Add the drained noodles and beans; cook 5 minutes longer. Taste for seasoning.

Serves 6–8.

Gevetsch

(MEAT CASSEROLE, YUGOSLAVIAN STYLE)

3 tablespoons vegetable oil
1 pound boneless beef, cut into 1-inch cubes
½ pound boneless veal, cut into 1-inch cubes
1 pound boneless pork, cut into 1-inch cubes
½ cup raw rice
12 small white onions, peeled

1½ cups beef broth
2 cups peeled sliced potatoes
2 carrots, sliced
2 tomatoes, cut in eighths
1 green pepper, cut julienne
2 teaspoons salt
½ teaspoon freshly ground black pepper

Heat the oil in a casserole or Dutch oven; brown the meats in it. Remove. To the fat remaining, add the rice and onions; cook until golden, stirring frequently. Add the broth and bring to a boil. Return the meat with the potatoes, carrots, tomatoes, green pepper, salt, and pepper. Bake in a 350° oven 2 hours.
Serves 6–8.

Gulyás

(HUNGARIAN GOULASH)

6 tablespoons butter
2 pounds onions, chopped
3 pounds chuck or cross ribs of beef, cut into 2-inch cubes
2 tablespoons Hungarian-style paprika
2 teaspoons salt

½ teaspoon freshly ground black pepper
1 clove garlic, minced
1 8-ounce can tomato sauce
2 cups cooked egg barley
1 cup sour cream

Melt 4 tablespoons butter in a Dutch oven or heavy saucepan and sauté the onions 15 minutes, stirring frequently. Remove the onions and set aside. Melt remaining butter in the pan and brown the meat well on all sides; sprinkle with the paprika, salt, and pepper. Return onions to pan with garlic and tomato sauce. Cover and cook over low heat 2½ hours, stirring occasionally. Add the egg barley. Mix in sour cream; heat but do not boil.

Serves 6.

Arroz à la Valenciana

(CLASSIC SPANISH RICE DISH, VALENCIA STYLE)

1 pound round steak	2 cups raw rice
3½-pound frying chicken	4 cups boiling chicken
½ cup olive oil	broth
2 cups chopped onions	1¼ teaspoons salt
2 green peppers, cut	½ teaspoon freshly
julienne	ground black pepper
2 cloves garlic, minced	¾ teaspoon saffron
¼ pound smoked ham,	1 pound cooked lobster
cut into strips	meat, cut into pieces
1 pound tomatoes, sliced	1 16-ounce can tiny peas
1 Spanish or other spicy	3 pimientos, cut julienne
sausage, sliced	8 canned asparagus tips

Cut the steak into ¾-inch squares; have the chicken cut up, bone and all, into small pieces. Wash and dry.

Heat the oil in a *paella* pan or Dutch oven; sauté the onions and peppers 10 minutes. Add the garlic, chicken, steak, and ham. Cook over low heat 10 minutes, stirring frequently. Add the tomatoes; cook 5 minutes. Add the sausage and rice.

135

Cook over low heat 5 minutes, shaking the pan frequently. Add the broth, salt, pepper, and saffron. Bring to a boil and cook over high heat 3 minutes; cover and cook over low heat 15 minutes. Watch carefully and add a little more boiling broth if pan becomes dry. Add the lobster and peas and arrange the pimientos and asparagus on top. Place uncovered in a 350° oven for 10 minutes.

Serves 6–8.

Three Meat Goulash

4 tablespoons butter
3 cups thinly sliced onions
1 cup sliced green peppers
1 pound boneless beef,
   cut into 1-inch cubes
1 pound boneless veal, cut
   into 1-inch cubes
1 pound boneless pork, cut
   into 1-inch cubes

2 teaspoons salt
½ teaspoon freshly
   ground black pepper
1 tablespoon paprika
2 tablespoons tomato
   paste
1 cup beef broth
1½ cups sour cream
2 cups cooked egg barley

Melt the butter in a casserole; sauté the onions 10 minutes. Add the peppers, beef, veal, and pork; cook over medium heat until browned. Stir in the salt, pepper, paprika, tomato paste, and ¼ cup broth. Cover and cook over low heat 30 minutes. Add the remaining broth and cook 1½ hours longer. Stir the sour cream into the pan juices, then the egg barley. Heat, but do not let boil.

Serves 6–8.

Boeuf a la Malaga

(BEEF STEW WITH RICE)

3 pounds rump or chuck
of beef

3 slices salt pork, cut into
small pieces

1½ cups sliced onions

2 teaspoons salt

½ teaspoon freshly
ground black pepper

1 cup dry white wine

2 cups beef broth

2 teaspoons finely chopped
bay leaves

½ teaspoon thyme

2 cloves garlic, minced

⅛ teaspoon saffron

1½ cups peeled chopped
tomatoes

3 tablespoons olive oil

1 cup raw rice

Cut the beef into slices 1 inch thick, then into 2-inch squares.
Brown the salt pork in a Dutch oven; pour off all but 2 tablespoons fat; add the meat and onions. Cook over medium heat
until browned. Add the salt, pepper, wine, broth, bay leaves,
thyme, garlic, and saffron. Bring to a boil, cover and bake in a
325° oven 1 hour. Mix in the tomatoes; recover and bake 1½
hours longer.

Heat the oil in a skillet; add the rice; cook, stirring until rice
is translucent. Place the meat over direct heat; lightly stir in
the rice, and a little boiling water if necessary. (At this point
there should be about 2½ cups liquid.) Recover and cook over
low heat 20 minutes or until rice is tender. Taste for seasoning.

Serves 6–8.

✳ ✳ ✳ ✳ ✳ ✳ ✳ ✳ ✳ ✳ ✳ ✳ ✳ ✳ ✳

Arroz con Carne

(RICE AND MEAT)

4 tablespoons olive oil
1 clove garlic, minced
2 cups chopped onions
2 green peppers, sliced
3 pounds boneless beef,
    cut into 1½-inch
    cubes
2 teaspoons salt
½ teaspoon freshly
    ground black pepper

1 teaspoon Spanish
    paprika
4 cups boiling water
1½ cups raw rice
1 Spanish-style sausage,
    sliced
½ cup sliced stuffed
    olives
3 tablespoons chopped
    parsley

Heat the oil in a Dutch oven or heavy saucepan; sauté the
garlic, onions, green peppers, and beef over high heat until meat
is browned on all sides. Mix in the salt, pepper, paprika, and 1
cup water. Cover and cook over low heat 1½ hours. Mix in the
rice, sausage, and remaining water, and cook 30 minutes, stirring occasionally. Mix in the olives and parsley, taste for seasoning, and serve.

Serves 6–8.

Meat, Sweet Potato, and Pineapple Casserole

3 pounds brisket of beef
1 tablespoon vegetable oil
½ cup chopped onions
2 teaspoons salt
¼ teaspoon freshly
    ground black pepper

4 sweet potatoes, peeled
    and sliced 1 inch thick
⅓ cup brown sugar
2½ cups water
1 15-ounce can pineapple
    chunks

Cut the meat into 1-inch slices. Heat the oil in a casserole; brown the meat and onions in it. Mix in the salt, pepper, sweet potatoes, sugar, and water. Bring to a boil over direct heat. Cover and bake in a 350° oven 2½ hours. Add a little water from time to time if necessary, and shake casserole to keep ingredients from sticking. Add the undrained pineapple; bake 20 minutes longer.

Serves 6–8.

Braised Short Ribs and Lentils

2 cups dried lentils
3 pounds short ribs, cut
    into serving-sized pieces
3 cups boiling water
2 teaspoons salt
¼ teaspoon freshly
    ground black pepper

1 bay leaf
1 cup chopped onions
1 clove garlic, minced
1½ cups sliced celery
½ teaspoon basil

Wash the lentils, discard any bruised ones, and cover with hot water. Let soak while preparing the meat.

Lightly brown the short ribs in a Dutch oven or heavy saucepan; add the water, salt, pepper, bay leaf, onions, garlic, and celery. Cover and cook over low heat 2 hours.

Drain the lentils and add to the meat with the basil and cook, stirring frequently, 30 minutes longer or until the lentils are tender. Discard any loose bones and the bay leaf. Taste for seasoning.

Serves 4–6.

Exeter Beef Stew

4 tablespoons vegetable oil

2½ pounds top round of beef, cut into 6 pieces

1½ cups chopped onions

1 cup flour

2 cups beef broth

2 tablespoons vinegar

½ teaspoon thyme

½ teaspoon freshly ground black pepper

2½ teaspoons salt

¾ teaspoon baking powder

¼ teaspoon marjoram

1 tablespoon chopped parsley

Dash of cayenne pepper

3 tablespoons butter

2 tablespoons ice water

1½ cups sliced carrots

Heat the oil in a Dutch oven or deep skillet; lightly brown the meat in it. Remove. In the oil remaining in the pan, sauté the onions 10 minutes. Blend in 3 tablespoons of the flour until smooth. Gradually add the broth, stirring steadily to the boiling point. Add the vinegar, thyme, pepper, 2 teaspoons salt, and the meat. Cover and cook over low heat 2 hours.

Sift the remaining flour, salt, and the baking powder into a bowl. Add the marjoram, parsley, and cayenne pepper, mixing well. Cut in the butter with a pastry blender or 2 knives until well blended. Add the ice water and toss lightly until a ball of dough is formed. Shape into 6 balls and drop into the stew with the carrots. Cover and cook over low heat 35 minutes. Serves 6.

Boeuf Bourguignonne

(BEEF, BURGUNDY STYLE)

3 pounds rump or cross rib
of beef, cut into 2-inch
cubes
½ cup flour
2 teaspoons salt
½ teaspoon freshly
ground black pepper
3 tablespoons olive oil
3 tablespoons butter
¼ cup warm cognac
2 slices bacon, diced
2 cups diced onions

¾ cup grated carrots
2 cloves garlic, minced
3 cups dry red wine
3 tablespoons minced
parsley
1 bay leaf
½ teaspoon thyme
12 small white onions,
lightly browned
12 mushroom caps,
sautéed

Roll the meat in a mixture of the flour, salt, and pepper. Heat the oil and butter in a skillet; brown the meat very well on all sides. Transfer to a Dutch oven or casserole; pour the warm cognac over it and set aflame.

Lightly brown the bacon in the skillet; pour off most of the fat. Add the diced onions, carrots, and garlic; cook 5 minutes, stirring frequently. Add to the meat with the wine, parsley, bay leaf, and thyme. Cover and bake in a 350° oven 2 hours. Add the onions and mushrooms; recover and bake 30 minutes longer.

Serves 6–8.

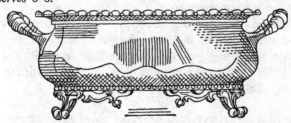

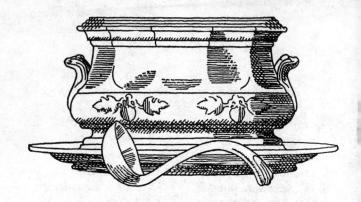

Guisada de Lentejas

(LENTIL-MEAT STEW, SPANISH STYLE)

2 cups dried lentils
2 teaspoons salt
¼ cup olive oil
1 cup chopped onions
2 pounds boneless beef,
    cut into 1-inch cubes
1 clove garlic, minced

2 cups diced tomatoes
¼ teaspoon freshly
    ground black pepper
3 chorizos (Spanish
    sausage), sliced
2 pimientos, cut julienne

Wash the lentils, cover with water, bring to a boil, and cook over low heat 45 minutes, or until tender. Add 1 teaspoon of the salt after 15 minutes' cooking time. Drain thoroughly. Prepare the meat meanwhile.

Heat the oil in a skillet; sauté the onions 5 minutes. Add the meat and brown well. Add the garlic, tomatoes, pepper, sausage, and remaining salt; cook over low heat 45 minutes. Mix in the lentils and pimientos; cook 15 minutes, stirring frequently. Taste for seasoning. Serves 6–8.

Vaca a la Catalane

(BEEF STEW, BARCELONA STYLE)

3 pounds rump or eye
   round of beef
4 slices salt pork
3 tablespoons olive oil
2 teaspoons salt
½ teaspoon freshly
   ground black pepper
1½ cups sliced onions
1 cup raw rice
1 cup dry white wine

2 cups beef broth
1 bay leaf, finely crushed
½ teaspoon thyme
2 cloves garlic, minced
⅛ teaspoon saffron
1½ cups peeled chopped
   tomatoes
1 package frozen peas,
   thawed

Cut the beef into pieces about 1 inch thick and 2 inches square. Brown the salt pork in a skillet; drain and transfer to a Dutch oven or casserole. Pour off the fat from the skillet. Heat the oil in the skillet; brown the meat in it. Add to the salt pork. Sprinkle with the salt and pepper. In the fat remaining in the skillet, sauté the onions 5 minutes. Add to the meat. To the fat remaining in the skillet, add the rice. Cook over medium heat, stirring constantly, until rice is yellow. Remove rice and reserve.

Add the wine to the skillet; bring to a boil, scraping any browned particles from the bottom. Add to the meat with the broth, bay leaf, thyme, garlic, and saffron. Bring to a boil, cover, and bake in a 325° oven 1 hour. Mix in the tomatoes; recover and bake 1½ hours longer.

Place the pan over direct heat; lightly stir in the rice and peas. Recover and cook over low heat 20 minutes or until rice is tender. Watch carefully and add a little boiling water if necessary. Taste for seasoning. *Serves 6–8.*

Ragoût de Boeuf Bordelaise

(MARINATED BEEF STEW, BORDEAUX STYLE)

2 cups dry red wine
1 clove garlic, minced
2 teaspoons salt
½ teaspoon freshly
   ground black pepper
1 bay leaf
2 cloves
¼ teaspoon thyme
3 pounds rump or chuck
   of beef, cut into 2-inch
   cubes

¼ cup olive oil
½ cup beef broth
3 sprigs parsley
12 small white onions
3 carrots, cut into 2-inch
   pieces
12 mushroom caps,
   sautéed
1 cup cooked or canned
   green peas
2 cups cooked potato balls

Combine the wine, garlic, salt, pepper, bay leaf, cloves, and thyme in a glass or pottery bowl. Marinate the meat in the mixture 4 hours at room temperature or overnight in the refrigerator. Drain, reserving the marinade.

Heat the oil in a casserole or Dutch oven; brown the meat in it very well. Add the marinade, broth, and parsley. Bring to a boil and cook over high heat 15 minutes. Cover and cook over low heat 30 minutes. Add the onions and carrots. Cover and cook over low heat 1½ hours. Add the mushrooms, peas, and potatoes. Heat, taste for seasoning, and serve.

Serves 6–8.

IN THE SOUTHWESTERN CORNER OF FRANCE, where it borders Spain along the Atlantic Ocean, there is a region called the Pyrénées. The month of May is a lovely one in this province, the fields covered with wildflowers, the thick white clouds scudding along a background of brilliant Technicolor blue, and a gentle feeling of approaching summer. The sun shines brightly, and it is pleasant enough to be outdoors without a coat.

But not the May when I was there! It rained all morning, and even my good-tempered husband had his lips pursed as he drove slowly and with difficulty along the narrow roads. By 11:30 in the morning, driving became increasingly difficult, and the rain seemed to change direction. Instead of falling down from the sky, it appeared to come at us horizontally. Upon reaching the small village of Ascain, we stopped in front of the first restaurant we saw; Etchola, I believe it was called. All we wanted was some steaming hot coffee, for we were both chilled to the bone. The interior of the restaurant was deserted, because no one eats lunch in that portion of France until at least 1 P.M. I heard muffled voices in the rear of the restaurant, and wandered toward the kitchen. There I found three women busily engaged in preparing food; at my approach, the conversation ceased suddenly, and there were inquiring looks on the fresh, plump faces of all three. I explained that we wanted coffee because we were cold and wet, and soon I was trying to cope with three simultaneous conversations, all expressing sympathy and hopes that I would not catch a cold. My husband joined the group, drawn by the voices. We must take our coats off and dry out before the fire; we must wait until some fresh coffee could be made, because the breakfast coffee was "tired." It was all so friendly and comfortable that we began asking about the dishes being prepared. In particular, I asked about a braised-beef dish to which the eldest woman was adding garlic with complete abandon. We remained, needless to say, for a heart-warming, stomach-filling lunch of the braised-beef dish, called *Le Hachua* in the Pyrénées region. In the recipe which follows, I have substantially decreased the amount of garlic, so have no fear. Two hours later, warmed and dry, we said our farewells, with many requests to return again.

It would be so charming and have a happy ending if I could tell you the rain stopped and sun came out. It didn't, and what's more, it rained the next day too.

Le Hachua

(BRAISED BEEF, MOUNTAIN STYLE)

3 pounds rump or chuck of beef, cut into 1-inch cubes
4 tablespoons flour
¼ cup olive oil
2 cups chopped onions
2 cloves garlic, minced
1½ cups finely diced ham
3 sprigs parsley
1 bay leaf
½ teaspoon basil
2 teaspoons salt
½ teaspoon freshly ground pepper
1 cup beef broth
1½ cups dry white wine
3 green peppers, cut julienne
1 package frozen Lima beans, thawed

Toss the meat with the flour. Heat the oil in a Dutch oven or casserole; brown the beef in it. Add the onions, garlic, ham, parsley, bay leaf, basil, salt, and pepper. Cook 5 minutes, stirring frequently. Stir in the broth and wine. Cover tightly and bake in a 275° oven 2 hours. Add the green peppers and Lima beans; recover and bake 30 minutes longer or until the meat is tender.

Serves 6–8.

La Carbonnade

(FRENCH BEEF STEW, TOULOUSE STYLE)

3 tablespoons butter
3 pounds sirloin or rump steak, cut into ½-inch cubes
1 cup sliced onions
2 tomatoes, peeled and sliced thin
2 teaspoons salt
¼ teaspoon freshly ground pepper

1 cup raw rice
1 8-ounce can corn kernels, drained
1 cup finely sliced green peppers
¼ teaspoon saffron
1 teaspoon brown sugar
1 cup dry white wine
1 cup beef broth
⅛ teaspoon cinnamon

Melt the butter in a Dutch oven or casserole; brown the steak in it. Add the onions, tomatoes, salt, and pepper; cover and cook over medium heat 10 minutes, shaking pan frequently. Mix in the rice, corn, green peppers, saffron, sugar, wine, broth, and cinnamon. Cover and cook over low heat 20 minutes or until rice is tender. Taste for seasoning.

Serves 6–8.

West Indian Beef Stew

3 pounds chuck or rump of beef, cut into 1½-inch cubes
½ cup flour
2 teaspoons salt
½ teaspoon freshly ground black pepper
⅓ cup vegetable oil

¾ cup chopped onions
1 clove garlic, minced
1 29-ounce can tomatoes
¾ teaspoon powdered ginger
1 package frozen okra, thawed
2 cups half-cooked rice

Toss the beef in a mixture of the flour, salt, and pepper. Heat the oil in a casserole; brown the meat in it very well. Pour off the fat. Add the onions and garlic; cook until onions begin to brown, stirring frequently. Mix in the tomatoes and ginger; cover and cook over low heat 1¾ hours. Add the okra and rice; cook 20 minutes longer. *Serves 6–8.*

Estouffat Catalan

(BEEF STEW, CATALAN MANNER)

4 pounds eye round of beef
Salt pork
1 clove garlic
¼ cup dry sherry
¼ cup flour
2 slices bacon, minced
1½ cups chopped onions
1 cup coarsely grated carrots
2 small white turnips, peeled and quartered
1½ cups peeled chopped tomatoes
¼ cup chopped parsley
1 bay leaf, finely crushed
½ teaspoon thyme
1 clove garlic, minced
2 cloves
1 teaspoon salt
½ teaspoon freshly ground black pepper
1 bottle dry red wine
3 cups cooked or canned kidney beans

Have the meat wrapped with salt pork. Cut the garlic in slivers; make some cuts in the meat and insert the garlic. Brush all over with sherry and roll in the flour. In a Dutch oven, spread the bacon, onions, carrots, turnips, tomatoes, parsley, bay leaf, thyme, minced garlic, cloves, salt, and pepper. Put the meat over it. Add the wine, cover pan tightly and bake in a 300° oven 3½ hours. Add the beans and bake uncovered 20 minutes longer.

Serves 8–10.

Pepperpot, Jamaica Style

1 cup packaged fine-grated coconut	1 package frozen okra
3 packages frozen kale	1 quart water
2 pounds beef, cut into 1-inch cubes	½ cup sliced green onions
½ pound dried chipped beef	½ cup raw rice
1½ cups coarsely chopped onions	1 teaspoon salt
	⅛ teaspoon cayenne pepper
	½ teaspoon thyme

Rinse the coconut under cold running water and combine in a deep saucepan with the kale, cubed and chipped beef, the onions, okra, and water. Bring to a boil and cook over low heat 1 hour. Remove kale and okra and force through a sieve. Return to pan with the green onions, rice, salt, cayenne pepper, and thyme; cook 15 minutes, or until the meat is tender. Taste for seasoning. *Serves 6.*

Boeuf en Daube

(MARINATED BEEF STEW)

4 pounds chuck or rump of beef	1½ teaspoons salt
3 slices salt pork, cut julienne	½ teaspoon freshly ground black pepper
3 tablespoons minced parsley	⅛ teaspoon nutmeg
2 cloves garlic, minced	3 tablespoons olive oil
2 cups dry red wine	12 small white onions
¼ cup cognac	4 carrots, sliced
3 tablespoons flour	½ cup beef broth
	½ teaspoon thyme
	1 bay leaf

Cut the beef into 2-inch cubes. Dip the salt-pork strips in a mixture of the parsley and garlic, then lard (or cover) the cubes of meat with them. Marinate the meat in a mixture of the wine and cognac 2 hours. Drain and dry. Reserve the marinade. Toss the meat with a mixture of the flour, salt, pepper, and nutmeg. Heat the oil in a Dutch oven or heavy casserole. Add the onions, carrots, and beef; cook over medium heat until well browned. Bring the marinade and broth to a boil; add to the meat with the thyme and bay leaf. Bring to a boil, cover tightly, and cook over low heat 2½ hours or until meat is very tender. Discard the bay leaf.

Serves 8–10.

Boeuf en Miroton

(PEASANT BEEF STEW WITH LEFTOVER MEAT)

2 tablespoons butter	2 tablespoons minced parsley
2 tablespoons flour	¼ teaspoon thyme
2 cups dry red wine	1 bay leaf
1 teaspoon salt	4 cups cooked beef, cut into ¼-inch cubes
½ teaspoon freshly ground black pepper	1 package frozen French-style green beans, thawed
½ cup peeled chopped tomatoes	
12 small white onions	
6 potatoes, peeled and quartered	

Melt the butter in a saucepan; blend in the flour until browned. Gradually mix in the wine, stirring steadily to the boiling point. Add the salt and pepper, tomatoes, onions, potatoes, parsley, thyme, and bay leaf. Cook over low heat 45 minutes. Add the beef and beans. Cook 15 minutes longer. Discard the bay leaf. *Serves 6.*

Ragoût de Boeuf

(BEEF STEW, FRENCH STYLE)

3 pounds chuck or rump of beef, cut into 2-inch cubes

2 teaspoons salt

½ teaspoon freshly ground black pepper

1 clove garlic, minced

2 tablespoons olive oil

2 cups sliced onions

1 cup boiling water

½ cup Madeira or sweet sherry

1½ cups diced tomatoes

¼ teaspoon marjoram

3 carrots, quartered

2 green peppers, cut in strips

4 potatoes, peeled and quartered

Season the meat with the salt, pepper, and garlic. Heat the oil in a heavy deep skillet or Dutch oven and brown the meat in it. Add the onions; cook until browned. Add the water, wine, and tomatoes. Cover and cook over low heat 2 hours. Add the marjoram, carrots, green peppers, and potatoes. Cook 30 minutes longer. *Serves 8–10.*

Beef Cholent

2 cups dried Lima beans

3 tablespoons vegetable oil

3 pounds brisket of beef

1½ cups diced onions

2 teaspoons salt

¼ teaspoon pepper

1 cup pearl barley

2 tablespoons flour

2 teaspoons paprika

Wash the beans; cover with water; bring to a boil and let soak 1 hour. Drain.

In a Dutch oven or heavy saucepan, heat the oil; brown the meat and onions in it. Sprinkle with the salt and pepper. Add the beans, barley, flour, paprika, and boiling water to reach one inch above the ingredients. Cover tightly. Bake in a 350° oven 4½ hours. Slice the meat.

Serves 8–10.

Estouffat

(SPANISH BRAISED BEEF AND BEANS)

4 pounds rump or eye
   round of beef
2 tablespoons wine
   vinegar
½ cup flour
¼ pound salt pork, diced
4 onions, quartered
3 carrots, cut in eighths
2 cloves garlic, minced
1½ cups peeled chopped
   tomatoes
2 teaspoons salt

½ teaspoon freshly
   ground black pepper
2 cloves
2 teaspoons finely
   chopped bay leaves
¼ teaspoon marjoram
4 cups dry red wine
2 cups cooked or canned
   dried white beans
2 tablespoons minced
   parsley

Cut the beef into 2-inch cubes, then toss with the vinegar
and roll in the flour.

Brown the salt pork in a Dutch oven or casserole; drain off all
but 3 tablespoons fat. Add the beef, onions, and carrots; brown
lightly. Mix in the garlic, tomatoes, salt, pepper, cloves, bay
leaves, marjoram, and wine. Cover and bake in a 300° oven 3
hours. Add the beans and parsley. Taste for seasoning and bake
30 minutes longer.

Serves 6–8.

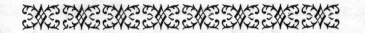

Beef and Lima Bean Curry

3 tablespoons butter
¾ cup chopped onions
1½ pounds ground beef
½ cup beef broth
1 package frozen Lima
beans, thawed
1½ teaspoons salt

½ teaspoon freshly
ground black pepper
1 tablespoon curry
powder
1½ cups cooked rice
2 eggs
1 cup yogurt

Melt the butter in a skillet; sauté the onions 10 minutes. Stir in the beef until browned. Add the broth, Lima beans, salt, pepper, and curry powder. Cover and cook over low heat 15 minutes. Stir in the rice.

Beat the eggs in a bowl; stir in the yogurt. Add a little of the meat mixture, stirring steadily. Return to skillet. Cook over low heat 5 minutes, stirring almost steadily, but do not let boil.
Serves 6–8.

Fa-Sool-Ya Ib Zeyt

(MEAT AND BEAN STEW, ARABIC STYLE)

1 cup dried white beans
3 pounds boneless beef,
cut into 2-inch cubes
1½ cups chopped onions
3 tablespoons vegetable
oil
2 teaspoons salt
½ teaspoon freshly
ground black pepper

¼ teaspoon cinnamon
1 bay leaf
4 cups hot beef broth
¾ cup raw rice
1½ cups peeled diced
tomatoes

Wash the beans. Cover with water, bring to a boil, and let soak 1 hour. Drain. Add fresh water to cover, bring to a boil, and cook over low heat 1 hour. Drain. Brown the beef and onions in the hot oil. Add the beans, salt, pepper, cinnamon, bay leaf, and hot beef broth. Cover and cook over low heat 1½ hours. Stir in the rice and tomatoes; recover and cook 25 minutes longer or until meat and beans are tender.

Serves 6–8.

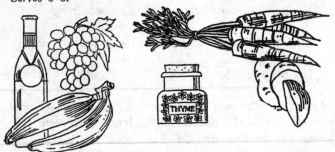

Boeuf aux Pruneaux

(BEEF WITH PRUNES)

1 pound prunes	1½ teaspoons salt
2 cups dry red wine	1 bay leaf
2 tablespoons vegetable oil	1 tablespoon wine vinegar
1¼ cups chopped onions	2 tablespoons brown sugar
3 pounds eye round, chuck, etc., cut into 2-inch cubes	1 teaspoon cinnamon
	4 potatoes, peeled and quartered

Wash the prunes and soak in the wine for 1 hour. Drain and reserve the wine. Heat the oil in a Dutch oven or in a casserole; brown the onions and meat in it. Add the salt, bay leaf, vinegar, sugar, cinnamon, and reserved wine. Cover and cook over low heat 1½ hours. Add the prunes and potatoes; cook 30 minutes longer. Discard bay leaf.

Serves 6–8.

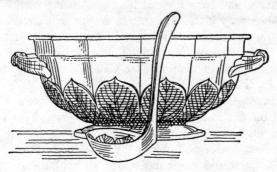

Skillet Steak and Vegetables

3 pounds sirloin steak,
cut ½ inch thick
4 tablespoons butter
3 cups peeled, cubed
potatoes
4 tablespoons olive oil
1½ cups chopped onions
1½ cups tomatoes

2 teaspoons salt
½ teaspoon ground dried
chili peppers
2 tablespoons wine
vinegar
1 8-ounce can green peas,
drained

Cut the steak into narrow strips. Melt the butter in a skillet;
sauté the potatoes until browned. Remove.

Heat the oil in the skillet; cook the steak in it over high heat
3 minutes, shaking the pan frequently. Remove steak. In the
oil remaining in the skillet, sauté the onions 5 minutes. Mix in
the tomatoes, salt, and chili peppers; cook over low heat 10
minutes. Mix in the vinegar, then the peas, steak, and potatoes.
Cook over low heat 10 minutes, mixing occasionally. Taste for
seasoning.

Serves 6–8.

LATE ONE OCTOBER, my husband and I were in Santiago, the attractive capital of Chile. It was just the beginning of spring-time (the seasons being reversed from ours) and Santiago was like a flower shop; everywhere we turned there were shrubs and bushes in bloom, and every house and store had plants and cut flowers in the windows. After several pleasant days in Santiago, we took the train to Viña del Mar, Chile's resort at the edge of the Pacific.

We wandered about Viña (literally translated, it means Vine-yard of the Sea) and found it a delightful place, filled with summer villas and the usual resort attractions.

There was service north along the coast to the coastal vil-lage of Concon, and we climbed aboard a local bus one sunny morning. The road followed the rugged, winding coast, which greatly resembled that of California, particularly near the Mon-terey peninsula. After a half hour, we began to notice small restaurants, featuring shellfish dishes, built onto the rocks. Just before Concon, we decided to get off the bus and have a seafood lunch, and we walked back a few hundred yards to a simple but attractive-looking restaurant. We wandered in and took seats at the water's edge; soon the proprietor came to our table holding a menu in his hand. We were very welcome, he as-sured us, and would we not like a little cool white wine with which to refresh ourselves? We would. And we also would like some shellfish, we said. Ah, it was such a shame, we were in-formed. The ocean had been very rough for the past week, and none of the fishing boats had been able to put to sea. There simply was no seafood of any sort, no shrimp, no clams, no lobster, not even *locos* (giant scallops). But there was a delicious *cazuela*, he told us, with a big smile. Of course we agreed. Actually, there was no choice, for we could only get another bus and ride back to Viña, some two hours away. The *cazuela*

156

turned out to be a marvelous dish, filled with meat and vegetables, and we ate an enormous portion of it, and drank a bottle of fine Chilean red wine.

We finished the entire *cazuela de vaca y legumbres*, and the entire bottle of wine, and an entire long loaf of bread. That salt air! We reached our hotel after five in the afternoon. I fell on my bed, kicked off my shoes, and slept for four solid hours.

Cazuela de Vaca y Legumbres

(BEEF-VEGETABLE STEW, CHILEAN STYLE)

4 tablespoons olive oil
3 pounds eye round or chuck of beef, cut into 1-inch cubes
1 cup chopped onions
¾ cup chopped green peppers
3½ cups water
2 cups cubed yellow squash
2 cups cubed white potatoes

2 cups cubed sweet potatoes
1 cup corn kernels
1 cup sliced carrots
2½ teaspoons salt
½ teaspoon freshly ground black pepper
2 tablespoons minced parsley

Heat the oil in a Dutch oven or casserole; brown the meat in it. Mix in the onions and green peppers until browned. Add half the water; cook over low heat 30 minutes. Add the squash, white potatoes, sweet potatoes, corn, carrots, salt, pepper, and remaining water. Cover and cook over low heat for 2 hours. Watch carefully and add a little boiling water to keep from burning. The resulting stew should have very little gravy. Taste for seasoning and sprinkle with the parsley.

Serves 4–6.

Beef with Cauliflower and Peas, Chinese Style

2 pounds sirloin steak,
cut ¼ inch thick
¼ cup vegetable oil
1 whole clove garlic
1 cup diced onions
1½ teaspoons salt
¼ teaspoon freshly
ground black pepper

1½ cups beef broth
2 cups cooked drained rice
2 packages frozen
cauliflower, thawed
2 packages frozen green
peas, thawed
2 tablespoons cornstarch
2 tablespoons soy sauce

Cut the beef into narrow strips. Heat the oil in a skillet; brown the garlic in it and discard. Add the meat and let brown, stirring frequently. Add the onions, salt, and pepper; cook 30 seconds. Add ¾ cup of the broth, the rice, cauliflower, and peas. Bring to a boil and cook 3 minutes. Mix the cornstarch and soy sauce with the remaining broth. Add to the skillet, stirring steadily until thickened. *Serves 4–6.*

Beef and Mixed Vegetables

3 pounds top round or
   top sirloin
5 tablespoons butter
¼ cup warm cognac
3 celery hearts, quartered
12 small white onions
6 small white turnips,
   scraped
6 small carrots, scraped
½ pound mushrooms,
   quartered

1 teaspoon tomato paste
2½ teaspoons salt
½ teaspoon freshly
   ground black pepper
2 tablespoons flour
1 cup dry red wine
¾ cup beef broth
1 bay leaf

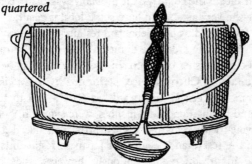

Cut the meat into 1-inch cubes. Melt 2 tablespoons of the
butter in a Dutch oven or casserole; brown the meat in it. Set the
cognac aflame in a ladle and pour it over the meat. When
flames die, remove the meat.

Melt the remaining butter in the pan; add the celery hearts,
onions, turnips, and carrots. Sauté until lightly browned. Add
the mushrooms; cook 2 minutes. Mix together the tomato paste,
salt, pepper, flour, wine, and broth. Add to the pan, stirring
steadily to the boiling point. Return the meat and add the bay
leaf; cover and cook over low heat 1 hour, or until the meat is
tender. Discard bay leaf.

Serves 6–8.

Mост people who come to Japan on their first trip visualize a country of stylized Japanese landscapes, with Mount Fuji in the background, and the ringing of temple bells. This preliminary dream is soon destroyed if they arrive in Tokyo by plane, for the outskirts of that giant city are quite nondescript (if not homely), and the traffic is heavier and worse than New York. Tokyo has its great attractions, but the atmosphere of old Japan is not one of them. For that, the traveler must head to the southwest to Kyoto, the old capital.

Kyoto, although a large, busy city, still retains many of its ancient manners and customs, and of almost all cities of Japan, helps to re-create the country as it probably was many centuries ago. We were very anxious to have some local specialties, and a Japanese friend told us of a delightful restaurant in the suburbs; he would personally order the dinner, which would feature the great and classic dishes of Kyoto. In the early evening, we went to see the famous Cherry Dance, performed by the *maiko*, the young apprentice geisha. Afterward, we took a taxi to the restaurant, and having removed our shoes, were shown into a small room, covered with straw mats. Each little room faced a lovely garden in the restaurant's center. In Japanese restaurants, most diners eat in private rooms; curiously, however, they like to bathe in mixed groups in public. We do just the opposite. A waitress began the meal by serving a clear fish soup, which was so fishy that we tasted just a few spoonfuls. Then came a fish dish, surrounded by slices of cucumber and tomatoes. It was *completely* raw, and although we ate a little of it, that was that. The next dish was chicken, but in the Japanese fashion was again almost completely uncooked; it wasn't raw, but it wasn't far from being raw. To be brief, we ate almost nothing.

We left the restaurant and walked toward the taxi stand. On the way, we walked past a restaurant that seemed quite busy, and being very hungry, I suggested that we go in. It was a happy decision.

There were no menus, but the waitress suggested *sukiyaki*, the famous dish of sliced beef and vegetables so popular with foreign visitors to Japan. The *sukiyaki* was prepared by our waitress at the table in a sort of chafing dish and had a fresh, slightly salty, delicious taste. It made up for the previous uneaten meal we had not enjoyed. My advice to Americans visiting Kyoto (unless they like raw fish and uncooked chicken)—don't order Kyoto specialties.

Sukiyaki

2 pounds sirloin steak	1 cup sliced celery
4 tablespoons sesame or vegetable oil	1 cup sliced bamboo shoots
½ cup beef broth	½ pound mushrooms, sliced thin
¾ cup soy sauce	
¼ cup sugar	1 cup shredded spinach
2 tablespoons dry white wine or sherry	4 green onions, sliced
	1 pound vermicelli, cooked and drained
2 cups thinly sliced onions	

Have the steak cut paper-thin and into pieces about 2 inches by 3 inches. (If you do it yourself, partially freeze the meat to facilitate cutting.)

Heat the oil in a large skillet. Add the meat and brown on all sides. Combine the broth, soy sauce, sugar, and wine in a bowl. Add half of this mixture to the meat. Push the meat to one side of the skillet. Add the onions and celery; cook over low heat for 3 minutes. Add the remaining soy mixture, the bamboo shoots, mushrooms, and spinach. Cook over low heat 3 minutes. Add the green onions and cook for 1 minute. Heap the vermicelli on one side of a platter and the *sukiyaki* on the other, and serve immediately.

This dish is particularly suited for preparation at the table in a chafing dish. *Serves 4–6.*

Beef and Red Cabbage Stew

2 tablespoons vegetable oil	1 teaspoon caraway seeds
3 pounds chuck or rump of beef, cut into 2-inch cubes	2 cups boiling water
	¼ cup wine vinegar
1½ cups thinly sliced onions	3 tablespoons brown sugar
2 teaspoons salt	4 cups coarsely shredded red cabbage
½ teaspoon freshly ground black pepper	¼ cup gingersnap crumbs

Heat the oil in a Dutch oven; brown the meat and onions in it. Add the salt, pepper, caraway seeds, and water; cover and cook over low heat 1 hour. Mix in the vinegar, sugar, cabbage, gingersnaps, and a little more water if necessary. Recover and cook 1 hour longer or until meat is tender. Taste for seasoning.
Serves 6–8.

Boeuf et Aubergine Gratiné

(BEEF WITH EGGPLANT)

2 pounds fillet of beef	¼ teaspoon freshly ground black pepper
1 medium-sized eggplant	
¼ cup flour	¼ teaspoon basil
⅓ cup olive oil	2 tablespoons chopped parsley
2 cups chopped tomatoes	
1 clove garlic, minced	¼ cup dry bread crumbs
1½ teaspoons salt	

Cut the beef into ¼-inch-thick slices. Peel the eggplant and slice ¼ inch thick. Dip the eggplant in the flour. Heat ¼ cup of the oil in a skillet; brown the eggplant in it. Arrange on the bottom of a greased casserole or baking dish with the beef on top. To the oil remaining in the skillet, add the tomatoes, garlic, salt, pepper, basil, and parsley. Cook over low heat 10 minutes, stirring frequently. Spoon over the beef; sprinkle with the bread crumbs and remaining oil. Bake in a 350° oven 35 minutes. *Serves 6–8.*

Cubed Beef, Chinese Style

3 tablespoons vegetable oil
1½ pounds eye round of beef, cut into 1-inch cubes
1 clove garlic, minced
¼ cup soy sauce
½ teaspoon salt
⅓ cup bottled Chinese Oyster Sauce

2 teaspoons sugar
1 tablespoon dry sherry
1 cup boiling water
½ cup sliced mushrooms
1½ cups cooked drained fine noodles
¼ cup thinly sliced green onions

Heat the oil in a skillet; brown the beef and garlic in it, stirring frequently. Add a mixture of the soy sauce, salt, Oyster Sauce, sugar, and sherry. Cook over medium heat 5 minutes, stirring almost constantly. Add the water; cover and cook over low heat 30 minutes, stirring occasionally. Mix in the mushrooms and noodles; cook 5 minutes. Add the green onions; cook 1 minute. *Serves 4–6.*

Beef Pie

PASTRY:

1½ cups sifted flour
¾ teaspoon salt
½ teaspoon thyme

½ cup shortening
4 tablespoons ice water (approx.)

Sift the flour and salt into a bowl; stir in the thyme. Cut in the shortening with a pastry blender or two knives. With a fork, toss in just enough of the water to make a dough. Form into a ball, wrap, and chill while preparing the meat.

FILLING:

- 2 pounds chuck or top round, cut into 1-inch cubes
- ¼ cup flour
- 2 teaspoons salt
- ½ teaspoon freshly ground black pepper
- 3 tablespoons butter
- 1 cup canned tomatoes
- 1½ cups water
- 1 bay leaf
- 1 teaspoon Worcestershire sauce
- 8 small white onions, peeled
- 3 cups peeled cubed potatoes
- 2 cups sliced celery
- 1 package frozen green peas, thawed

Toss the meat in a mixture of the flour, salt, and pepper. Melt the butter in a Dutch oven; brown the meat in it. Add the tomatoes, water, bay leaf, and Worcestershire sauce. Bring to a boil, cover, and cook over low heat 1¼ hours. Add all the vegetables; cook 30 minutes longer. Discard bay leaf, taste for seasoning, and turn into a 2½-quart casserole. Cool 15 minutes.

Roll out the pastry to fit the top of the casserole; place over the top, sealing the edges. Cut two slits on the top. Bake in a preheated 425° oven 25 minutes or until pastry is browned.

Serves 4–6.

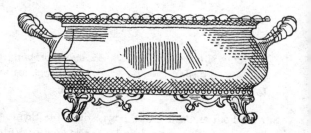

Potato-Beef Pie

1½ pounds ground beef
3 tablespoons melted
   butter
2½ teaspoons salt
½ teaspoon freshly
   ground black pepper
¼ teaspoon marjoram

1 cup sliced carrots
12 small white onions,
   lightly browned
2 cups thinly sliced
   potatoes
1 cup grated cheddar
   cheese

Mix together the beef, butter, 1½ teaspoons salt, ¼ teaspoon pepper, and the marjoram. Spread half the mixture in a buttered casserole. Arrange the carrots, onions, and potatoes over it, and cover with the remaining meat mixture. Sprinkle with the remaining salt and pepper. Bake in a 325° oven 45 minutes. Sprinkle the cheese on top and bake 15 minutes longer.

Serves 6–8.

Chipped Beef and Vegetables

1 pound dried chipped
   beef
2 tablespoons olive oil
1 cup chopped onions
¼ teaspoon dried ground
   red peppers
1 cup diced tomatoes

2 teaspoons paprika
2 packages frozen mixed
   vegetables, cooked and
   drained
3 cups cubed potatoes,
   cooked and drained

Cover the chipped beef with boiling water; let stand 1 hour. Drain and shred.

Heat the oil in a saucepan; sauté the onions 10 minutes. Add the red peppers, tomatoes, and paprika. Cook over low heat 5 minutes. Mix in the beef and cook 5 minutes, stirring frequently. Add the vegetables and potatoes; cook 3 minutes.

Serves 4–6.

Wild Rice-Beef Casserole

1½ cups wild rice
4 tablespoons butter
1 cup chopped onions
1 cup chopped celery
¼ pound mushrooms,
   sliced
1 pound ground beef

1 pimiento, chopped
1½ teaspoons salt
¼ teaspoon freshly
   ground black pepper
5 cups beef broth
   (approx.)

Wash the rice under cold running water until the water runs clean. Cover with boiling water and let stand 1 hour. Drain well.

Melt the butter in a 1½-quart casserole; sauté the onions, celery, and mushrooms 5 minutes. Add the beef; sauté 5 minutes. Mix in the rice, pimiento, salt, pepper, and 4 cups beef broth. Cover and bake in a 375° oven 45 minutes, or until the rice is tender. Add more of the reserved broth from time to time if casserole becomes dry.

Serves 4–6.

Veal

DURING LATE OCTOBER of one year, when the days were growing shorter and the slanting rays of the sun brought little warmth, my husband and I were driving in a region to the northwest of Vienna. This portion of Austria is called the Wachau, and every view is enchanting, precisely what tourists look for when abroad. The entire district has a romantic feeling, reminiscent of medieval madrigals, and the scenery and old-world houses seem ideally suited to the area. We reached the very small town of Dürnstein, which has some of the narrowest streets I have ever seen. We were riding in a small European car but nevertheless found it difficult to maneuver through the streets. Suddenly our engine coughed (or did it hiccup?) and finally stopped. We blocked traffic for a while, but the good-natured inhabitants of Dürnstein merely gathered around and gently pushed us to a repair shop. The verdict: at least several hours work, and that was all the traveling for that day. We found pleasant, old-fashioned rooms at the nearby Gasthof Zum Richard Lowenherz. At dinnertime, we descended to the hotel's dining room and enjoyed a delicious veal goulash with dumplings; *Kalbsgulyás mit Knödel*, as the menu listed it. After dinner, we fell into conversation with some English-speaking Austrians out on a vacation trip. Did we know that in the year 1193, after the disasters of the Crusades, England's Richard the Lion-hearted was returning on foot from the Holy Land? He was recognized and captured by his enemy, the Duke Leopold; during his imprisonment, his faithful minstrel, Blondel, sang to him. The very hotel we were staying in, the Gasthof Zum Richard Lowenherz was named for the fearless king. It was a fascinating story but it didn't make the veal goulash taste better; nothing could, it was so good to begin with.

Kalbsgulyás mit Knödel

(VEAL GOULASH WITH DUMPLINGS)

4 tablespoons butter
1½ cups chopped onions
2 pounds boneless veal,
    cut into ½-inch cubes
½ cup tomato sauce
¾ cup beef broth
2½ teaspoons salt
2 teaspoons paprika
¼ teaspoon black pepper

1 cup sour cream
1½ cups sifted flour
2 teaspoons baking powder
¼ teaspoon thyme
2 tablespoons minced
    parsley
3 tablespoons shortening
¾ cup milk (approx.)

Melt the butter in a skillet; sauté the onions and veal until browned. Mix in the tomato sauce, broth, 1¾ teaspoons salt, the paprika, and pepper. Cover and cook over low heat for 45 minutes or until the veal is tender. Stir in the sour cream gradually. Heat and taste for seasoning.

Sift together the flour, baking powder, and remaining salt. Mix in the thyme and parsley; then cut in the shortening. Stir in just enough of the milk to make a batter thick enough to hold its shape. Drop from a teaspoon around the edge of the goulash. Cover tightly and cook over low heat 15 minutes.

Serves 6–8.

Lombatina con Verdure

(VEAL CHOPS WITH VEGETABLES)

6 veal chops, cut 1 inch
thick
¼ cup flour
2 teaspoons salt
¼ teaspoon freshly
ground black pepper
2 tablespoons olive oil
4 tablespoons butter

½ cup Marsala or sweet
sherry
½ teaspoon thyme
2 tablespoons heavy cream
1 cup sautéed sliced
mushrooms
18 cooked asparagus
2 cups cooked green peas

Dip the chops into a mixture of the flour, salt, and pepper. Heat the oil and 2 tablespoons butter in a skillet or casserole; brown the chops in it on both sides. Add the wine and thyme; cover and cook over low heat 15 minutes. Stir in the cream. Spread the mushrooms over the chops and arrange the asparagus on top. Dot with the remaining butter and surround with the peas. Cover and bake in a 450° oven 10 minutes.
Serves 6.

Scaloppine with Rice and Vegetables

1¼ pounds veal scaloppine
(about 12 pieces)
¼ cup flour
2½ teaspoons salt
½ teaspoon freshly
ground black pepper
4 tablespoons olive oil
1½ cups chopped onions
2 green peppers, cut in
julienne strips

1 cup raw rice
1½ cups peeled chopped
tomatoes
2½ cups beef broth
1 pound green peas,
shelled
2 carrots
½ teaspoon basil

Dip the veal slices in a mixture of the flour, 1 teaspoon salt, and ¼ teaspoon pepper.

Heat 2 tablespoons of the olive oil in a skillet; sauté the onions and green peppers 5 minutes. Add the rice; cook 5 minutes, stirring almost constantly. Add the tomatoes, broth, green peas, carrots, basil, and remaining salt and pepper. Cook over low heat for 10 minutes, stirring occasionally.

Heat the remaining olive oil in a skillet; sauté the veal until browned on both sides. Add to the vegetable mixture. Cook 10 minutes, or until rice is tender. Taste for seasoning.

Serves 4–6.

Veal Gumbo

2 quarts water
¾ pound spinach, shredded or 1 package frozen
2 cups shredded green cabbage
2 cups chopped watercress
1 cup chopped parsley
2 cups chopped green onions
3 tablespoons butter
1½ pounds boneless veal, cut into ½-inch cubes
¼ pound smoked ham, diced

1 cup chopped onions
2 teaspoons salt
½ teaspoon freshly ground black pepper
¼ teaspoon cayenne pepper
½ teaspoon ground allspice
½ teaspoon thyme
1 bay leaf, finely chopped
1 cup raw rice
1 tablespoon filé powder (optional)

Combine the water, spinach, cabbage, watercress, parsley, and green onions; bring to a boil and cook over medium heat 1 hour. Purée the undrained mixture in an electric blender or force through a sieve.

Melt the butter in a Dutch oven or heavy, deep saucepan; sauté the veal, ham, and onions until browned. Mix in the salt, pepper, cayenne pepper, allspice, thyme, and bay leaf. Add the puréed mixture. Bring to a boil, cover, and cook over low heat 30 minutes. Add the rice; cook 30 minutes longer. Taste for seasoning. Gradually mix in the *filé* powder, but do not reheat after *filé* is added. Serve with rice.

Serves 6–8.

Ground Veal Ragoût

3 tablespoons vegetable
   oil
1 cup chopped onions
2 pounds ground veal
1½ teaspoons salt
½ teaspoon freshly
   ground black pepper
¼ teaspoon cumin seeds

1 tablespoon flour
1 8-ounce can tomato
   sauce
2 packages frozen mixed
   vegetables, thawed
1 cup sour cream
2 tablespoons minced
   parsley

Heat the oil in a skillet; sauté the onions 5 minutes. Add the veal; cook over medium heat, stirring almost steadily, until the meat is browned. Mix in the salt, pepper, cumin, and flour, then the tomato sauce. Cover and cook over low heat 20 minutes. Add the vegetables; cook 10 minutes longer. Mix in the sour cream; heat, but do not let boil. Taste for seasoning; sprinkle with the parsley.

Serves 6–8.

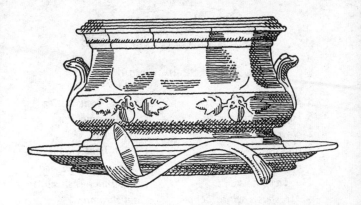

Veal and Black Olive Ragoût

3 pounds boneless leg of
  veal, cut into 1½-inch
  cubes
½ cup flour
2½ teaspoons salt
½ teaspoon freshly
  ground black pepper
4 tablespoons olive oil
¾ cup sliced onions
1 clove garlic, minced

½ teaspoon thyme
1 cup dry white wine
1 tablespoon tomato
  paste
½ cup chicken broth
2 cups potato balls or
  cubes
3 tablespoons butter
1 cup sliced black olives

Toss the veal in a mixture of the flour, salt, and pepper. Heat the oil in a casserole or deep skillet with ovenproof handle; brown the veal in it. Mix in the onions and garlic; cook until onions brown. Add the thyme, wine, tomato paste, and broth. Cover and bake in a 325° oven 2 hours.

While the meat is cooking, lightly brown the potatoes in the butter. Add the potatoes and olives and bake 15 minutes longer.
Serves 6–8.

Veal Fricassee in Cream Sauce

3 pounds boneless veal	2 tablespoons butter
5 cups chicken broth	3 tablespoons flour
2 cloves	2 egg yolks
2 onions	½ cup light cream
1 carrot, quartered	1½ cups cooked rice
1½ teaspoons salt	1 cup sautéed sliced
¼ teaspoon white pepper	mushrooms
½ teaspoon thyme	12 small white onions,
1 bay leaf	sauteed

Cut the veal into 2-inch cubes; place in a saucepan and add cold water to cover. Bring to a boil, cook 2 minutes, then drain and rinse under cold water. Return to the pan and add the broth. Bring to a boil and skim the top. Stick the cloves into the onions and add with the carrot, salt, pepper, thyme, and bay leaf. Cover and cook over medium heat 1 hour or until tender. Drain the meat. Strain the stock and reserve 2½ cups.

Melt the butter in a saucepan; blend in the flour and gradually add the reserved stock, stirring steadily to the boiling point. Cook over low heat 10 minutes. Beat the egg yolks and cream in a bowl; gradually add a little of the hot sauce, stirring steadily to prevent curdling. Return to balance of sauce and cook, stirring steadily until thickened. Add the meat, rice, mushrooms, and onions; taste for seasoning. Cook over very low heat 10 minutes, but do not let boil.

Serves 6–8.

Veau à l'Ancienne

(VEAL, OLD-FASHIONED STYLE)

1 breast of veal
2 tablespoons olive oil
2 tablespoons butter
¾ cup chopped onions
¼ cup chopped celery
2 cups peeled cubed
  tomatoes
2 teaspoons salt
½ teaspoon freshly
  ground black pepper

½ teaspoon marjoram
½ cup hot beef broth
2 cups peeled cubed
  potatoes
1 package frozen peas and
  carrots, thawed
2 tablespoons minced
  parsley

Have the veal cut up into 2-inch pieces, bone and all. Heat
the oil and butter in a Dutch oven or heavy casserole; sauté the
onions and celery 5 minutes. Add the veal; cook until browned.
Add the tomatoes, salt, pepper, and marjoram. Cover and bake
in a 300° oven 1½ hours, adding the broth from time to time.
Skim the fat. Add the potatoes, peas and carrots; recover and
bake 20 minutes longer. Sprinkle with the parsley.

Serves 4–5.

Veal Stew in Red Wine

3 slices salt pork, diced
3 pounds boneless veal,
  cut into 1½-inch cubes
12 small white onions
3 carrots, sliced
1½ teaspoons salt
½ teaspoon white pepper
1 clove garlic, minced
3 tablespoons flour

2 cups dry red wine
2 teaspoons finely
  chopped bay leaves
¼ teaspoon thyme
2 cups potato balls
½ pound mushrooms,
  sliced and sautéed
2 tablespoons minced
  parsley

Brown the salt pork in a deep skillet or casserole; remove the browned pieces and reserve. Pour off all but 3 tablespoons fat. In the fat remaining, brown the veal, onions, and carrots. Sprinkle with the salt, pepper, garlic, and flour; add the wine, bay leaves, and thyme. Cover and cook over low heat 1 hour. Add the potatoes; cook 15 minutes. Skim the fat. Add the pork bits, mushrooms, and parsley. Cook 5 minutes longer. Taste for seasoning.

Serves 6–8.

Veal Paprika and Vegetables

3 pounds boneless veal
½ cup flour
2 teaspoons salt
½ teaspoon freshly ground black pepper
4 tablespoons butter
2 cups sliced onions
2 cups boiling water

2 teaspoons paprika
1 package frozen cauliflower, thawed
¼ pound mushrooms, sliced and sautéed
1 cup sour cream
2 tablespoons minced parsley

Cut the veal into 1½-inch cubes and toss in a mixture of the flour, salt, and pepper. Melt the butter in a casserole; brown the veal in it. Add the onions; cook 5 minutes. Pour off the fat and add the water and paprika; cover and cook over low heat 1½ hours. Add the cauliflower and mushrooms; cook 5 minutes. Stir in the sour cream and parsley gently; heat, but do not let boil.

Serves 6–8.

Poitrine de Veau à l'Etuvée

(BRAISED BREAST OF VEAL)

3 pounds breast of veal	12 small white onions
2 teaspoons salt	1 clove garlic, minced
½ teaspoon freshly	¾ cup water
ground black pepper	3 cups raw shoestring
4 tablespoons butter	potatoes
2 tablespoons warm	1¼ pounds green beans,
cognac	cut in half
½ pound sausage meat	

Have the veal cut up into serving-sized pieces; season with the salt and pepper. Melt the butter in a Dutch oven; brown the veal in it. Set the cognac aflame, and pour it over the veal. When flames die, add the sausage meat, onions, and garlic. Cover and cook over low heat 30 minutes, shaking the pan frequently. Pour off the fat and add ½ cup water. Cover and cook 45 minutes. Add potatoes, beans, and remaining water. Recover and cook 20 minutes.

Serves 4–6.

Vitello alla Genovese

(VEAL WITH RICE, GENOA STYLE)

3 tablespoons olive oil	¼ teaspoon rosemary
2 tablespoons butter	2 tablespoons minced
1 cup chopped onions	parsley
1 cup chopped celery	¾ cup dry white wine
1 cup grated carrots	3 cups water
1½ pounds ground veal	1½ cups raw rice
2½ teaspoons salt	Grated Parmesan cheese
½ teaspoon freshly	
ground black pepper	

Heat the oil and butter in a saucepan; sauté the onions, celery, and carrots 10 minutes. Mix in the veal, 1 teaspoon salt, the pepper, rosemary, and parsley; sauté 5 minutes, stirring frequently. Add the wine; cover and cook over low heat 45 minutes.

Prepare the rice meanwhile. Combine the water, rice, and remaining salt in a saucepan; bring to a boil, cover, and cook over low heat 15 minutes. Drain, if any water remains. Add to the meat; cook 5 minutes. Taste for seasoning. Serve with grated Parmesan cheese.

Serves 4–6.

❋❋❋❋❋❋❋❋❋❋❋❋❋❋❋❋

Blanquette de Veau au Riz

(VEAL STEW WITH RICE, FRENCH STYLE)

¼ pound butter	2 sprigs parsley
2 pounds boneless veal, cut into 1½-inch cubes	1 bay leaf
	½ teaspoon marjoram
2 cups chopped onions	½ pound mushrooms, sliced
¼ cup flour	
1 cup dry vermouth	3 cups firm-cooked rice
2 teaspoons salt	1 egg yolk
½ teaspoon white pepper	1 teaspoon lemon juice
2 cups boiling water	¾ cup heavy cream

Melt the butter in a Dutch oven; brown the veal in it. Add the onions; cook 5 minutes. Stir in the flour until browned. Add the vermouth; cook over high heat 5 minutes. Add the salt, pepper, boiling water, parsley, bay leaf, and marjoram. Cover and cook over low heat 1¼ hours. Add the mushrooms and rice; cook 15 minutes.

Beat together the egg yolk, lemon juice, and cream. Gradually add to the pan, stirring steadily. Taste for seasoning and heat, but do not let boil. *Serves 4–6.*

Veal and Green Rice

3 tablespoons chili sauce
3 tablespoons soy sauce
1 tablespoon vinegar
¼ teaspoon freshly
  ground black pepper
½ cup vegetable oil
2 pounds veal steak, cut
  ¼ inch thick

1 cup raw rice
1 cup shredded spinach
1 cup chopped green
  onions
½ cup minced parsley
2 cups chicken broth
1 8-ounce can green peas,
  drained

Mix together the chili sauce, soy sauce, vinegar, pepper, and half the oil. Cut the veal into serving-sized pieces and marinate it in the previous mixture 2 hours at room temperature, or overnight in the refrigerator. Baste and turn occasionally.

Drain the veal. Heat 2 tablespoons of the remaining oil in a skillet. Add the veal; cook over low heat until tender and browned on both sides.

Heat the remaining oil in a casserole; stir in the rice until translucent. Add the spinach, green onions, and parsley; cook 3 minutes. Add the broth and peas. Cover, bring to a boil, and cook over low heat 10 minutes. Taste for seasoning. Arrange the veal on top; recover and cook 5 minutes longer or until the rice is tender and fairly dry.

Serves 4–6.

Kalbnuss Elsasser Art

(VEAL WITH SAUERKRAUT, AUSTRIAN FASHION)

2 pounds sauerkraut
1 cup dry white wine
½ teaspoon caraway
seeds
3 pounds boned loin of
veal
4 tablespoons butter
1 cup chopped onions

1½ teaspoons salt
½ teaspoon freshly
ground black pepper
½ cup water
1 egg yolk
3 cups seasoned mashed
potatoes

Combine the sauerkraut, wine, and caraway seeds in a casserole. Cover and cook over low heat 1½ hours, stirring frequently. While the sauerkraut is cooking, prepare the veal.

Cut the veal into ½-inch-thick slices. Melt the butter in a skillet; brown the veal on both sides. Add the onions, salt, and pepper, and cook 5 minutes. Add the water; cover and cook over low heat 25 minutes, or until the veal is tender. When the sauerkraut is cooked, arrange the veal over it, and pour pan juices on top. Beat the egg yolk into the potatoes, and make a border around the edge of the casserole. Place under a hot broiler until potatoes are delicately browned.

Serves 6–8.

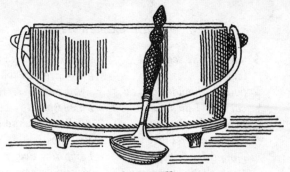

Sformato de Vitello

(VEAL AND ZUCCHINI CASSEROLE)

1½ pounds small
  zucchini
2½ teaspoons salt
12 veal scallops
¾ teaspoon freshly
  ground black pepper

6 tablespoons butter
¼ teaspoon nutmeg
¾ cup grated Parmesan
  cheese
2 cups cooked rice
½ cup light cream

Scrub the zucchini and slice very thin. Sprinkle with 1½ teaspoons salt and let stand 1 hour. Drain well. Season the veal with ¼ teaspoon pepper and the remaining salt. Lightly brown the veal in 2 tablespoons of the butter.

In a 13 by 9-inch buttered baking dish or 2-quart casserole, spread ⅓ the zucchini; sprinkle with a little pepper and nutmeg. Arrange 6 pieces of veal over it; sprinkle with ¼ cup cheese and dot with 1 tablespoon butter. Spread half the rice over it. Cover with ½ the remaining zucchini, sprinkle with a little seasoning, arrange remaining veal over it, sprinkle with ¼ cup cheese, and dot with 1 tablespoon of the butter. Spread remaining rice over it. Cover with the remaining zucchini, sprinkle with the remaining cheese, and dot with remaining butter. Add the cream. Bake in a 350° oven 45 minutes.

Serves 4–6.

Veal with Cashew Nuts

3 tablespoons vegetable
oil
2 pounds shoulder of veal,
cut into 1-inch cubes
2 teaspoons salt
½ teaspoon freshly
ground black pepper
½ cup chopped onions

1 clove garlic, minced
1 8-ounce can tomato
sauce
1 tablespoon
Worcestershire sauce
2½ cups boiling water
1 cup raw rice
¾ cup cashew nuts

Heat the oil in a Dutch oven; brown the veal in it. Add
the salt, pepper, onions, and garlic; cook 5 minutes. Stir in the
tomato sauce, Worcestershire, and ½ cup boiling water. Bring
to a boil, cover, and cook over low heat 45 minutes. Add the
remaining boiling water, the rice, and nuts. Recover and cook
25 minutes longer, or until veal and rice are tender.

Serves 4–6.

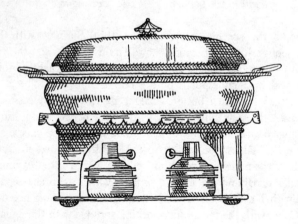

Lamb

Every visitor to India is almost duty-bound to visit the Taj Mahal, one of the most famous buildings in the world. From New Delhi to Agra, where the Taj is located, is a drive of several hours over good roads, and quite a fascinating trip. The road passes through primitive villages, junglelike scenery with monkeys hanging from the trees, brilliantly colored parrots cawing, and also hot climate much of the year. When we reached Agra, the temperature could hardly have been much under 100°, and there was nothing I yearned for so much as a place to wash up and a cooling drink. The British hotel provided both of those things, and after a rest on the airy terrace, I was ready for lunch.

What a letdown! One of the wonderful things about the British is that they take their culture and way of life with them wherever they go, and are quite stubborn about it. They were so stubborn that they didn't know they were licked during the war years and went on to win. In any British outpost around the world, British food is served, and customs are still followed. But in a climate of about 100°, it does seem pretty ridiculous to offer a menu of steaming hot consommé, roast leg of lamb and potatoes, and no alternative choices. My woebegone expression caused the Indian waiter to ask me if anything was wrong. I told him nothing was wrong, except that I didn't want hot consommé and roast leg of lamb. He looked suitably distressed but then paused for a moment and hesitatingly asked if I wouldn't like an Indian lamb dish that the waiters were going to eat. It was a mixture of lamb, rice, and vegetables made with yogurt, but perhaps not to *memsahib's* taste? He was wrong— it was to *memsahib's* taste, and yours too. And if you ever go to Agra, and they try to serve you hot consommé and roast leg of lamb when the temperature is near 100°, don't eat it. Instead, order lamb *biriani*.

Lamb Biriani

(INDIAN LAMB-VEGETABLE CASSEROLE)

4 tablespoons butter
1½ cups thinly sliced
   onions
2 pounds boneless lamb,
   cut into ½-inch cubes
1 cup raw rice
1 cup yogurt
2 teaspoons ground cumin
1 pound green beans, or 1
   package frozen, thawed
1 pound green peas,
   shelled, or 1 package
   frozen, thawed

1 cup diced carrots
1 clove garlic, minced
¼ teaspoon powdered
   ginger
2 tablespoons tomato
   paste
2 cups boiling water
2 teaspoons salt
½ teaspoon freshly
   ground black pepper

Melt the butter in a casserole; sauté the onions and lamb 10 minutes. Mix in the rice, yogurt, and cumin; cook over low heat 5 minutes. Add the beans, peas, and carrots; cook over low heat 10 minutes, shaking the pan frequently. Mix in the garlic, ginger, tomato paste, water, salt, and pepper. Cover and cook over low heat 20 minutes. Watch carefully and add a little more water if necessary.

Serves 4–6.

Indian Lamb-Vegetable Curry

2 pounds boneless lamb,
cut into 1-inch cubes
3 teaspoons salt
¾ teaspoon freshly
ground black pepper
¾ pound green beans, or
1 package frozen,
thawed
1 pound green peas,
shelled, or 1 package
frozen, thawed
4 carrots, diced
1½ pounds potatoes,
peeled and quartered

4 tablespoons butter
1½ cups thinly sliced
onions
½ teaspoon dried mint
1 cup yogurt
2 teaspoons ground cumin
1 clove garlic, minced
¼ teaspoon powdered
ginger
2 tablespoons tomato paste
1½ cups boiling water

Brown the lamb in a skillet; drain and toss with half the salt and pepper.

Combine the beans, peas, carrots, and potatoes in a bowl. Cover with boiling water. Cover the bowl and let stand 10 minutes; then drain.

Melt the butter in a casserole; sauté the onions 10 minutes. Mix in the mint, yogurt, and cumin; cook over low heat 5 minutes. Add the vegetables and lamb; cook over low heat 10 minutes, shaking the pan frequently. Mix in the garlic, ginger, tomato paste, water, and remaining salt and pepper. Cover and cook over low heat 20 minutes.

Serves 4–6.

Curried Lamb

3 tablespoons butter
¾ cup finely chopped
  onions
3 pounds boneless lamb,
  cut into ¾-inch cubes
2 teaspoons salt
2 tablespoons curry
  powder

¼ cup chopped
  preserved ginger
1½ cups beef broth
2 tablespoons lime or
  lemon juice
½ cup packaged fine-
  grated coconut
1 cup light cream

Melt the butter in a deep skillet or casserole; brown the onions and lamb in it. Stir in the salt, curry powder, ginger, and
broth. Cover and cook over low heat 1 hour. Stir the lime juice
into the pan juices, then add the coconut and cream. Cook 10
minutes, but do not let boil. Serve with rice.

Serves 6–8

Baked Lamb Curry

4 tablespoons butter
1½ cups chopped onions
2 pounds boneless lamb,
  cut into 1-inch cubes
1½ teaspoons salt
¼ teaspoon freshly
  ground black pepper
1 tablespoon curry powder

1 tablespoon flour
2 cups beef broth
1 teaspoon drained capers
1 cup milk
4 cups cooked, drained rice
2 tablespoons flaked
  coconut

Melt the butter in a saucepan; sauté the onions, lamb, salt,
pepper, and curry powder 15 minutes, stirring frequently. Blend
in the flour. Gradually add the broth, stirring constantly to the

boiling point. Cook over low heat 45 minutes or until the lamb is tender. Add the capers and milk. Cook 5 minutes, stirring occasionally. Taste for seasoning.

Spread the rice in a buttered baking dish. Pour the lamb mixture over it. Sprinkle the coconut on top. Bake in a 375° oven 10 minutes.

Serves 4–6.

Lancashire Hot Pot

4 tablespoons butter	4 onions, sliced
6 shoulder lamb chops	¼ pound mushrooms,
3 teaspoons salt	sliced
1 teaspoon freshly ground	½ pound string beans, cut
black pepper	in half
6 potatoes, peeled and	1 cup stock
sliced	½ cup light cream

Melt 2 tablespoons butter in a skillet and brown chops well on both sides. Transfer to a baking dish or casserole and sprinkle with 1½ teaspoons salt and ½ teaspoon pepper. Arrange a layer of half the potatoes over the chops. Add successive layers of onions, mushrooms, and string beans. Combine the broth, cream, and remaining salt and pepper, and pour over the vegetables. Arrange the remaining potatoes in an even overlapping design on top. Dot with the remaining butter. Cover and bake in a 350° oven 2½ hours. Remove cover and bake 20 minutes longer or until potatoes are brown on top. Serve directly from the dish.

Serves 6.

Braised Lamb, Swedish Style

6 shoulder lamb chops, cut
  1 inch thick
2 tablespoons butter
1½ cups sliced onions
1 cup sliced carrots
1½ teaspoons salt

½ teaspoon freshly
  ground black pepper
2 teaspoons sugar
1¼ cups brewed coffee
½ cup heavy cream
6 potatoes, peeled and
  quartered

Trim the fat off the chops. Melt the butter in a deep skillet; brown the lamb and onions in it. Pour off the fat. Add the carrots, salt, pepper, and sugar; cook 5 minutes. Mix in the coffee and cream; cover, bring to a boil and cook over low heat 45 minutes. Add the potatoes; cook 20 minutes longer. Skim the fat and taste for seasoning. *Serves 6.*

Irish Stew

8 shoulder lamb chops, cut
  1 inch thick
2½ teaspoons salt

¾ teaspoon freshly
  ground black pepper
16 small potatoes, peeled
16 small white onions

Trim off all the fat from the chops and arrange them in a Dutch oven or heavy saucepan. Sprinkle with some of the salt and pepper. Make layers of the potatoes and onions, sprinkling the layers with salt and pepper. Add water to almost reach the top of the ingredients. Bring to a boil, cover, and cook over low heat 1½ hours. *Serves 4.*

Braised Lamb Shanks with Rice

4 lamb shanks
3 tablespoons vegetable oil
12 small white onions
2 teaspoons salt
½ teaspoon freshly
  ground black pepper
¼ teaspoon marjoram

½ cup chopped tomatoes
3 cups boiling water
1 cup raw rice
1 pound whole green beans
2 tablespoons minced
  parsley

Have the shanks sawed into serving-sized pieces. Heat the oil in a Dutch oven or heavy saucepan; brown the shanks in it. Pour off the fat. Add the onions; let brown. Add the salt, pepper, marjoram, tomatoes, and 1 cup of the water. Cover and cook over low heat 1¼ hours. Skim the fat; add the remaining boiling water, the rice and green beans. Recover and cook over low heat 30 minutes. Sprinkle with the parsley. *Serves 4–6.*

Haricot de Mouton

(LAMB WITH WHITE BEANS, FRENCH STYLE)

1 pound dried navy beans
6 tablespoons butter
2 pounds boneless lamb,
  cut into 1-inch cubes
1 cup chopped onions
2 tablespoons flour

1 tablespoon tomato paste
2 cloves garlic, minced
2½ teaspoons salt
½ teaspoon freshly
  ground black pepper
Boiling water

Wash the beans, cover with water, and bring to a boil. Let soak 1 hour. Drain, add fresh water to cover, bring to a boil, and cook over low heat 1½ hours. Drain.

While the beans are cooking, melt the butter in a Dutch oven or heavy saucepan; brown the lamb in it. Add the onions; cook 5 minutes. Stir in the flour until browned. Add the tomato paste, garlic, salt, pepper, and boiling water to barely cover. Cover and cook over low heat 1½ hours. Add the beans and cook 30 minutes longer, or until the meat and beans are tender.

Serves 4–6.

Fassolia Me Arni

(GREEK BEAN AND LAMB STEW)

2 *cups dried white beans*	1 *bay leaf*
2 *tablespoons olive oil*	1½ *cups peeled chopped*
1½ *cups chopped onions*	*tomatoes*
2 *pounds boneless lamb,*	2 *cloves garlic, minced*
cut into 2-inch cubes	1 *package frozen French-*
1½ *cups boiling water*	*style green beans,*
2 *teaspoons salt*	*thawed*
½ *teaspoon freshly*	2 *tablespoons minced*
ground black pepper	*parsley*

Wash the dried beans, cover with water, and bring to a boil. Cook 5 minutes, remove from the heat, and let stand 1 hour. Drain. Add fresh water to cover, bring to a boil and cook over low heat 1½ hours. Drain.

Heat the oil in a Dutch oven or casserole; brown the onions in it. Add the lamb and cook until browned. Add the beans, the 1½ cups boiling water, the salt, pepper, and bay leaf. Cover and cook over low heat 1 hour. Add the tomatoes and garlic; recover and cook 45 minutes. Add the green beans; cook 15 minutes longer. Sprinkle with the parsley.

Serves 6–8.

Cassoulet

4 cups pea beans
2 quarts water
2 cloves garlic, minced
2 onions
2 cloves
½ teaspoon thyme
1 bay leaf
⅛ pound salt pork, diced
2 tablespoons vegetable
    oil
1 pound lamb, cubed

1½ pounds pork, cubed
1½ cups chopped onions
1 6-ounce can tomato
    sauce
1 cup dry white wine
1 tablespoon salt
Confit d'oie or 1 roast
    duck cut into pieces
    and boned (see NOTE)
2 garlic sausages, sliced

Wash the beans, add the 2 quarts water, and bring to a boil.
Cook 2 minutes, remove from heat, and let soak 1 hour. Add
the garlic, onions stuck with the cloves, thyme, bay leaf, and
salt pork. Bring to a boil and cook over medium heat 1 hour.

Heat the oil in a skillet; brown the lamb and pork in it. Add
to the beans. In oil remaining in the skillet, brown the onions.
Add to the bean mixture with the tomato sauce, wine, and salt.
Cover and cook over low heat 1 hour. Transfer to a large
casserole. Add the confit d'oie or duck to the beans with the
sausages. Mix lightly. Taste for seasoning. Bake in a 325° oven
50 minutes.

Serves 8–10.

NOTE: Confit d'oie (preserved goose) is available in cans in
specialty food shops.

Gormeh Sabzee

(LAMB AND BEAN STEW, IRANIAN STYLE)

3 pounds boneless lamb
⅓ cup sesame or
vegetable oil
2 cups chopped green
onions
8 cups chopped parsley
2½ teaspoons salt

¾ teaspoon freshly
ground black pepper
⅓ cup lemon juice
1 lemon, quartered
3 cups boiling water
2 16-ounce cans kidney
beans

Trim the fat off the lamb and cut into 1-inch cubes. Heat 2 tablespoons of the oil in a Dutch oven; brown the lamb in it. Remove. Heat the remaining oil in the pan; add the green onions and parsley; cook 5 minutes, stirring frequently. Return the meat and add the salt, pepper, lemon juice, lemon, and boiling water. Cover and cook over low heat 1¼ hours. Skim the fat; add the undrained beans. Taste for seasoning and cook 15 minutes longer. *Serves 6–8.*

Cassoulet Toulousain

(FRENCH BEANS, LAMB, AND DUCK)

1½ pounds dried white
pea beans
1½ pounds garlic sausage
(French, if available)
4 tablespoons rendered
chicken fat or butter
¾ cup chopped onions
2 cloves garlic, minced
2 pounds boneless lamb,
cubed

1 4-pound duck, disjointed
1 8-ounce can tomato
sauce
2 bay leaves
1 tablespoon salt
½ teaspoon freshly
ground black pepper
¼ cup dry bread crumbs

193

Wash the beans, cover with water, and bring to a boil; remove from heat and let stand 1 hour. Drain. Cover with fresh water; add the sausage. Bring to a boil and cook 30 minutes. Remove the sausage and cook the beans 1½ hours longer, or until almost tender. Prepare the meat while the beans are cooking.

Melt the fat in a deep skillet; brown the onions, garlic, lamb, and duck in it. Pour off the fat. Add the tomato sauce, bay leaves, salt, and pepper. Cover and cook over low heat 45 minutes or until tender. Drain the beans. In a large casserole, arrange several layers of the beans and undrained meat mixture, starting and ending with the beans. Slice the sausage and arrange on top. Sprinkle with the bread crumbs. Bake in a 450° oven 25 minutes.

Serves 10–12.

Agneau aux Flageolets

(DRIED GREEN BEANS AND LAMB)

1½ cups dried flageolets	1 cup chopped onions
1 clove	1 clove garlic, minced
1 whole onion	2 cups peeled chopped
1 bay leaf	tomatoes
2 sprigs parsley	3 tablespoons minced
4 tablespoons butter	parsley
3 pounds shoulder of	2½ teaspoons salt
lamb, cut into serving-	½ teaspoon freshly
sized pieces	ground black pepper

Wash the beans, cover with water, bring to a boil, cook 2 minutes, then let soak 1 hour. Stick the clove into the whole onion and add to the beans with the bay leaf and parsley. Bring to a boil again, and cook over low heat 1½ hours. Drain.

While the beans are cooking, melt the butter in a Dutch oven or casserole; brown the lamb in it. Add the onions and garlic; cook 5 minutes. Add the tomatoes, cook 10 minutes. Add the beans, parsley, salt, and pepper. Cover and cook over low heat 30 minutes longer, or until the beans and lamb are tender.

Serves 6–8.

Israeli Meat and Beans

2 cups dried Lima beans	¼ cup barley
6 tablespoons rendered chicken fat or butter	3 cups beef broth
	2 teaspoons salt
1½ cups chopped onions	½ teaspoon freshly ground black pepper
2 pounds boneless lamb, cubed	
	2 teaspoons paprika
1 2-pound chicken, disjointed	1 tablespoon flour
	3 frankfurters, sliced ½ inch thick
2 tomatoes, peeled and chopped	

Wash the Lima beans. Place in a saucepan with water to cover, bring to a boil, then remove from heat and let soak 2 hours. Drain well; add fresh water to cover. Bring to a boil, cover saucepan, and cook over low heat 1½ hours. Drain.

Melt 4 tablespoons fat in a skillet. Sauté the onions 10 minutes; remove from skillet. Brown the lamb and chicken in the fat remaining in the skillet. Combine the beans, onions, browned meats, tomatoes, barley, broth, salt, pepper, paprika, and flour in a 4-quart Dutch oven or casserole. Dot with the remaining fat; cover and bake in a 325° oven 2 hours. Add a little boiling water from time to time if pan becomes too dry. Taste for seasoning. Remove cover, arrange frankfurters on top, and bake 20 minutes longer.

Serves 6–8.

Lamb and Wheat, Middle East Style

1½ cups cracked wheat
2 pounds boneless lamb,
　 cut into 2-inch cubes
2 teaspoons salt
½ teaspoon freshly
　 ground black pepper
2 tablespoons olive oil
1 cup chopped onions

2 cups canned drained
　 tomatoes
½ teaspoon orégano
4 cups boiling water
2 packages frozen
　 French-style green
　 beans, thawed

Wash the wheat (available in health-food or gourmet shops) under water. Drain well, then knead until fairly dry.

Toss the lamb with the salt and pepper. Heat the oil in a Dutch oven or casserole; brown the lamb in it. Stir in the onions and let brown. Add the tomatoes and orégano; cover and cook over low heat 40 minutes. Add the wheat, boiling water, and beans. Cook 20 minutes longer or until all the liquid is absorbed. Taste for seasoning. *Serves 6–8.*

Daoud Basha

(LAMB BALLS WITH RICE, PERSIAN STYLE)

2 pounds ground lamb
2 teaspoons salt
½ teaspoon freshly
　 ground black pepper
3 tablespoons minced
　 parsley
¼ cup cold water
4 tablespoons vegetable
　 oil

2 cups chopped onions
1 8-ounce can tomato
　 sauce
1 cup raw rice
3 cups boiling water
¼ cup pine nuts or sliced
　 almonds

Mix together the lamb, salt, pepper, parsley, and water. Form into 1-inch balls.

Heat the oil in a large, deep skillet or Dutch oven. Brown the meat balls on all sides. Add the onions and tomato sauce. Cover and cook over low heat for 15 minutes, stirring occasionally. Add rice, water, and nuts, and cook 20 minutes longer.

Serves 6–8.

Rice à la Grecque

4 tablespoons butter
1½ pounds boneless lamb, cut into ½-inch cubes
1 cup chopped onion
1 clove garlic, minced
1 cup shredded lettuce
3 pork sausages, sliced
¾ cup sliced mushrooms
1½ cups peeled diced tomatoes
1½ cups raw rice
3 cups boiling water
1½ teaspoons salt
¼ teaspoon freshly ground black pepper
1 cup cooked or canned peas
¼ cup chopped pimientos
3 tablespoons raisins

Melt 2 tablespoons of the butter in a Dutch oven or large saucepan; brown the lamb in it. Remove. Add the remaining butter; sauté the onions 10 minutes. Add the garlic, lettuce, sausages, mushrooms, and tomatoes; cook 3 minutes, stirring steadily. Return the lamb; cook over low heat 30 minutes. Mix in the rice, then add the boiling water, salt, and pepper. Cover tightly and cook over low heat 20 minutes. With a fork, stir in the peas, pimientos, and raisins.

Serves 6–8.

Couscous

(ALGERIAN SEMOLINA-MEAT STEW)

1 pound couscous
(falofel), or cracked
wheat

½ cup water

½ cup sesame or olive oil

2 pounds boneless leg of
lamb, cut into 1½-inch
cubes

3-pound chicken,
disjointed

2½ teaspoons salt

½ teaspoon freshly
ground black pepper

¼ teaspoon cayenne
pepper

½ teaspoon ground cumin

2 teaspoons ground
caraway seeds

3 tablespoons tomato
paste

2 cloves garlic, minced

2 quarts chicken broth

12 small white onions

6 carrots, cut in eighths

3 turnips, cut in eighths

2 small zucchini, sliced

1 small cabbage, cut into
8 wedges

1 can chick-peas, drained

1 green pepper, cut into
12 pieces

2 hard-cooked eggs, cut in
sixths

There are special *couscousières* available, consisting of a large,
deep saucepan with a colander type of arrangement which fits
over the bottom. The *couscous* is placed in the colander with
the meat and vegetables under it. Or you may use a colander
placed over a Dutch oven.

In either case, spread the *couscous* on a flat surface, and
sprinkle with the water. Using the fingers, knead lightly until
the grains are moistened.

Heat the oil in the bottom of the *couscousière* or Dutch oven;
add the lamb, chicken, salt, and pepper. Cook until browned,

stirring frequently. Mix in the cayenne pepper, cumin, caraway seeds, and tomato paste. Add the garlic and broth. Bring to a boil, cover and cook over low heat 35 minutes. Put the *couscous* in the colander portion of the *couscousière* or an ordinary colander. Place over the stew. Cover the pan with the cover or a large piece of foil, tucking in the sides to seal in the steam. Cook 15 minutes. Lift up the colander and add the onions, carrots, and turnips. Replace colander and recover; cook 15 minutes. Lift up the colander and add the zucchini, cabbage, chick-peas, and pepper. Replace colander, stir the *couscous* with a fork, and cover again. Cook 20 minutes longer. Taste the stew for seasoning. Spread the *couscous* on a large platter. Gradually add the gravy from the stew, stirring until it is absorbed. Cover and let stand 5 minutes.

Heap the *couscous* in a deep serving dish. Arrange the meat, chicken, vegetables, and eggs over it.

Serves 8–10.

Lamb, Turkish Style

2 cups raw rice	½ teaspoon cinnamon
6 shoulder lamb chops, cut 1 inch thick	¼ teaspoon ground cloves
2 teaspoons salt	½ teaspoon saffron
½ teaspoon freshly ground black pepper	3 cups boiling water
¼ pound butter	¼ cup seedless raisins
1 cup chopped onions	1 16-ounce can green peas, drained
1 clove garlic, minced	¼ cup sliced, blanched almonds

Soak the rice in cold water for 2 hours; drain. Brown the chops in a skillet. Drain and season with 1½ teaspoons salt and ¼ teaspoon pepper. While the chops are cooking, prepare the rice.

Melt the butter in a casserole or Dutch oven; sauté the onions and garlic 5 minutes. Add the rice; cook 5 minutes, stirring frequently. Add the cinnamon, cloves, saffron, water, and remaining salt and pepper. Cover and cook over low heat 15 minutes. With a fork, stir in the raisins, peas, and almonds. Arrange the chops on top. Cook 5 minutes longer.

Serves 6.

Tas Kebab

(LAMB STEW, MIDDLE EAST STYLE)

3 *pounds boneless lamb, cut into 2-inch cubes*	2 *tablespoons butter*
2½ *teaspoons salt*	2 *tablespoons vegetable oil*
¾ *teaspoon freshly ground black pepper*	3 *cups water*
½ *teaspoon cinnamon*	1 *8-ounce can tomato sauce*
½ *teaspoon crushed coriander*	1 *8-ounce can tiny peas, drained*
1 *cup thinly sliced onions*	1½ *cups raw rice*
2 *cups diced eggplant*	

Season the lamb with the salt, pepper, cinnamon, and coriander. Mix in the onions. Cover and let marinate for 2 hours at room temperature.

Sauté the eggplant in the butter until browned. Heat the oil in a Dutch oven or heavy skillet; brown the lamb and onions in it. Add ½ cup water; cook over low heat 1½ hours. Add the tomato sauce, eggplant, peas, rice, and remaining water. Cook 20 minutes.

Serves 6–8.

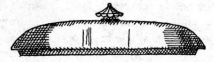

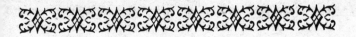

Lamb and Barley Stew

½ cup medium barley
2 cups water
3 tablespoons vegetable
   oil
2 pounds boneless lamb,
   cut into 1-inch cubes
1 cup sliced onions
½ cup sliced green
   peppers

2 teaspoons salt
¼ teaspoon white pepper
2 cups diced potatoes
1 cup sliced carrots
2 tablespoons minced
   parsley

Wash the barley and soak in the 2 cups water for 1 hour. Heat the oil in a Dutch oven or casserole; brown the lamb in it; mix in the onions and let brown. Pour off the fat; add the green peppers, salt, pepper, and undrained barley. Bring to a boil, cover, and cook over low heat 1½ hours, adding a little boiling water from time to time if necessary. Add the potatoes and carrots, recover, and cook 30 minutes longer. Sprinkle with the parsley. *Serves 4–6.*

Navarin aux Pommes

(LAMB STEW, FRENCH COUNTRY STYLE)

3 pounds boneless lamb,
   cut into 1½-inch cubes
2½ teaspoons salt
½ teaspoon freshly
   ground black pepper
4 tablespoons butter
3 tablespoons flour
Boiling water
3 tablespoons canned
   tomato sauce

2 cloves garlic, minced
3 sprigs parsley
1 bay leaf
½ teaspoon thyme
1½ pounds small
   potatoes, peeled
4 turnips, scraped and
   sliced
24 small white onions

Season the lamb with the salt and pepper. Melt the butter in a Dutch oven or casserole; brown the lamb in it. Add the flour and let it brown, stirring constantly. Add enough water to barely cover the meat. Bring to a boil and skim the top. Add the tomato sauce, garlic, parsley, bay leaf, and thyme. Cover and cook over low heat 1 hour. Discard the parsley and bay leaf.

Add the potatoes, turnips, and onions; recover and cook 45 minutes longer. Taste for seasoning.

Serves 6–8.

Gedünstete Lammkeule

(LAMB STEW, AUSTRIAN STYLE)

4 tablespoons butter
3 pounds boneless lamb, cut into 1½-inch cubes
2 teaspoons salt
½ teaspoon freshly ground black pepper
½ teaspoon caraway seeds
1½ cups sliced carrots
1 cup dry white wine
1 cup water
1 bay leaf

2 cups peeled diced tomatoes
16 small white onions
2 cups potato balls or cubes
2 packages frozen cauliflower flowerets, half cooked and drained
2 tablespoons minced dill or parsley

Melt the butter in a Dutch oven or casserole; brown the lamb in it. Add the salt, pepper, caraway seeds, carrots, wine, water, and bay leaf. Bring to a boil, cover, and cook over low heat 30 minutes. Add the tomatoes and onions; recover and cook 45 minutes. Add the potatoes and a little water if necessary; cook 20 minutes. Add the cauliflower; cook 5 minutes longer. Taste for seasoning and sprinkle with the dill or parsley. *Serves 6–8.*

Scotch Soup-Stew

3 pounds shoulder of
   lamb
3 quarts water
½ cup barley
½ cup split peas
4 teaspoons salt
½ teaspoon white pepper
1 pound onions, peeled
   and quartered

2 carrots, cut julienne
3 leeks, sliced
1 small turnip, cut
   julienne
6 small potatoes, cut in
   half

Cut the meat into serving-sized pieces and combine with the water in a kettle or heavy large casserole. Bring to a boil and skim the top. Add the barley, split peas, salt, and pepper. Cover and cook over low heat 1½ hours. Add all the vegetables; cook 30 minutes longer. Serve in bowls.

Serves 6–8.

Baked Lamb-Rice Casserole

1½ cups raw rice
3 pounds boneless lamb,
   cut into 1½-inch cubes
2 pounds tomatoes, peeled
   and sliced
3 teaspoons salt
¾ teaspoon freshly
   ground black pepper

½ teaspoon orégano
1 medium eggplant,
   peeled and sliced thin
2 green peppers, cut in
   eighths lengthwise
1½ cups puréed canned
   tomatoes
3 tablespoons olive oil

Wash the rice, cover with boiling water, and let soak 5 minutes. Drain. Brown the lamb cubes in a skillet; drain off all the fat.

In a greased casserole, spread half the tomatoes; sprinkle with a little of the salt, pepper, and orégano. Make layers of half the eggplant, green peppers, and lamb, sprinkling each layer with seasoning. Repeat the layers, then spread the rice on top. Add the puréed tomatoes, and sprinkle with the olive oil. Cover and bake in a 400° oven 1¼ hours, adding a very little boiling water if necessary to keep from burning. Remove cover and bake 10 minutes longer.

Serves 6.

Agneau à la Provençal

(BAKED LAMB, PROVENCE STYLE)

6 loin lamb chops, cut 1 inch thick	1 medium eggplant, peeled and sliced thin
1½ pounds tomatoes, sliced	2 green peppers, cut in eighths lengthwise
3 teaspoons salt	1 cup raw rice
¾ teaspoon freshly ground black pepper	1 cup puréed canned tomatoes
1 clove garlic, minced	1 cup beef broth
½ teaspoon basil	3 tablespoons olive oil

Brown the chops on both sides in a skillet; drain.

In a greased Dutch oven or casserole, spread half the tomatoes; sprinkle with a little of the salt, pepper, garlic, and basil. Make layers of half the eggplant and green peppers, sprinkling each layer with seasoning. Repeat the sequence, then spread rice over all. Arrange chops over the rice and season. Add the puréed tomatoes and broth and sprinkle with the olive oil. Cover and bake in a 400° oven 1¼ hours, adding a very little boiling water if necessary to keep from burning. Remove cover and bake 10 minutes longer. *Serves 6.*

Lamb and Prunes, Balkan Style

24 prunes
1½ cups fine egg noodles
3 pounds boneless lamb,
   cut into 2-inch cubes
¼ cup flour
2 teaspoons salt
½ teaspoon freshly
   ground black pepper

3 tablespoons butter
1½ cups coarsely chopped
   onions
¼ teaspoon cinnamon
¼ teaspoon nutmeg
Dash ground allspice
3½ cups chicken broth

Wash the prunes. Cover with water and let soak 4 hours. Cover the noodles with boiling water and let stand while preparing the meat.

Toss the lamb in a mixture of the flour, salt, and pepper. Melt the butter in a Dutch oven or heavy skillet; brown the lamb in it. Add the onions; cook 15 minutes. Add the cinnamon, nutmeg, allspice, and 2½ cups chicken broth. Bring to a boil, cover, and cook over low heat 1¼ hours. Add the drained prunes, drained noodles, and remaining broth. Cook 15 minutes longer. Taste for seasoning. *Serves 6–8.*

Abbacchio Pasticciare
(LAMB AND EGGPLANT CASSEROLE)

6 loin lamb chops, cut 1
   inch thick
3 teaspoons salt
¾ teaspoon freshly
   ground black pepper
¾ teaspoon basil
⅓ cup olive oil
1 medium eggplant,
   peeled and sliced thin

1½ pounds tomatoes,
   sliced
2 green peppers, cut in
   eighths lengthwise
1 cup raw rice
1 cup puréed canned
   tomatoes

Brown the chops on both sides in a skillet; drain. Season with a little of the salt, pepper, and basil. Heat 2 tablespoons of the oil in the skillet; lightly brown the eggplant in it.

In a greased casserole, spread half the tomatoes, sprinkle with a little of the salt, pepper, and basil. Make layers of half the eggplant and green peppers, sprinkling each layer with seasoning. Repeat the sequence, then spread rice over all. Arrange chops over the rice. Add the puréed tomatoes and sprinkle with the remaining olive oil. Cover and bake in a 400° oven 2 hours, adding a very little boiling water if necessary to keep from burning. Remove cover and cook 10 minutes longer.

Serves 6.

Aush Bhogar

(LAMB CURRY WITH DUMPLINGS, INDIAN STYLE)

3 pounds boneless lamb	2½ teaspoons salt
2½ cups chopped onions	4 tablespoons butter
3 cloves garlic, minced	2 cups water
1 teaspoon ground cumin	2 egg yolks
2 teaspoons ground coriander	2 tablespoons melted butter
1½ teaspoons turmeric	½ cup cracker meal
½ teaspoon powdered ginger	2 egg whites, stiffly beaten
½ teaspoon dried ground chili peppers	1 16-ounce can green peas, drained

Cut the lamb into 1-inch cubes. Pound or chop to a paste the onions, garlic, cumin, coriander, turmeric, ginger, chili peppers, and 2 teaspoons salt. Toss the meat in the mixture until coated; let stand 30 minutes. Melt the 4 tablespoons butter in a casserole or Dutch oven; cook the meat in it, stirring frequently until browned. Add half the water; cover, and cook over low heat 45 minutes, adding the remaining water from time to time. Prepare the dumplings meanwhile.

Beat together the egg yolks, melted butter, and remaining salt; stir in the cracker meal. Fold in the egg whites. Chill 10 minutes and shape into walnut-size balls. Add the peas to the meat, then arrange the dumplings around the top; cover and cook over low heat 25 minutes. *Serves 6–8.*

Kofta Curry-Stew

2 pounds lean ground
   lamb
½ cup finely chopped
   onions
2 cloves garlic, minced
2½ teaspoons salt
6 tablespoons butter
¾ cup thinly sliced onions

1½ tablespoons curry
   powder
1 tablespoon tomato paste
2 cups yogurt
1 package frozen mixed
   vegetables, thawed
1½ cups cubed potatoes
¼ cup ground almonds

With the hand, mix together the lamb, chopped onions, garlic, and 1½ teaspoons salt. Shape into 1-inch balls.

Melt the butter in a heavy saucepan; brown the sliced onions in it. Add the meat balls, sauté 5 minutes. Mix in the curry powder, tomato paste, yogurt, and remaining salt. Cook over low heat 10 minutes, stirring frequently. Add the vegetables, potatoes, and almonds; cover and cook over low heat 20 minutes, adding a little water if necessary. *Serves 6–8.*

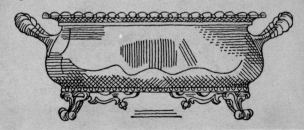

Lamb Pulao

2 cups rice	1 teaspoon powdered
¼ pound butter	ginger
2 pounds boneless lamb,	1 teaspoon cinnamon
cut into 1-inch cubes	1 bay leaf
1½ cups sliced onions	3 cups yogurt
2 cloves garlic, minced	¼ teaspoon saffron
2 teaspoons salt	¼ cup slivered blanched
⅛ teaspoon ground	almonds
cardamom	¼ cup pistachio nuts
2 cloves	¼ cup seedless raisins

Wash the rice, then soak in cold water for 20 minutes. Drain thoroughly.

In a Dutch oven or heavy saucepan, melt the butter. Brown the lamb and onions in it very well. Sprinkle with the garlic, salt, cardamom, cloves, ginger, and cinnamon. Mix well, then add the bay leaf and yogurt. Bring to a boil, cover, and cook over low heat 1 hour. Dissolve the saffron in a little boiling water and add to the lamb with the rice. If liquid doesn't cover the rice, add boiling water to barely cover. Recover the pan and cook 20 minutes longer or until the rice is almost tender. Mix in the nuts and raisins; cook 5 minutes longer or until all the liquid is absorbed.

Serves 4–6.

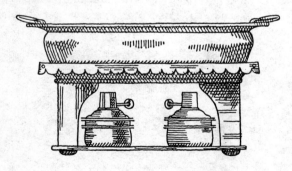

Pork

Wʜɪʟᴇ ᴡᴇ ᴡᴇʀᴇ ɪɴ ʟɪᴍᴀ, ᴘᴇʀᴜ, about two years ago, we decided to make a side trip to Cuzco, the ancient capital of the Incas. Very very early one morning we flew up to Cuzco, sitting with oxygen pipes in our mouths, because the plane was not pressurized and the altitude was so great. Once the plane put down in Cuzco on a grassy runway, we started to walk into the airport building but both suddenly felt shaky, and our knees buckled under us. "The altitude," we simultaneously gasped. (Cuzco is a mere 11,024 feet above sea level.) In the customs shed, everyone was kindness itself. We were not to move, we were to sit down, everything would be done for us. And it was. We were helped into a taxi, driven to the government hotel, and then we dragged ourselves upstairs (no elevator!) to our room. By this time it was dark, and the temperature had nose-dived to below freezing. Our room was the temperature of the interior of a refrigerator, or perhaps of a Deepfreeze. We decided not to bother changing our clothes, but rather to add some extra layers. Gradually I became somewhat accustomed to the great altitude, but the slightest exertion was enough to make my heart beat with the firmness of a hammer striking a solid surface.

At dinnertime, we slowly trudged toward the dining room. On the way, we passed the hotel desk where the assistant manager watched our slow progress with some concern. He wanted to know how we felt and warned us to eat lightly, because food took longer to digest at Cuzco's elevated altitude. In the dining room, my eyes fell upon a dish on the menu that I had pursued relentlessly, but with no success, all over Peru. It was *sopa seca*, a fascinating kind of pork stew, and a great specialty of the country. Specialty or not, it had never appeared on any menu I had previously encountered in Peru, and I wasn't going to pass up the opportunity now. I ordered it, to the consternation of my husband, who cautiously ordered some hot soup. When the orders came, I ate my delicious stew with relish, but my husband found his soup rather dull. After dinner we trudged upstairs, undressed, and quickly jumped under the covers.

I now wish to report, that I slept like a log (with my pork stew), and my husband reported that he had tossed for hours, unable to sleep (with his cautiously ordered and very light soup).

Sopa Seca

(PORK STEW, PERUVIAN STYLE)

½ cup olive oil
2½ cups chopped onions
1½ pounds ground pork
2 cloves garlic, minced
1½ cups chopped fresh
  tomatoes
2 cans chick-peas, drained
3½ teaspoons salt
¼ teaspoon dried ground
  chili peppers

2 cups raw rice
½ cup chopped green
  peppers
1 16-ounce can tomatoes
2 cups boiling water
½ teaspoon freshly
  ground black pepper
½ teaspoon orégano
½ cup seedless raisins
½ cup sliced almonds

Heat half the oil in a saucepan; brown half the onions in it.
Mix in the pork and half the garlic until browned. Add the
fresh tomatoes, chick-peas, 1½ teaspoons salt, and the chili
peppers. Cover and cook over low heat 45 minutes. Prepare the
rice meanwhile.

Heat the remaining oil in a saucepan; sauté the rice, green
peppers, and remaining onions until browned. Mix in the canned
tomatoes, boiling water, pepper, orégano, and the remaining
garlic and salt. Cover and cook over low heat for 25 minutes.
Mix in the raisins and almonds. Combine with the chick-pea
mixture. *Serves 6–8.*

Rôti de Porc à la Boulangère

(ROAST PORK WITH POTATOES AND APPLES)

8-rib loin of pork
1 clove garlic, minced
4 teaspoons salt
1 teaspoon freshly ground
  black pepper
1½ pounds potatoes,
  peeled and sliced thin

1 cup diced onions
2 tablespoons minced
  parsley
2 tablespoons butter
½ cup boiling water
4 apples, quartered

Rub the pork with a mixture of the garlic, 2½ teaspoons salt, and ¾ teaspoon pepper. Place the pork on a rack in a roasting pan or casserole. Roast in a 425° oven 1 hour. Remove the pork and rack from pan. Pour off all the fat. To the pan, add the potatoes, onions, parsley, and remaining salt and pepper. Dot with the butter, add the water, then place pork over the potatoes. Reduce the heat to 400°. Roast 20 minutes. Arrange the apples around the pork. Roast 40 minutes longer, or until the pork is tender. *Serves 4.*

Rôti de Porc en Cidre

(PORK IN CIDER)

8 pounds loin of pork
1 tablespoon salt
¾ teaspoon freshly
  ground black pepper
8 baking apples, cored

8 small potatoes, peeled
8 large onions
1½ cups cider
2 tablespoons flour
¼ cup cognac

Rub the pork with the salt and pepper; place in a roasting pan. Roast in a 375° oven 1½ hours. Pour off the fat. Arrange the apples, potatoes, and onions around the pork, and add 1 cup cider. Reduce heat to 325° and roast 1¼ hours longer, basting frequently.

Place the pork, apples, potatoes, and onions on a serving platter. Skim the fat from the gravy. Place pan on direct low heat and stir in the flour. Gradually add the cognac and remaining cider, stirring constantly and scraping the bottom. Cook over low heat 5 minutes.

Serves 8.

Rôti de Porc Pôelé

(ROAST MARINATED PORK)

5-pound boned rolled loin
  or leg of pork
1 tablespoon salt
½ cup wine vinegar
1 cup dry white wine
¼ cup olive oil
2 cloves garlic, split
½ cup sliced onions
½ cup sliced carrots
8 peppercorns
1 teaspoon thyme
2 bay leaves
3 tablespoons vegetable
  oil
1 cup sliced onions
½ cup beef broth
4 potatoes, quartered
1 package frozen green
  peas
1 package frozen green
  beans, thawed

Rub the meat with the salt. Combine the vinegar, wine, olive oil, garlic, onions, carrots, peppercorns, thyme, and bay leaves in a bowl (not metal). Marinate the pork in the mixture 24 hours in the refrigerator, basting and turning the meat frequently. Drain the meat and dry with paper towels. Strain the marinade.

Heat the vegetable oil in a casserole; brown the pork in it on all sides. Pour off all but 2 tablespoons of the fat. Add the onions; cover and bake in a 325° oven 2 hours, basting and turning meat a few times. Pour off the fat; add the broth and ¾ cup of the marinade, the potatoes, peas, and green beans. Recover and bake 30 minutes longer.

Serves 8–10.

Lentejas con Puerco

(LENTILS AND PORK, CUBAN STYLE)

1½ cups lentils	¼ cup boiling water
4 cups water	2½ teaspoons salt
1 tablespoon olive oil	¾ teaspoon freshly
2 pounds boneless pork,	ground black pepper
cubed	4 firm bananas, cut into
¾ cup chopped onions	1-inch pieces
2 cloves garlic, minced	3 tablespoons parsley
1½ cups peeled chopped	
tomatoes	

Wash the lentils well and cook in the 4 cups water for 40 minutes.

While the lentils are cooking, prepare the pork. Heat the oil in a Dutch oven or casserole; brown the pork in it. Mix in the onions and garlic until browned. Add the tomatoes and boiling water, salt, and pepper; cover and cook over low heat for 40 minutes. Add the undrained lentils to the pork. Mix well, cover and cook over low heat for 30 minutes. Taste for seasoning. Add the bananas and parsley; cook 5 minutes longer.

Serves 6–8.

Baked Pork and Beans

6 pork chops, cut ½ inch thick	1 clove garlic, minced
1½ teaspoons salt	¼ teaspoon dry mustard
½ teaspoon freshly ground black pepper	½ cup chili sauce
1 tablespoon vegetable oil	1 20-ounce can Lima beans, drained
1 cup chopped onions	1 20-ounce can kidney beans, drained

Trim the fat off the chops; season with the salt and pepper. Heat the oil in a skillet, add the chops, and cook over low heat until browned on both sides. Remove the chops. Pour off all but 2 tablespoons fat. In the fat remaining, sauté the onions and garlic 5 minutes. Stir in the mustard, chili sauce, and beans; taste for seasoning. Arrange the chops on top, cover, and bake in a 350° oven 45 minutes.

Serves 6.

Pork Chops, Tampa Style

6 pork chops, cut 1 inch thick	2 large onions, cut into ½-inch slices
2 tablespoons vegetable oil	6 slices lime
2½ teaspoons salt	3½ cups tomato juice
1½ cups raw rice	½ teaspoon Tabasco
½ cup chili sauce	1 package frozen okra, thawed

Trim the fat off the chops. Heat the oil in a Dutch oven or deep skillet; brown the chops in it. Remove the chops and sprinkle with 1½ teaspoons of the salt.

Stir the rice into the fat remaining in the pan until translucent. Arrange the chops over it. Spread some chili sauce on each chop, then the onions, and place a slice of lime on each. Add a mixture of the tomato juice, Tabasco, and remaining salt. Cover and bake in a 325° oven 50 minutes. Add the okra; recover and bake 15 minutes longer, or until the chops are tender.

Serves 6.

Heete Bliksem

(SPICY PORK CHOPS WITH APPLES, DUTCH STYLE)

4 cups beef broth
2 pounds apples, peeled,
   cored, and cubed
1½ pounds potatoes,
   peeled and cubed
1½ cups diced onions

1 teaspoon freshly ground
   black pepper (or less, if
   you wish)
6 pork chops, 1 inch
   thick
2 teaspoons salt
12 pork sausages

Combine the broth, apples, potatoes, onions, and half the pepper in a saucepan; cook over medium heat 45 minutes, or until liquid is absorbed. Prepare the chops meanwhile.

Sprinkle the chops with the salt and remaining pepper. Place in a heated skillet and cook over low heat until tender and well browned on both sides, about 30 minutes. Remove. Fry the sausages in the skillet until brown. Drain well. Heap the apple mixture in the center of a platter. Arrange chops and sausages around it. *Serves 6.*

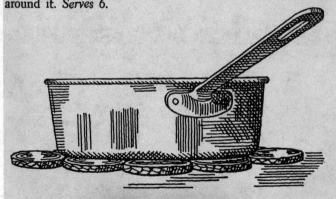

Baked Pork Chops, Creole Style

6 pork chops, cut 1½
inches thick
3½ teaspoons salt
¾ teaspoon freshly
ground black pepper
2 tablespoons vegetable
oil
2 cups thinly sliced
potatoes

1 cup thinly sliced onions
1 cup thinly sliced green
peppers
1 clove garlic, minced
1 20-ounce can tomatoes
½ teaspoon thyme
1 bay leaf
3 tablespoons minced
parsley

Wash and dry the pork chops; rub with 2 teaspoons salt and
½ teaspoon pepper. Rub a deep skillet or casserole with the oil.
Arrange the potatoes on the bottom; season with a little salt.
Arrange the chops over them. Spread the chops with the onions
and green peppers, and add the garlic, tomatoes, thyme, bay
leaf, parsley, and remaining salt and pepper. Cover and bake in
a 375° oven 1½ hours, or until chops are tender. Discard the
bay leaf. Serve from the casserole.

Serves 6.

Côtelettes de Porc aux Choux Rouge

(PORK CHOPS WITH CHESTNUTS AND RED CABBAGE)

6 loin pork chops, cut 1½
inches thick
2½ teaspoons salt
¼ teaspoon freshly
ground black pepper
1 egg, beaten
2 tablespoons butter

2 tablespoons flour
1 pound chestnuts, cooked
and peeled
3 pounds red cabbage,
coarsely shredded
1 cup dry red wine

Season the chops with 1½ teaspoons salt and the pepper, then dip into the egg. Heat the butter in a heavy skillet, and brown the chops 5 minutes on each side. Sprinkle with the flour. Cover and cook over low heat 25 minutes, turning the chops twice.

While the chops are cooking, combine the chestnuts, cabbage, wine, and remaining salt in a Dutch oven or deep skillet. Cook over medium heat 15 minutes. Arrange the chops on top; cook 5 minutes longer.

Serves 6.

Braised Shoulder of Pork with Beans

1 *pound dried white beans*	1½ *cups sliced onions*
2 *cloves*	2 *green peppers, thinly*
1 *onion*	*sliced*
1 *bay leaf*	1½ *cups beef broth*
3 *teaspoons salt*	2 *cloves garlic, minced*
¾ *teaspoon freshly*	¼ *teaspoon rosemary*
ground black pepper	1 *tablespoon tomato*
3 *pounds shoulder of*	*paste*
pork, cut into 2-inch	2 *tablespoons minced*
cubes	*parsley*

Wash the beans, cover with water, and bring to a boil. Let soak 1 hour. Drain, add fresh water to cover; add the cloves, stuck in the onion, and the bay leaf. Bring to a boil, cover, and cook over low heat 1½ hours. Add 1½ teaspoons salt and ¼ teaspoon pepper after 1 hour. While the beans are cooking, prepare the pork.

Toss the pork with the remaining salt and pepper. Brown it in a Dutch oven or heavy saucepan. Pour off the fat. Add the sliced onions and green peppers; cook 5 minutes. Add the broth, garlic, and rosemary; cover and cook over low heat 1 hour. Add the beans and ½ cup bean liquid. Recover and cook 1 hour longer. Stir in the tomato paste and parsley; cook 10 minutes longer.

Serves 6–8.

Spiced Pork in Peanut Sauce

3 pounds boneless pork
¼ cup olive oil
3 cups chopped onions
2 cloves garlic, minced
3 tablespoons raw rice
2½ cups chopped
    tomatoes
2 teaspoons salt
½ teaspoon freshly
    ground black pepper
¼ teaspoon dried ground
    chili peppers

¼ teaspoon saffron
¼ teaspoon cinnamon
1 clove
1½ cups beef broth
4 potatoes, peeled and
    quartered
½ cup ground peanuts
½ cup heavy cream
1 tablespoon molasses
2 green bananas, peeled
    and quartered

Cut the meat into ¾-inch cubes.

Heat the oil in a Dutch oven or large saucepan; sauté the onions and garlic 5 minutes. Add the pork and rice; cook over high heat until meat is browned. Mix in the tomatoes, salt, pepper, chili peppers, saffron, cinnamon, clove, and broth. Cover and cook over low heat 30 minutes. Add the potatoes and cook 15 minutes. Stir in the peanuts, cream, and molasses, then add the bananas and cook 15 minutes longer, or until the meat and potatoes are tender. Taste for seasoning.

Serves 6–8.

Guisado de Puerco y Calabaza

(PORK AND SQUASH STEW, SPANISH STYLE)

3 pounds boneless pork,
  cut into 1-inch cubes
2½ teaspoons salt
½ teaspoon freshly
  ground black pepper
3 tablespoons olive oil
1½ cups sliced onions

1 teaspoon paprika
1½ pounds yellow squash,
  peeled and sliced
1½ cups diced tomatoes
3 cups hot beef broth
1 cup raw rice
3 pimientos, cut julienne

Toss the pork with the salt and pepper. Heat the oil in a deep skillet; brown the pork and onions in it. Add the paprika, squash, and tomatoes; cook over low heat 10 minutes. Add 1 cup of the broth; cover and cook over low heat 30 minutes. Add the rice and remaining broth; cook 15 minutes. Mix in the pimientos; cook 5 minutes longer. Taste for seasoning.

Serves 6–8.

Rôti de Porc Grand'mère

(PORK WITH TURNIPS AND ONIONS)

5-pound loin of pork
2 teaspoons salt
½ teaspoon freshly
  ground black pepper
¼ teaspoon powdered
  bay leaf
¼ teaspoon thyme
1 clove garlic, minced

2 tablespoons vegetable oil
1 cup sliced carrots
12 small white onions
4 potatoes, peeled and
  quartered
4 turnips, peeled and
  quartered lengthwise
½ cup dry vermouth

Rub the pork (boned, if you like) with a mixture of the salt, pepper, bay leaf, thyme, and garlic. Let stand 2 hours at room temperature.

Heat the oil in a Dutch oven or heavy skillet; brown the pork in it on all sides. Pour off all but 2 tablespoons fat and turn meat fat side up and add the carrots. Cover and roast in a 325° oven 1½ hours, basting frequently. Meanwhile, pour boiling water over the onions, potatoes, and turnips. Let stand 10 minutes, then drain. Add to the pork with the vermouth. Recover and roast 1 hour longer, basting frequently. Skim the fat.

Serves 6–8.

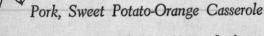

Pork, Sweet Potato-Orange Casserole

6 pork chops, cut 1 inch thick	⅓ cup firmly packed brown sugar
1¾ teaspoons salt	¼ cup melted butter
¼ teaspoon freshly ground black pepper	2 tablespoons rum
2 pounds sweet potatoes, cooked and peeled	2 oranges, peeled and diced
	¼ cup chopped nuts

Season the chops with 1¼ teaspoons salt and the pepper. Brown on both sides in a skillet. Drain and arrange in a 2½-quart baking dish or casserole.

Mash the sweet potatoes very smooth, then beat in ¼ cup of the brown sugar, half the butter, the remaining salt, and the rum. Fold in the oranges. Heap over the chops.

Mix together the nuts and the remaining brown sugar and butter; sprinkle over the top. Bake in a 375° oven 30 minutes.

Serves 6.

Pork and Green Beans, Taiwan Style

1½ pounds string beans
3 tablespoons vegetable oil
1½ pounds ground pork
1 clove garlic, minced
¾ teaspoons salt
2 tablespoons soy sauce

1 cup sliced water
  chestnuts
1½ cups water
1 cup bean sprouts
2 teaspoons cornstarch
1 cup shredded lettuce
¼ cup sliced green onions

Wash the fresh beans and cut crosswise into ¼-inch slices. Heat the oil in a skillet; add the pork and garlic. Cook over medium heat, stirring constantly until browned. Add the salt, soy sauce, and water chestnuts. Cook 1 minute. Add 1 cup water; bring to a boil and carefully stir in the green beans and bean sprouts. Cook 1 minute, cover, and cook 2 minutes.

Mix the cornstarch with the remaining water and stir into the skillet until thickened. Spread the lettuce in a hot deep serving dish and pour the meat mixture over it. Sprinkle with the green onions. *Serves 4–6.*

Pork and Bean Sprouts, Chinese Style

2 pounds boneless pork
4 tablespoons vegetable or
  peanut oil
1 cup sliced onions
1½ cups chicken broth
2 cups cooked rice
½ cup thinly sliced celery
¼ pound mushrooms,
  sliced

1 can bean sprouts,
  drained
1 tablespoon cornstarch
¾ teaspoon salt
¼ teaspoon freshly
  ground black pepper
½ teaspoon sugar
3 tablespoons soy sauce
2 tablespoons dry sherry

Cut the pork into matchlike pieces. Heat the oil in a skillet or chafing dish; sauté the pork in it for 15 minutes. Add the onions; cook 3 minutes. Mix in the chicken broth, rice, celery, mushrooms, and bean sprouts; bring to a boil and cook over low heat 5 minutes.

Blend together the cornstarch, salt, pepper, sugar, soy sauce, and sherry. Stir into the pan until thickened.

Serves 4–6.

Braised Pork with Beans

3 cups dried white or black beans

4 teaspoons salt

2 pounds boneless pork, cut into 2-inch squares

¼ teaspoon freshly ground black pepper

2 cups boiling water

½ cup olive oil

2 cups chopped onions

2 cloves garlic, minced

¼ teaspoon dried ground red peppers

¼ cup chopped onion

½ cup grated cheddar cheese

Wash the beans. Cover with water and bring to a boil. Let soak 1 hour; drain, add fresh water to cover, and bring to a boil. Cook over low heat 2 hours or until tender, adding 2 teaspoons salt after 1 hour of cooking time. Drain if any liquid remains.

While the beans are cooking, brown the pork lightly; season with the pepper and remaining salt, and add the 2 cups boiling water. Cover and cook over low heat 20 minutes.

Heat the oil in a Dutch oven or casserole; sauté the chopped onions 10 minutes. Add the undrained pork, the garlic, beans, and the red peppers. Cover and cook over low heat 30 minutes. Sprinkle with the onions and grated cheese.

Serves 4–6.

Baked Pork and Sauerkraut

2 tablespoons vegetable oil
1 cup sliced onions
6 pork chops, cut 1 inch thick
1½ teaspoons salt
½ teaspoon freshly ground black pepper
1 pound sauerkraut
2 cups canned puréed apricots
¼ teaspoon caraway seeds

Heat the oil in a skillet; sauté the onions 5 minutes. Remove the onions; in the oil remaining, brown the chops. Season with the salt and pepper. Rinse the sauerkraut under cold running water; drain well. Mix with the apricots, caraway seeds, and sautéed onions. Spread in a greased 2-quart baking dish, and arrange the chops over the mixture. Cover and bake in a 350° oven 1¼ hours, removing the cover for the last 15 minutes.
Serves 6.

Pork-Cabbage Casserole

8 pork chops, cut ¾ inch thick
1½ teaspoons salt
½ teaspoon freshly ground black pepper
½ pound Italian or Spanish sausages, sliced
2 slices salt pork, diced
1 cup thinly sliced onions
1½ cups sliced green peppers
1 tablespoon flour
1½ cups dry white wine
1 bay leaf
3-pound head of cabbage
3 potatoes, peeled and quartered

Season the pork chops with the salt and pepper. Lightly brown the sausages in a Dutch oven or heavy casserole. Remove the sausages and pour off all the fat. Lightly brown the salt pork in the same pan. Pour off half the fat. Add the onions and green peppers; sauté 5 minutes. Add the chops; brown lightly on both sides. Sprinkle with the flour and add the browned sausages, the wine, and bay leaf; cover and cook over low heat 1¼ hours.

While the pork is cooking, cut the cabbage in eighths; cook in boiling salted water 5 minutes. Drain very well. Add to the casserole with the potatoes; recover and cook 30 minutes longer. Taste for seasoning.

Serves 6–8.

Maiale e Cavolo

(PORK AND CABBAGE, NAPLES STYLE)

3-pound head of cabbage
8 pork chops, cut ¾ inch thick
1½ teaspoons salt
½ teaspoon freshly ground black pepper
2 slices salt pork, diced
1½ cups thinly sliced onions

1½ cups diced carrots
1 tablespoon flour
½ pound Italian sausages, sliced
1½ cups dry white wine
1 bay leaf

Wash the cabbage, cut the head in eighths, cover with boiling water, and let stand while preparing the pork. Drain well.

Rub the pork chops with the salt and pepper. Lightly brown the salt pork in a Dutch oven or deep skillet. Pour off half the fat. Add the onions and carrots; sauté 5 minutes. Add the chops; brown lightly on both sides. Sprinkle with the flour and add the sausages, wine, and bay leaf; cover and cook over low heat 45 minutes. Add the cabbage; cook 30 minutes longer. Taste for seasoning and discard the bay leaf.

Serves 8.

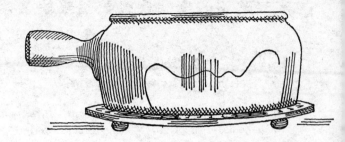

Tocana do Porc

(PORK WITH SAUERKRAUT, HUNGARIAN STYLE)

4 tablespoons vegetable
  oil
2 pounds boneless pork,
  cut into 1½-inch cubes
1½ pounds onions,
  peeled and sliced
1 pound sauerkraut,
  drained
1 clove garlic, minced
2 teaspoons salt
½ teaspoon freshly
  ground black pepper

1 teaspoon thyme
2 tablespoons chopped
  parsley
1 tablespoon chopped dill
2 teaspoons caraway seeds
2 cups beef broth
3 potatoes, peeled and
  quartered
1 tablespoon paprika
1 cup sour cream

Heat the oil in a Dutch oven; brown the pork in it. Remove. In the remaining oil, sauté the onions 10 minutes, stirring frequently. Add the sauerkraut; cook over medium heat 5 minutes, stirring almost constantly. Return the pork and add the garlic, salt, pepper, thyme, parsley, dill, caraway seeds, and broth. Cover and cook over low heat 1 hour. Add the potatoes and cook 30 minutes longer or until the pork is tender. Stir in the paprika and sour cream; cook 5 minutes. Taste for seasoning.
  Serves 4–6.

Szekely Gulyas

(HUNGARIAN PORK AND SAUERKRAUT)

2 pounds sauerkraut
3 tablespoons vegetable oil
2 cups chopped onions
2 cloves garlic, minced
1 tablespoon paprika
2 tablespoons caraway
  seeds
3 pounds boneless pork,
  cut into 1½-inch cubes

2 teaspoons salt
½ teaspoon freshly
  ground black pepper
2 cups chopped canned
  tomatoes
½ cup water
3 potatoes, peeled and
  quartered
1 cup sour cream

Rinse the sauerkraut under cold running water, then drain thoroughly.

Heat the oil in a casserole; sauté the onions and garlic 10 minutes, stirring frequently. Mix in the paprika and caraway seeds, then the pork. Cook 5 minutes, stirring almost constantly. Add the salt, pepper, tomatoes, and water. Cover and cook over low heat 30 minutes. Mix in the sauerkraut gently. Recover and cook 1 hour. Add the potatoes; cook 30 minutes. Stir in the sour cream and heat.

Serves 6–8.

Pork Hocks with Vegetables

2 cloves
8 small white onions
4 pork hocks
2 teaspoons salt
½ teaspoon freshly
  ground black pepper

1 clove garlic, sliced
1 bay leaf
4 sweet potatoes, peeled
  and quartered
4 carrots

228

Stick the cloves into one of the onions.

Wash and scrub the pork hocks, then combine in a saucepan with the salt, pepper, garlic, bay leaf, and water to cover. Bring to a boil, cover, and cook over low heat 2 hours or until almost tender. Add the potatoes, carrots, and onions; cook 30 minutes longer. Drain the hocks and pull off the skin. Arrange on a serving dish with the vegetables around them.

Serves 4.

Wienereintopf

(PORK STEW, VIENNA STYLE)

2 pounds boned shoulder of pork, cut into 1-inch cubes	1½ pounds potatoes, peeled and sliced
3 teaspoons salt	¾ teaspoon caraway seeds
¾ teaspoon freshly ground black pepper	3 carrots, cut julienne
¼ pound butter	2 cups finely shredded cabbage
2 cups thinly sliced onions	3 cups chicken broth

Season the pork with 1½ teaspoons salt and ¼ teaspoon pepper. Melt 2 tablespoons butter in a skillet; lightly brown the pork in it. Remove. Melt 2 tablespoons butter in the skillet; sauté the onions until golden. Remove. Melt the remaining butter in the skillet and reserve.

Arrange half the potato slices on the bottom of a buttered 3-quart casserole. Sprinkle with a little salt, pepper, and caraway seeds. Arrange alternate layers of the pork, onions, carrots, and cabbage, sprinkling each layer with salt, pepper, and caraway seeds. Cover with the remaining potatoes, and sprinkle with salt, pepper, caraway seeds, and the melted butter. Pour in enough of the broth to reach the top layer. Cover the casserole and bake in a 375° oven 1½ hours, removing the cover for the last 15 minutes.

Serves 4–6.

Ají de Puerco

(SPICED PORK STEW)

3 pounds boneless pork
½ cup olive oil
3 cups chopped onions
2 cloves garlic, minced
½ cup raw rice
1½ cups chopped
    tomatoes
2 cups beef broth
2 teaspoons salt
½ teaspoon freshly
    ground black pepper

¼ teaspoon dried ground
    red peppers
¼ teaspoon saffron
4 potatoes, peeled and
    quartered
3 firm bananas, cut into
    2-inch lengths
½ cup ground peanuts
½ cup heavy cream
1 tablespoon molasses

Cut the pork into 1-inch cubes.

Heat the oil in a casserole; sauté the onions 5 minutes. Add the pork and garlic; cook until browned, stirring frequently. Add the rice and tomatoes; cook for 10 minutes. Stir in the broth, salt, pepper, red peppers, and saffron. Cover and cook over medium heat for 30 minutes. Add the potatoes; cook for 15 minutes. Add the bananas, peanuts, cream, and molasses; cook 15 minutes longer. Taste for seasoning.

Serves 6–8.

Karjalanpaisti

(FINNISH MEAT STEW)

1 pound boneless pork
1 pound boneless lamb
1 pound chuck of beef
1 cup chopped onions
1½ cups boiling beef broth
1 teaspoon ground allspice

1 bay leaf
½ teaspoon powdered ginger
2 teaspoons salt
2 cups cubed potatoes
1 package frozen peas and carrots, thawed

Cut the meat into 1-inch cubes.

In a 2-quart baking dish, combine the meat, onions, broth, allspice, bay leaf, ginger, and salt. Bake in a 475° oven 20 minutes. Cover dish tightly, reduce heat to 325° and bake 2 hours. Add the potatoes and peas and carrots. Recover and bake 20 minutes longer or until the potatoes are tender.

Serves 6–8.

Pörkölt

(HUNGARIAN STEW)

4 pounds pork or beef
2 tablespoons butter
2 cups sliced onions
2 tablespoons paprika
2 teaspoons salt
½ teaspoon freshly ground black pepper
2 cloves garlic, minced

1 cup chopped green peppers
1 tablespoon lemon juice
2 tablespoons tomato paste
½ teaspoon basil
2 cups boiling water
1 cup egg barley

Leave the fat on the meat and cut into 1½-inch cubes. Melt the butter in a Dutch oven; sauté the onions until golden. Remove from the heat and stir in the paprika, salt, and pepper. Add the meat, garlic, green peppers, lemon juice, tomato paste, basil, and 1 cup of the boiling water. Cover and cook over low heat 3 hours. Skim the fat, add the remaining water and egg barley; cook 3 minutes longer. Taste for seasoning.

Serves 6–8.

Estofado de Puerco y Garbanzos

(PORK-CHICK-PEA STEW)

2 cups dried chick-peas or 2 cans chick-peas, drained	1 cup diced green peppers
4 tablespoons olive oil	4 Spanish or Italian sausages, sliced
2 pounds boneless pork, cut into 1-inch cubes	1 tablespoon chili powder
1 cup chopped onions	1 29-ounce can tomatoes
3 cloves garlic, minced	½ cup dry red wine
	2 teaspoons salt

If dried chick-peas are used, wash and cover with water; bring to a boil and let soak 1 hour. Drain and cover with fresh water; bring to a boil and cook over low heat 1½ hours. Drain.

Heat the oil in a casserole or Dutch oven; brown the pork, onions, garlic, and green peppers in it. Brown the sausages in a skillet; drain and add to the stew with the chili powder, tomatoes, wine, and salt. Cover and bake in a 350° oven 1 hour, stirring occasionally. Add the cooked or canned chick-peas. Recover and bake 1 hour longer. Taste for seasoning.

Serves 6–8.

Trinidad Pepperpot

4-pound pullet, disjointed
2 pounds pickled spareribs,
  cut into individual ribs
2 pounds boneless pork,
  cut into 1-inch cubes
2 cups water
1 clove garlic, minced
1½ cups sliced onions
2 tablespoons dark brown
  sugar

2 tablespoons
  Worcestershire sauce
½ teaspoon dried ground
  chili peppers
½ teaspoon thyme
½ teaspoon freshly
  ground black pepper
3 cups peeled cubed
  potatoes
2 packages frozen okra

Combine the chicken, spareribs, pork, and water in a saucepan; cover and cook over medium heat 2 hours. Add the garlic, onions, sugar, Worcestershire sauce, chili peppers, thyme, pepper, potatoes, and okra. Recover and cook over low heat 30 minutes longer. Taste for seasoning.

Serves 8–10.

Mauffay

(PORK AND FISH, VIRGIN ISLANDS STYLE)

½ pound salt pork, cubed
1 pound boneless beef,
  cut into 1-inch cubes
1 pound boneless pork,
  cut into 1-inch cubes
2 cups chopped onions
7 cups water
1 cup corn meal

3 fillets of fish, cut into 1-
  inch pieces
2 cups peeled chopped
  tomatoes
1 teaspoon salt
¾ teaspoon thyme
½ teaspoon freshly
  ground black pepper

Cook the salt pork in a saucepan over low heat until it begins to brown. Pour off the fat. Add the beef, pork, and onions, and brown well. Add the water and cook over medium heat 30 minutes. Gradually mix in the corn meal, stirring steadily, then add the fish, tomatoes, salt, thyme, and pepper. Cook over low heat 30 minutes. Taste for seasoning.

Serves 6–8.

Ham Steak and Wild Rice, Creole Style

1 cup wild rice
1 ham steak, cut
  1¼ inches thick
  (about 3 pounds)
2 cups thinly sliced onions
3 cups thinly sliced green
  peppers
½ pound mushrooms,
  sliced
1 29-ounce can tomatoes
1 clove garlic, minced
1 cup sliced green olives

½ teaspoon
  thyme
8 sprigs parsley   tied
1 stalk celery,   together
  with the leaves
1 bay leaf
⅛ teaspoon ground cloves
1 teaspoon salt
¾ teaspoon freshly
  ground black pepper
2 tablespoons butter

Wash the rice thoroughly, cover with boiling water, and let stand until needed

Score the fat of the ham. Place in a skillet, cover with water, bring to a boil, and cook over medium heat 5 minutes. Drain well.

Put the ham in a greased baking dish. Add the onions, green peppers, mushrooms, tomatoes, garlic, olives, herb bundle, cloves, salt, and pepper. Cover and bake in a 350° oven 1 hour, basting occasionally. Discard the herb bundle. Add the drained wild rice and broth; recover and bake 30 minutes longer, or until rice is tender. Stir in the butter and taste for seasoning.

Serves 4–6.

Carolina Ham Casserole

4 tablespoons butter
4 tablespoons flour
2 cups milk
1 teaspoon salt
¼ teaspoon freshly
 ground black pepper
½ cup chopped green
 pepper

1 pound cooked ham,
 diced
2 cups cooked rice
3 apples, peeled and
 sliced thin
⅓ cup brown sugar

Melt the butter in a saucepan; blend in the flour until smooth. Gradually add the milk, stirring constantly to the boiling point. Mix in the salt, pepper, and green pepper; cook over low heat 5 minutes. Mix in the ham and rice. Taste for seasoning. Pour into a buttered 1½-quart casserole and arrange the apple slices on top. Sprinkle with the brown sugar. Place the casserole in a shallow pan of water. Bake in a 350° oven for 30 minutes.
 Serves 4.

I LIKE TO DRIVE AROUND ITALY and do so as frequently as possible. Distances between towns are not great, there is much to see in almost every region, and even if there weren't, the food, wine, and coffee would be worth the journey. On this occasion, I was driving from Rimini to Venice. It became obvious that I wouldn't make Venice in time for lunch, because the car must be left on the mainland and then a motorboat or gondola taken for the trip to a hotel, all very time-consuming. The cup of coffee I'd had for breakfast wasn't very filling, and I was just about starved.

I headed toward Chioggia, a small town south of Venice, and I've never been sorry. First of all, Chioggia turned out to be a miniature Venice, filled with canals and old buildings and laden with atmosphere. There was a small neighborhood restaurant in the narrow street where I parked. Everyone seemed to be eating a rice preparation in which I could see bits of meat, mushrooms, and sausages. The waiter told me it was the house specialty, *risotto e prosciutto*, and I soon learned why the local residents were eating it with such abandon. After lunch, I found it absolutely necessary to take a short nap in the car before proceeding on toward Venice.

Risotto e Prosciutto
(BAKED RICE AND HAM)

6 tablespoons butter
1 cup finely chopped onions
1 cup raw rice
3 cups hot chicken broth
¼ teaspoon white pepper
⅛ teaspoon saffron

1 pound sweet Italian sausages, cut into 1-inch pieces
1 pound mushrooms, sliced
1 pound prosciutto or cooked ham, diced

Melt the butter in a casserole; sauté the onions 10 minutes. Stir in the rice until coated with the butter and translucent. Add the broth, pepper, and saffron; bring to a boil, then cover and bake in a 350° oven 10 minutes.

While the rice is baking, brown and drain the sausages. In the same skillet, sauté the mushrooms 5 minutes. Drain. Mix the sausages, mushrooms, and ham into the rice with two forks. Re-cover and bake 30 minutes longer, removing the cover for the last 10 minutes. Serve with grated Parmesan or Romano cheese.

Serves 4–6.

Baked Ham with Lima Beans and Mushrooms

2-pound cooked ham steak	3 tablespoons flour
½ cup dry white wine	1 cup tomato juice
½ teaspoon ginger	1 4-ounce can sliced
1 teaspoon dry mustard	mushrooms
2 tablespoons vegetable oil	1 20-ounce can green Lima
3 tablespoons butter	beans
½ cup minced onions	

Marinate the ham steak in a mixture of the wine, ginger, and mustard for 1 hour, turning the ham a few times. Drain well; reserve the marinade.

Heat the oil in a large skillet; brown the ham in it on both sides. Remove. Pour off the fat. Add the butter to the skillet and let it melt; sauté the onions 5 minutes. Blend in the flour; gradually add the tomato juice and liquid from the canned mushrooms, stirring steadily to the boiling point; then cook over low heat 5 minutes. Stir in the reserved marinade, the mushrooms, and the Lima beans. Return the ham steak. Bake in a 350° oven 20 minutes.

Serves 4–6.

✳ ✳ ✳ ✳ ✳ ✳ ✳ ✳ ✳ ✳ ✳ ✳ ✳ ✳ ✳ ✳

Fave Fresche Stufato

(LIMA BEANS WITH HAM, ITALIAN STYLE)

6 ham steaks, cut ¼ inch
   thick
3 tablespoons butter
½ cup finely chopped
   onions
1 cup shredded lettuce

2 pounds Lima beans,
   shelled or 2 packages
   frozen, thawed
1 teaspoon salt
¼ teaspoon freshly
   ground black pepper
¾ cup boiling water

Brown the ham on both sides in a skillet; remove the ham and pour off the fat.

Melt the butter in the skillet; sauté the onions 5 minutes. Mix in the lettuce, beans, salt, pepper, and water. Bring to a boil, cover, and cook over low heat 5 minutes for fresh, 6 for frozen beans. Drain, add the ham, and cook 5 minutes longer.

Serves 6.

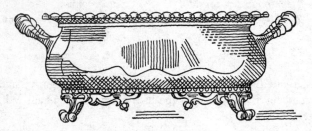

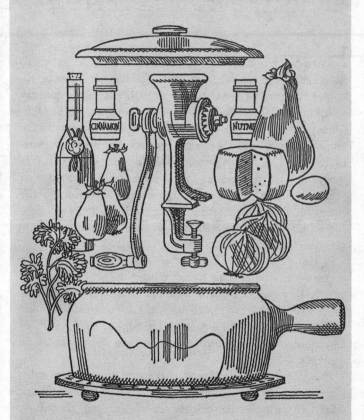

Ground Beef

Hong kong, one of the most fascinating cities in the world, features Chinese cooking at its best. The reasons are quite obvious. Ordinarily, Chinese people cook with a very large quantity of vegetables and noodles, flavored with just a little meat or fish. China is a tremendous country with an almost astronomical number of people, and wages are low and food prices comparatively high. The average person thinks in terms of an ounce or two of meat or fish per day, when he is fortunate enough to obtain it. Often it is beyond his means. The cuisine of the country has been built around filling foods, skillfully prepared and artfully flavored with exceedingly small amounts of expensive ingredients like meat, poultry, or seafood.

In Hong Kong, the Chinese chefs find the situation greatly improved. Instead of being forced to make use of scraps of meat or fish, they have reasonable quantities available to them for the first time, and the superb food to be found in the homes and restaurants of Hong Kong bears witness to the skill of Chinese chefs when there is a comparative abundance of ingredients.

Hong Kong is an island, and a very attractive one scenically. On the far side of the island there is a small Chinese fishing village, somewhat inappropriately called Aberdeen, charmingly situated on the edge of a bay. Anchored in the center of the bay are several large, floating restaurants built on houseboats. To reach these delightful restaurants, it is necessary to take a *sampan*, a small, shallow boat. It is usually poled out to the floating restaurants by women, inevitably the wives of the fishermen who go out to sea in order to bring in the catch that you will eat on the decks of the floating restaurants. There I also had Beef and Noodles, a succulent affair made with bean sprouts.

Beef and Noodles, Chinese Style

3 tablespoons vegetable
  oil
1½ pound ground beef
1½ teaspoons salt
½ teaspoon freshly
  ground black pepper
1 clove garlic, minced
2 cups bean sprouts

2 tablespoons sugar
1½ cups beef broth
1 tablespoon cornstarch
2 tablespoons water
½ pound fine noodles,
  cooked, drained, and
  chilled
½ cup sliced green onions

Heat the oil in a deep skillet; add the meat and cook, stirring almost constantly, until browned. Add the salt, pepper, garlic, bean sprouts, sugar, and broth. Bring to a boil. Mix together the cornstarch and water; stir into the meat until mixture thickens. Stir in the noodles and cook 3 minutes.

Sprinkle with the green onions.

Serves 6–8.

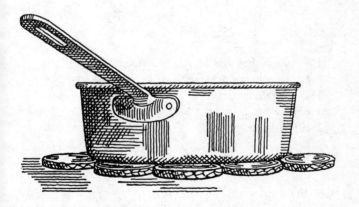

Baked Meat Loaf and Vegetables

2 pounds ground beef
2 eggs
¼ cup fresh bread crumbs
½ cup heavy cream
2 tablespoons chili sauce
2 teaspoons salt
½ teaspoon freshly
  ground black pepper
½ cup finely chopped
  onion

2 tablespoons minced
  parsley
2 tablespoons butter
1 package frozen mixed
  vegetables, thawed
2 cups diced potatoes
¾ cup hot beef broth

Mix together the beef, eggs, bread crumbs, cream, chili sauce, salt, pepper, onion, and parsley. Shape into a loaf. Melt the butter in a Dutch oven or heavy saucepan; place the loaf in it. Bake in a 375° oven 30 minutes. Add the mixed vegetables, potatoes, and broth. Cover and bake 30 minutes longer or until the vegetables are tender.

Serves 6–8.

Chili con Carne

1½ pounds boneless beef
3 tablespoons vegetable oil
1½ cups thinly sliced
  onions
1 cup chopped green
  peppers
1 29-ounce can tomatoes

2 teaspoons salt
½ teaspoon freshly
  ground black pepper
2 tablespoons chili powder
1 clove garlic, minced
1 16-ounce can kidney
  beans

Cut the meat into ½-inch cubes.

Heat the oil in a saucepan; sauté the onions and green peppers 10 minutes. Add the meat; cook over medium heat, stirring frequently, until browned. Mix in the tomatoes, salt, pepper, chili powder, and garlic. Cover and cook over low heat 1½ hours. Add the beans, taste for seasoning, and cook 10 minutes longer. Serves 4–6.

AMERICANS LOVE GREECE. In fact, if a popularity contest of European countries were held, Italy, Denmark, and Greece would probably come out in a triple tie. But Greece might emerge the victor, and in any event there's a reason why. The Greeks dearly love visitors and especially Americans, because almost every Greek has a few relatives in the United States. They are frequently surprised when you claim that you don't know their cousin, or sister-in-law, or half brother. Your statement that New York (for example) is a large city does little to help the situation.

My husband and I are very fond of driving about in Greece, because there is so much to see. Several years ago, in late September, we decided to drive from Athens to Delphi, home of the Oracle. About lunchtime, we approached a town where the directions pointed to Thivai, which we knew was Thebes (in English). Just before reaching the town, while still in the open countryside, we saw a sign for a *taverna*, one of Greece's informal restaurants. The owner had arranged a group of tables attractively under the trees and was cooking food out-of-doors under a sort of lean-to shed. We were the first to arrive, and, as everyone does in a Greek *taverna*, went directly to where the food was being prepared, rather than sitting down at the table.

The owner (and chef) might have come from Central Casting in Hollywood. He had a large pink face, bald head, and wild handlebar mustaches of jet black color. He proudly showed us what he had prepared, but as soon as *pastitso* (the classic dish made of layers of macaroni and beef) was presented, I could not be swayed. What's more, I went back for an additional portion, to my husband's amazement. But I must have encouraged him, because he took a second helping too. Between us, we finished a bottle of the local red wine. All of which may help to explain why, when he reached the Oracle, my husband kept asking the Oracle about what the stock market was going to do. If he got an answer, he didn't tell me.

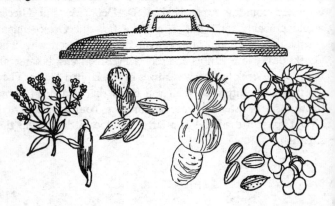

Pastitso, I

(GREEK BEEF AND MACARONI)

4 tablespoons butter
1 cup chopped onions
1½ pounds ground beef
1 cup peeled chopped
   tomatoes
2 teaspoons salt
½ teaspoon freshly
   ground black pepper

¼ teaspoon orégano
½ cup grated Parmesan
   cheese
1 pound small elbow
   macaroni, cooked and
   drained

Melt the butter in a skillet; add the onions and meat. Cook over high heat, stirring steadily, for 5 minutes. Mix in the tomatoes, salt, pepper, and orégano; cook over low heat 5 minutes. Mix in the cheese. Taste for seasoning.

In a buttered 13 by 9-inch baking dish, spread half the macaroni. Spread the meat mixture over it and cover with the remaining macaroni.

Cover with the following sauce.

2 tablespoons butter
2 tablespoons flour
½ teaspoon salt
⅛ teaspoon white pepper

1 cup milk
1 egg yolk
¼ cup grated Parmesan
   cheese

Melt the butter in a saucepan; blend in the flour, salt, and pepper. Gradually add the milk, stirring steadily to the boiling point. Cook over low heat 5 minutes. Beat the egg yolk and cheese in a bowl; add the hot sauce, stirring steadily to prevent curdling. Pour over the macaroni. Bake in a 375° oven 30 minutes. Cut into squares.

Serves 6–8.

Pastitso, II

(GREEK MACARONI AND BEEF CASSEROLE)

¼ cup olive oil
1½ cups chopped onions
1 pound ground beef
2 tomatoes, peeled and
chopped
1½ teaspoons salt
¼ teaspoon pepper
1 cup grated Parmesan
cheese

3 tablespoons butter
2 tablespoons flour
1 cup hot milk
1 egg, beaten
1 pound elbow macaroni,
cooked and drained

Heat the oil in a skillet. Cook the onions and beef over high heat 5 minutes, stirring constantly. Mix in the tomatoes, salt, and pepper. Cook over low heat 15 minutes. Stir in half the cheese.

Melt the butter in a saucepan; blend in the flour until smooth. Gradually add the milk, stirring constantly to the boiling point. Mix in the remaining cheese and cook over low heat 5 minutes. Beat the egg in a bowl. Gradually add the hot sauce, beating constantly to prevent curdling. Taste for seasoning.

Spread half of the macaroni on the bottom of a buttered 8 by 12-inch baking dish. Spread the meat mixture over it, and cover with the remaining macaroni. Pour the sauce over the top. Bake in a 375° oven 35 minutes.

Serves 4–6.

Spanish Rice with Beef

6 tablespoons olive oil
1½ cups chopped onions
2 cloves garlic, minced
1¼ cups raw rice
1½ pounds ground beef
½ cup chopped stuffed olives
1 green pepper, finely chopped

1 8-ounce can tomato sauce
2½ cups beef broth
1½ teaspoons salt
1 16-ounce can green peas, drained

Heat 3 tablespoons of the oil in a skillet; sauté the onions and garlic 5 minutes, stirring frequently. Remove from pan. Add the rice and remaining oil to the pan and cook until translucent, stirring frequently. Mix together the meat, onions, rice, olives, green pepper, tomato sauce, beef broth, and salt. Turn into a greased 1½-quart casserole. Cover and bake in a 325° oven 45 minutes. Mix in the green peas, bake 5 minutes longer, uncovered.

Serves 6–8.

Texas Casserole

3 tablespoons olive oil
½ cup chopped onion
1 pound ground beef
2 cups half-cooked rice
1 29-ounce can tomatoes
1 cup water
1 cup canned corn kernels
1 cup canned green peas

2 teaspoons salt
1 tablespoon chili powder
½ cup sliced black olives
1 cup grated cheddar cheese
1 pound noodles, cooked and drained

Heat the oil in a skillet, sauté the onion and beef 5 minutes, stirring frequently. Mix in the rice, tomatoes, water, corn, green peas, salt, chili powder, black olives, cheese, and noodles. Turn into a buttered casserole. Bake in a 350° oven 45 minutes.

Serves 4–6.

Moussaka à la Grecque

(MEAT-EGGPLANT LAYERS)

2 medium-sized eggplants	¼ teaspoon cinnamon
⅜ pound (1½ sticks) butter	¼ cup chopped parsley
	3 tablespoons flour
3½ teaspoons salt	3 cups hot milk
1½ cups chopped onions	1 cup ricotta or cottage cheese
1½ pounds ground lamb or beef	
	2 eggs, beaten
1 tablespoon tomato paste	⅛ teaspoon nutmeg
	¾ cup dry bread crumbs
⅓ cup dry red wine	¾ cup grated Parmesan cheese
½ teaspoon freshly ground black pepper	

Peel the eggplants and cut into slices ½ inch thick. Melt 4 tablespoons butter in a skillet; brown the eggplant slices on both sides. Remove and sprinkle with 1 teaspoon of the salt.

In the same skillet, melt 4 tablespoons of the remaining butter; sauté the onions 10 minutes. Add the meat; cook 10 minutes, stirring frequently. Stir in the tomato paste, wine, pepper, cinnamon, parsley, and 1½ teaspoons of the remaining salt. Cook over low heat, stirring frequently, until mixture is fairly dry. Taste for seasoning. Cool.

Melt the remaining butter in a saucepan. Blend in the flour and remaining salt. Add the milk, stirring steadily to the boiling point, then cook 5 minutes longer. Remove from the heat, cool 5 minutes, then mix in the ricotta cheese, eggs, and nutmeg.

Grease an 8 by 12-inch baking pan, and dust lightly with some bread crumbs. Arrange layers of the eggplant and meat, sprinkling each layer with bread crumbs and Parmesan cheese. Start and end with eggplant. Pour the sauce over the top. Bake in preheated 375° oven 1 hour, or until the custard top is set and golden brown. Let stand 30 minutes at room temperature before cutting into squares.

Serves 6–8.

Beef-Potato Bake

2 tablespoons butter
1 cup chopped onions
1½ pounds ground beef
1½ teaspoons salt
¼ teaspoon freshly
  ground black pepper
2 cups cooked or canned
  green peas

2 tablespoons minced
  parsley
½ cup chili sauce
3 cups seasoned mashed
  potatoes
1 egg, beaten

Melt the butter in a skillet; brown the onions in it. Mix in the meat and cook over medium heat until no red remains. Stir in the salt, pepper, peas, parsley, and chili sauce. Turn into a greased 1½-quart baking dish. Mix the potatoes with the egg; drop by tablespoons over the meat. Bake in a 350° oven 30 minutes or until the meat is very hot and the potatoes are browned.

Serves 6–8.

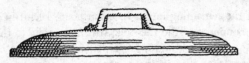

Beef and Green Beans, Singapore Style

3 tablespoons vegetable
oil
1½ cups thinly sliced
onions
1 cup thinly sliced green
peppers
1 pound ground beef
1 clove garlic, minced
1½ teaspoons salt

½ teaspoon freshly
ground black pepper
½ teaspoon powdered
ginger
3 tablespoons soy sauce
2½ cups beef broth
1 package frozen green
beans, thawed
1¼ cups raw rice

Heat the oil in a deep skillet; add the onions, green peppers, beef, and garlic. Cook over high heat 5 minutes, stirring almost constantly. Add the salt, pepper, ginger, soy sauce, broth, and beans. Bring to a boil, add the rice, cover, and cook over low heat 20 minutes. Taste for seasoning.

Serves 4.

Meat-Zucchini Custard

4 tablespoons butter
1½ cups chopped onions
1 pound zucchini, diced
1 pound ground beef
1½ teaspoons salt
½ teaspoon freshly
ground black pepper

¼ cup tomato juice
2 tablespoons minced
parsley
6 egg yolks, beaten
6 egg whites, stiffly beaten

Melt the butter in a skillet; sauté the onions 5 minutes. Add the zucchini and beef; cook over medium heat 10 minutes, stirring frequently. Add the salt, pepper, tomato juice, and parsley; cook over low heat 10 minutes. Cool 10 minutes, then beat in the egg yolks. Fold in the egg whites. Turn into a 2-quart baking dish or casserole. Bake in a preheated 375° oven 45 minutes, or until set.

Serves 4–6.

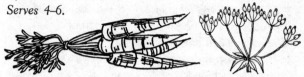

Carne e Melanzane Parmigiana

(MEAT AND EGGPLANT, PARMA STYLE)

3 tablespoons olive oil
1 medium-sized eggplant, peeled and sliced thin
2 teaspoons salt
½ teaspoon freshly ground black pepper
1½ pounds ground beef

2 hard-cooked eggs, diced
¼ cup grated Parmesan cheese
¼ pound mozzarella cheese, thinly sliced
2 tablespoons butter

Heat the oil in a skillet until it bubbles; brown the eggplant slices in it on both sides. Remove and season with 1 teaspoon salt and ¼ teaspoon pepper.

In the same skillet, sauté the meat 5 minutes, stirring almost constantly. Cool 5 minutes. Mix in the eggs, 1 tablespoon of the Parmesan cheese, and the remaining salt and pepper.

In a greased casserole, arrange successive layers of the eggplant, meat mixture, and mozzarella, starting and ending with the eggplant. Sprinkle with the remaining Parmesan cheese and dot with the butter. Bake in a 350° oven 30 minutes. Serve directly from the casserole.

Serves 4–6.

Beef-Eggplant Casserole

1 medium eggplant
4 teaspoons salt
¼ cup flour
3 tablespoons vegetable oil
2 pounds ground beef
½ cup chopped onions
½ teaspoon freshly
  ground black pepper
3 tablespoons minced
  parsley
½ teaspoon thyme
2 cups drained canned
  tomatoes

Peel the eggplant and cut in quarters, then into ½-inch slices. Sprinkle with 2 teaspoons salt and let stand 30 minutes. Drain well. Dip in the flour, then brown in the oil. Mix together the beef, onions, pepper, parsley, thyme, and remaining salt. In a greased 2-quart casserole, arrange successive layers of the eggplant, beef, and tomatoes, ending with the tomatoes. Bake in a 350° oven 1 hour.

Serves 6–8.

Spezzatino

(ITALIAN GROUND MEAT STEW)

1½ cups raw rice
2 slices bacon, diced
¾ cup chopped onions
1 carrot, sliced
1 pound ground beef
1 pound ground veal
1 teaspoon salt
¼ teaspoon freshly
  ground black pepper
1 teaspoon tomato paste
3 cups beef broth
1 cup chopped
  mushrooms
3 chicken livers, diced
¼ cup heavy cream

Wash the rice; cover with boiling water and let stand while preparing the meat.

Combine the bacon, onions, and carrot in a deep skillet; sauté until lightly browned. Add the beef and veal; cook over medium heat, stirring almost constantly until meat browns. Stir in the salt, pepper, and tomato paste; then add 1 cup of the broth. Cover and cook over low heat 1 hour, stirring frequently. Add the drained rice, mushrooms, livers, and remaining broth; recover and cook 15 minutes longer. Stir in the cream; taste for seasoning.

Serves 6–8.

Baked Ground Beef, Southern Style

3 tablespoons butter
1 cup chopped green
  pepper
1 cup chopped onions
1½ pounds ground beef
1½ teaspoons salt
¼ teaspoon freshly
  ground black pepper
¼ teaspoon marjoram

1 egg, beaten
1 16-ounce can cream-style
  corn
1 8-ounce can green peas,
  drained
3 tomatoes, thinly sliced
½ cup buttered bread
  crumbs

Melt the butter in a skillet; sauté the green pepper and onions 5 minutes. Add the beef; cook over high heat, stirring almost steadily, until browned. Mix in the salt, pepper, and marjoram. Cool slightly, then mix in the egg.

Spread half the corn in a greased 2-quart baking dish. Cover with half the meat mixture, half the peas, and half the tomato slices. Repeat the layers; sprinkle with the crumbs. Bake in a 350° oven 40 minutes.

Serves 6–8.

Surprise Casserole

1½ pounds ground beef
3 tablespoons melted
butter
2½ teaspoons salt
½ teaspoon freshly
ground black pepper
¼ teaspoon rosemary

1 cup sliced raw carrots
12 small white onions
2 cups thinly sliced raw
potatoes
1 cup grated cheddar
cheese

Mix together the beef, butter, 1½ teaspoons salt, ¼ teaspoon pepper, and the rosemary. Spread half the mixture in a buttered casserole. Arrange the carrots, onions, and potatoes over it, sprinkle with remaining salt and pepper, and cover with the remaining meat mixture. Bake in a 325° oven 30 minutes. Sprinkle the cheese on top and bake 30 minutes longer.
Serves 6–8.

Persian Meat Casserole

1 cup lentils
1 cup raw rice
3½ teaspoons salt
½ cup seedless raisins
6 tablespoons butter
½ cup chopped onions

1½ pounds ground beef
¼ teaspoon freshly
ground black pepper
½ teaspoon cinnamon
¼ teaspoon nutmeg
2 cups beef broth

Wash the lentils, cover with water, bring to a boil, and cook over low heat 1 hour. Drain.

Wash the rice and cook in boiling water 10 minutes. Drain and mix with the lentils and 2 teaspoons salt. Soak the raisins in warm water 10 minutes. Drain.

Melt 2 tablespoons butter in a skillet; sauté the onions 5 minutes. Mix in the beef, pepper, cinnamon, nutmeg, and remaining salt; cook over medium heat 5 minutes, stirring almost constantly.

In a buttered 3-quart casserole, spread half the lentil mixture. Spread with the meat and raisins. Cover with remaining lentil mixture. Add the broth, then dot with the remaining butter. Cover and bake in a 325° oven 45 minutes or until almost all the liquid is absorbed.

Serves 6–8.

Pfifferlinge Frikasse

(MUSHROOM-MEAT BALL FRICASSEE, GERMAN STYLE)

¾ cup white bread cubes
½ cup light cream
1 pound ground beef
½ cup grated onions
1 egg
2 teaspoons salt
½ teaspoon white pepper
2 cups beef broth
3 tablespoons butter
1 pound mushrooms, sliced
2 tablespoons flour
½ cup dry white wine
2 egg yolks
2 cups cooked, drained rice
2 tablespoons minced parsley

Soak the bread in the cream, drain, and mash smooth. Mix thoroughly with the beef, onions, egg, 1 teaspoon salt, and ¼ teaspoon pepper. Shape into walnut-sized balls. Bring 1 cup broth to a boil; cook the meat balls in it 10 minutes. Drain.

Melt the butter in a saucepan; sauté the mushrooms 5 minutes. Remove. Blend the flour and remaining salt and pepper into the butter remaining in the saucepan. Gradually add the remaining broth, stirring steadily to the boiling point. Stir in the wine; cook over low heat 5 minutes. Beat the egg yolks in a bowl; gradually add the hot sauce, stirring steadily to prevent curdling. Return to the saucepan with the meat balls, rice, and mushrooms. Taste for seasoning and heat, but do not let boil. Sprinkle with parsley. *Serves 4.*

Chinese Beef Casserole

3 tablespoons vegetable oil
¾ cup minced onions
1 pound ground beef
6 eggs
1¼ teaspoons salt
¼ teaspoon freshly ground black pepper

¼ teaspoon powdered ginger
1 1-pound can bean sprouts, drained
1½ cups cooked fine noodles

Heat the oil in a skillet; sauté the onions 10 minutes. Mix in the meat until no pink remains. Cool 10 minutes.

Beat the eggs, salt, pepper, and ginger in a bowl; stir in the meat mixture, bean sprouts, and noodles. Turn into a greased 2-quart casserole. Bake in a preheated 350° oven 30 minutes or until set. *Serves 4–6.*

Meat Ball-Vegetable Stew

1½ pounds ground beef
1½ teaspoons salt
½ teaspoon freshly ground black pepper
3 tablespoons vegetable oil
½ cup chopped green pepper
½ cup chopped onion

1 8-ounce can tomato sauce
½ cup water
1 tablespoon chili powder
2 cups canned or frozen corn kernels
1 package frozen green beans, thawed

256

Mix together the beef, salt, and pepper. Shape into 2-inch balls. Heat the oil in a deep skillet; brown the meat balls in it. Remove the meat balls. To the oil remaining, add the green pepper and onion; sauté 10 minutes. Return meat balls to the skillet, and add the tomato sauce, water, and chili powder. Cover and cook over low heat 10 minutes. Add the corn and green beans; recover and cook over low heat 10 minutes.

Serves 6.

Succotash and Meat Balls

1½ pounds ground beef
½ cup half-cooked rice
¼ cup grated onion
2 eggs, beaten
½ cup light cream
1½ teaspoons
  Worcestershire sauce
2 teaspoons salt
½ teaspoon freshly
  ground black pepper

2 tablespoons vegetable oil
1 cup thinly sliced green
  peppers
1 29-ounce can tomatoes
1 bay leaf
2 packages frozen
  succotash, thawed

Mix together the beef, rice, onion, eggs, cream, Worcestershire, 1 teaspoon salt, and ¼ teaspoon pepper. Shape into 1-inch balls.

Heat the oil in a skillet; brown the meat balls in it on all sides. Remove. Add the green peppers and tomatoes to the skillet. Cover and cook over low heat 10 minutes. Add the bay leaf, succotash, meat balls, and remaining salt and pepper; recover and cook 15 minutes longer or until vegetables are tender. Taste for seasoning, and discard the bay leaf.

Serves 6–8.

Beef Balls with Eggplant, Middle East Style

1 pound ground beef
½ cup half-cooked rice
1 egg, beaten
2 tablespoons water
1½ teaspoons salt
¼ teaspoon freshly
  ground black pepper
2 tablespoons minced
  parsley

¼ cup sliced almonds
2 tablespoons seedless
  raisins
½ cup vegetable oil
1 eggplant, peeled and
  cubed
2 8-ounce cans tomato
  sauce
1 cup potato balls

Mix together the beef, rice, egg, water, salt, pepper, parsley, almonds, and raisins. Chill 1 hour, then shape into 1-inch balls. Heat the oil in a skillet; brown the meat balls in it. Remove. In the oil remaining, brown the eggplant. Pour off the oil. Add the tomato sauce and potato balls, and return the meat balls. Bring to a boil and cook over low heat 15 minutes. Taste for seasoning.

Serves 4–6.

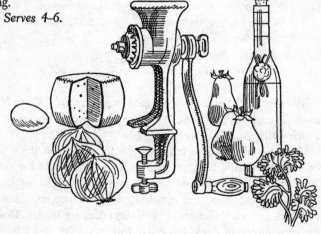

Other Combinations

TODAY'S SPECIALS

SPARERIBS

LIVER

KIDNEYS

❉❉❉❉❉❉❉❉❉❉❉❉❉❉❉❉

About the end of april several years ago, my husband and I were in Vienna, enjoying the worldly pleasures of that happy-but-sad city. One day we walked past the Hungarian Embassy and began to talk about the fact we had never visited that country. Suddenly, we simultaneously stopped walking, looked at one another, and retraced our steps. Inside the Hungarian Embassy we presented our passports, filled out several forms, and asked for visas. Several days later, they called to inform us that the visas had been issued. Delighted, we rented an automobile, obtained the necessary insurance, and armed with the visas (for ourselves) and a *carnet* (a set of papers for the car), we set out for the Hungarian border with mixed feelings of elation and a slightly disquieting feeling of nervousness.

From Vienna to the border is only a short distance. At the actual crossing I felt a dryness of the throat and a degree of restlessness, but everything was accomplished in a matter of fifteen minutes, in an atmosphere of correct coolness on the part of the Hungarian customs officials. Once inside Hungary, we headed toward Budapest. My husband and I, relieved of tension, felt lighthearted. The countryside was not particularly interesting, consisting mostly of farmland, but was pleasantly green. The road was passably good, there was no traffic whatsoever in either direction, and we drove steadily at a speed of sixty kilometers, roughly forty miles an hour. Suddenly, we noticed an alarming amount of steam escaping from the engine's hood, followed by a loud hissing sound. We stopped, and my husband reported that the radiator had boiled over because the fan belt had become loose; this he fixed in a moment. However, the radiator had to be refilled. But where? We hadn't seen a car on the road; there were no service stations and no telephones. I finally noticed the dull green roof of a farmhouse in the distance.

We left the car and walked over the fields toward the small building.

We found only a peasant woman, busily engaged in airing bedclothes in the yard adjacent to the farmhouse. We tried requesting water in English, French, and German, with no results. Sign language, however, did the trick, and we took away a large bucket filled with water, promising to return it (by means of more waving hands, and fingers pointing to the bucket). When the car's radiator was filled, we drove back to the farmhouse, returned the empty bucket, and offered money in repayment. The woman waved it aside and motioned us to come inside the kitchen. A delicious aroma filled the air, and, always curious, I wanted to know what was on the stove. But, it appeared, that was the very reason why we had been asked inside—to have something to eat. It was a meal-in-one-dish, a sausage stew made with potatoes and sauerkraut, hearty and delicious. We were embarrassed about eating her food, for it was obvious that the farm was a poor one, but we were very hungry, and she was watching us for expressions of enjoyment in the food. It was very good— delicious, in fact. We drank a light white wine with the stew and enjoyed both enormously.

My husband, who has his points, came up with the perfect method of repayment. The woman wouldn't take any money, of course, but my husband opened a suitcase and extracted a box of Viennese candy which we had brought along. He was right! She was ecstatic with pleasure and quickly and enthusiastically recited a list of names, apparently members of her family who would enjoy the candies. We left, amid many words of thanks on both sides, which she couldn't understand and which we couldn't understand, but which everyone did understand.

Hungarian Frankfurters

2 pounds sauerkraut
3 cups grated potatoes
2 cups sour cream
¼ teaspoon freshly
  ground black pepper

1½ pounds frankfurters,
  cut into 2-inch pieces

Rinse the sauerkraut under cold running water. Drain. Combine the sauerkraut, potatoes, sour cream, and pepper in a casserole. Cover and bake in a 385° oven 45 minutes. Mix in the frankfurters; bake 30 minutes, uncovered.

Serves 6–8.

Baked Beans, New England Style

1 pound dried navy beans
1 stalk celery
3 sprigs parsley
½ teaspoon thyme
8 thin slices salt pork
¼ cup brown sugar
⅔ cup molasses

2 teaspoons dry mustard
½ teaspoon freshly
  ground black pepper
1 cup chopped onions
1½ pounds Canadian-
  style bacon
1 cup dry sherry

Wash the beans, cover with water, and bring to a boil. Let soak 1 hour. Drain, cover with fresh water, and add the celery, parsley, and thyme. Bring to a boil, and cook over low heat 15 minutes. Drain, reserving 2 quarts liquid. Discard the celery and parsley.

In a 3-quart bean pot or casserole, make layers of the beans and salt pork, saving 2 slices pork for the top. Combine the brown sugar, molasses, mustard, pepper, onions, and bean liquid. Pour over the beans. Cover and bake in a 300° oven 5 hours. While the beans are baking, slice the Canadian bacon ½ inch thick. Lightly brown the slices in a skillet. Drain, and at the end of the 5 hours, bury the slices in the beans. Pour the sherry over the top. Recover and bake 1 hour longer or until the beans are tender. Serve with Boston brown bread.

Serves 6–8.

Baked Rice and Cheese

⅓ cup olive oil
1 cup chopped onions
1 clove garlic, minced
1 cup chopped green
  pepper
1½ cups raw rice
2½ cups boiling water
1½ teaspoons salt
½ teaspoon freshly
  ground black pepper

2 8-ounce cans tomato
  sauce
½ cup sliced black olives
2 cups cooked or canned
  green peas
2 cups grated mozzarella
  cheese

Heat the oil in a deep skillet; sauté the onions, garlic, green pepper, and rice until lightly browned, stirring almost constantly. Add the water, salt, pepper, and 1½ cups tomato sauce. Cover and cook over low heat until the liquid is almost absorbed; about 15 minutes.

Line a greased 1½-quart baking dish with half the rice. Spread the olives, peas, and 1½ cups cheese over it. Cover with the remaining rice; pour the remaining half cup tomato sauce over it, and sprinkle with the remaining cheese. Bake in a 375° oven 15 minutes, or until browned.

Serves 4–6.

Egg and Rice Casserole

3 tablespoons butter
3 tablespoons grated onion
3 tablespoons flour
2 cups milk
1 teaspoon salt
¼ teaspoon freshly
  ground black pepper
2 cups (½ pound) grated
  American cheese

4 cups cooked rice
1 can asparagus tips,
  drained
6 hard-cooked eggs, cut in
  half lengthwise
1 cup dry bread crumbs
4 tablespoons melted
  butter

Melt the 3 tablespoons butter in a saucepan; sauté the onion for 2 minutes. Blend in the flour; add the milk, stirring constantly to the boiling point, then cook over low heat 5 minutes. Mix in the salt, pepper, and cheese until the cheese melts.

Combine the rice with half of the sauce. Spread on the bottom of a buttered 1½-quart casserole. Arrange the asparagus and egg halves over the rice. Pour the remaining sauce on top, and sprinkle with the bread crumbs and melted butter. Bake in a 350° oven for 20 minutes. *Serves 4–6.*

Fabada Asturiana

(BEAN-SAUSAGE CASSEROLE, SPANISH STYLE)

1 pound dried white beans
1 pound boneless pork,
  diced
1 pound smoked ham,
  diced

½ pound chorizos
  (Spanish sausages),
  sliced
2 teaspoons salt
½ teaspoon freshly
  ground black pepper
½ teaspoon saffron

Wash the beans, cover with water, bring to a boil, and cook 2 minutes. Let soak 1 hour. Drain. Put in a bean pot or Dutch oven and add fresh water to cover. Bring to a boil and cook over medium heat 30 minutes. Lightly brown the pork and ham; drain. Lightly brown the sausages; drain. Add the pork, ham, sausages, salt, pepper, and saffron to the beans; recover and cook over low heat 2½ hours longer or until the beans are very tender. *Serves 4–6.*

Baked Sweetbreads and Chicken Livers

3 pairs sweetbreads	1 cup dry white wine
1 tablespoon vinegar	1½ cups cooked rice
1 pound chicken livers	½ pound mushrooms,
6 tablespoons butter	sliced and sautéed
2 teaspoons salt	1 16-ounce can green peas,
½ teaspoon freshly	drained
ground black pepper	

Wash the sweetbreads and soak in cold water 10 minutes. Drain; add fresh water to cover; add the vinegar. Bring to a boil and cook over low heat 15 minutes. Drain and cover with cold water; let stand 15 minutes. Drain, remove membrane, and cut each part in half crosswise. Wash the livers, removing any discolored areas.

Spread the butter in a 1½-quart baking dish. Arrange the sweetbreads in it and cover with the livers. Season with the salt and pepper and add the wine. Bake in a 425° oven 10 minutes. Mix in the rice, mushrooms, and peas; reduce heat to 325° and bake 10 minutes longer.

Serves 6.

Risotto alla Napolitana

(RICE WITH SAUSAGES)

1 pound sweet or hot
Italian sausages
3 tablespoons olive oil
3 tablespoons butter
1 cup chopped onions
1 clove garlic, minced
1½ cups raw rice

1½ cups canned Italian-
style tomatoes
1½ cups boiling water
1½ teaspoons salt
½ teaspoon basil
2 tablespoons grated
Parmesan cheese

Cut the sausages into 1-inch slices and brown. Drain.

Heat the oil and 1 tablespoon butter in a saucepan; sauté the onions and garlic 5 minutes. Stir in the rice until translucent. Add the tomatoes, half the water, the salt, and the basil. Cover and cook over low heat 20 minutes, adding the remaining water from time to time. Stir in the cheese, remaining butter, and the sausages. Cook 5 minutes longer. *Serves 6.*

Koru Ragu

(SWEDISH SAUSAGE STEW)

1 pound pork sausages
3 tablespoons butter
½ cup chopped onion
1 tablespoon flour
1 cup beef broth
1 pound potatoes, peeled
and cubed

2 cups sliced carrots
1. teaspoon salt
½ teaspoon freshly
ground black pepper
1 bay leaf

Lightly brown the sausages in a heavy saucepan. Remove and reserve. Pour off the fat. Melt the butter in the saucepan; sauté the onion 5 minutes. Blend in the flour, then stir in the broth until mixture boils. Add the sausages, potatoes, carrots, salt, pepper, and bay leaf. Bring to a boil, cover, and cook over low heat 20 minutes. *Serves 4.*

Zungen Ragout

(TONGUE RAGOÛT, GERMAN STYLE)

5-pound fresh beef tongue
1 onion
1 bay leaf
6 peppercorns
3 teaspoons salt
2 pair sweetbreads
6 tablespoons butter
½ pound ground pork
1 egg

3 tablespoons dry bread
    crumbs
⅛ teaspoon black pepper
2 cups peeled cubed
    potatoes
4 tablespoons flour
1 cup sliced mushrooms
¼ cup sweet sherry

Wash the tongue, cover with water, and bring to a boil. Add the onion, bay leaf, peppercorns, and 2 teaspoons salt. Cover, bring to a boil, and cook over low heat 2½ hours, or until tender. Drain, reserving the stock. Trim the tongue of the root ends, bones, and skin.

While the tongue is cooking, soak the sweetbreads in ice water for 30 minutes. Drain, cook in the tongue stock for 15 minutes. Drain, reserve stock; cover sweetbreads with cold water and let stand 15 minutes. Drain, remove the membranes and tubes, and cut into cubes. Melt 3 tablespoons butter in a skillet and lightly brown the cubes in it.

Mix together the pork, egg, bread crumbs, pepper, and ½ teaspoon salt. Shape into walnut-sized balls and add to the tongue stock with the potatoes; cook 20 minutes. Drain. Strain and reserve 3 cups stock.

Melt the remaining butter in a saucepan; blend in the flour. Gradually add the stock, stirring steadily to the boiling point. Add the mushrooms and remaining salt; cook over low heat 10 minutes. Mix in the sherry. Slice the tongue and add to the sauce with the pork balls, potatoes, and sweetbreads. Reheat.

Serves 8–10.

Kidney Stew

6 veal kidneys
2 cups water
2 tablespoons vinegar
⅓ cup flour
1½ teaspoons salt
½ teaspoon freshly
  ground black pepper
2 tablespoons vegetable
  oil
2 tablespoons butter
½ cup finely chopped
  onions

2 tablespoons minced
  parsley
½ cup dry red wine
⅛ teaspoon thyme
2 cups cubed potatoes,
  cooked
1 package frozen peas and
  carrots, cooked and
  drained

Wash the kidneys, trim the fat, and remove the membrane and core. Soak in the water mixed with the vinegar for 1 hour. Drain, dry, and slice. Toss in the flour mixed with the salt and pepper. Heat the oil and butter in a skillet; brown kidneys on both sides over high heat. Mix in the onions; cook 2 minutes. Add the parsley, wine, thyme, potatoes, and peas and carrots. Cook over medium heat 5 minutes.

Serves 6.

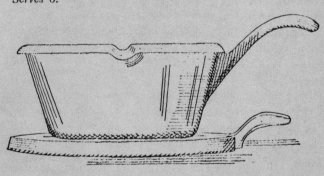

Frankfurter Goulash

2 tablespoons vegetable oil
3 cups chopped onions
3 cups julienne-cut green
  peppers
1 clove garlic, minced
1 29-ounce can tomatoes
1 teaspoon caraway seeds

1 teaspoon salt
½ teaspoon freshly
  ground black pepper
2 teaspoons paprika
3 cups cubed potatoes
1½ pounds frankfurters,
  cut into 2-inch pieces

Heat the oil in a deep skillet or Dutch oven; saute the onions until lightly browned. Add the green peppers and garlic; cook over low heat 5 minutes. Mix in the tomatoes, caraway seeds, salt, pepper, and paprika; bring to a boil, cover and cook over low heat 20 minutes, stirring occasionally. Add the potatoes, cook 10 minutes. Add the sliced frankfurters; cook 10 minutes longer. *Serves 6–8.*

Risotto con Fegato

(CALF'S LIVER WITH RICE, ITALIAN STYLE)

1½ pounds calf's liver
6 tablespoons butter
3 tablespoons olive oil
1 cup chopped onions
1 clove garlic, minced
1½ cups raw rice
4 cups chicken broth

1 teaspoon tomato paste
¼ teaspoon freshly
  ground black pepper
1 8-ounce can tiny green
  peas
2 tablespoons minced
  parsley

Cut the liver into finger-length strips. Melt the butter in a deep skillet or casserole; brown the liver in it. Remove the liver.

269

Heat the oil in the skillet; sauté the onions 5 minutes. Add the garlic and rice; cook over low heat 5 minutes, stirring frequently. Add the broth, tomato paste, and pepper; bring to a boil. Return the liver, cover and bake in a 350° oven 35 minutes. Add the peas; recover and bake 10 minutes longer or until the rice is tender and dry. Taste for seasoning. Sprinkle with the parsley. *Serves 4–6.*

Foie de Veau à la Campagne

(CALF'S LIVER, FRENCH COUNTRY STYLE)

2-pound piece of calf's liver	½ teaspoon freshly ground black pepper
8 thin strips salt pork or bacon	12 small white onions
2 tablespoons butter	8 carrots, cut in eighths, lengthwise
2 tablespoons flour	3 cups peeled cubed potatoes
1 cup dry white wine	2 tablespoons minced parsley
½ teaspoon thyme	
1 bay leaf	
¾ teaspoon salt	

Lard the liver by piercing the surface on one side with the point of a sharp knife and inserting the salt-pork strips. Melt the butter in a deep skillet or casserole, and brown liver on both sides. Remove from pan; mix the flour into the fat remaining in the pan, cooking until browned. Add the wine, stirring to the boiling point. Add the thyme, bay leaf, salt, pepper, onions, carrots, potatoes, and liver. Cover and bake in a 300° oven 1¼ hours. Discard the bay leaf and sprinkle with the parsley. *Serves 6–8.*

Baked Liver, Martinique Style

2-pound piece of calf's liver
½ cup flour
3 teaspoons salt
1 teaspoon freshly ground
  black pepper
3 tablespoons butter
1 cup thinly sliced onions
1 cup thinly sliced green
  peppers
1 cup sliced mushrooms

¼ cup chopped ham
1 20-ounce can tomatoes
1 clove garlic, minced
3 tablespoons minced
  parsley
½ teaspoon marjoram
1 bay leaf
⅔ cup dry white wine
2 cups cooked, drained
  rice

Leave the liver in one piece; rinse and dry. Dip the liver in a mixture of the flour, 2 teaspoons salt, and ½ teaspoon pepper. Melt the butter in a deep skillet or casserole; brown the liver in it on all sides. Add the onions, green peppers, mushrooms, ham, tomatoes, garlic, parsley, marjoram, bay leaf, wine, and the remaining salt and pepper. Cover and bake in a 375° oven 45 minutes. Add the rice; taste for seasoning; bake 15 minutes longer. Slice the liver and serve. *Serves 6–8.*

Pilaff de Foie de Veau

(CALF'S LIVER AND RICE, FRENCH STYLE)

1 pound calf's liver
¼ cup olive oil
6 slices eggplant
1 small zucchini, sliced
1 tomato, peeled and sliced
1 cup raw rice
1½ cups chicken broth

3 tablespoons butter
½ pound mushrooms,
  sliced
¼ cup port wine
1½ teaspoons salt
½ teaspoon freshly
  ground black pepper

Cut the liver into ½-inch cubes. Heat the oil in a deep skillet; add the eggplant, zucchini, and tomato; cook over medium heat 5 minutes. Stir in the rice until translucent. Add the broth; cover and cook over low heat 12 minutes. Meanwhile, melt the butter in another skillet; brown the liver in it. Remove. In the butter remaining, sauté the mushrooms 3 minutes. Remove. Pour the port into the skillet; cook over high heat 2 minutes. Add to the rice with the salt, pepper, liver, and mushrooms; mix lightly with two forks and cook over low heat 5 minutes, or until the rice is tender.

Serves 4.

Wieprzowina z Kapusta

(SPARERIBS WITH SAUERKRAUT, POLISH STYLE)

2 tablespoons vegetable oil

3 pounds spareribs, cut into individual pieces

2 cloves garlic, minced

1½ cups coarsely chopped onions

1 bay leaf

1½ teaspoons salt

½ teaspoon freshly ground black pepper

2 cups boiling water

1 apple, peeled, cored, and chopped

1 pound sauerkraut

½ cup fine barley

1 teaspoon caraway seeds

Heat the oil in a Dutch oven or large saucepan; brown the ribs in it over high heat. Add the garlic and onions; cook over low heat 10 minutes. Mix in the bay leaf, salt, pepper, and half the water and cook 30 minutes, stirring occasionally. Add the apple, undrained sauerkraut, barley, caraway seeds, and remaining water. Mix well and cook 1 hour longer. Taste for seasoning and discard the bay leaf. Serves 4–6.

IN LATE SEPTEMBER, when the weather was absolutely ideal, my husband and I drove from Frankfurt, Germany, westward to Paris. We reached Mainz, a history-laden city, and continued on to the medieval town of Bingen, where we crossed on the ferry to Rüdesheim, the center of Germany's wine industry.

Rüdesheim is a unique place. It has a magnificent situation on the Rhine River, and because of its wine trade the colorful town is filled with wine shops, atmospheric small bars selling wine, and bustling restaurants featuring wine. My husband thought we should stay overnight at a very quiet place, away from the Rüdesheim's music and noise, which (as we knew) can continue until the early hours of the morning. We drove to a hunting lodge turned hotel, some ten minutes outside of town at the edge of a forest, surrounded by meadows waving with grain. We were given a large, old-fashioned room facing the fields, and my husband exclaimed with pleasure at the thought of sleeping late the next morning.

At dinnertime we drove back into Rüdesheim and parked the car near the Drosselgasse, a very narrow street hemmed in on both sides by a score of lively restaurants featuring music, wine, and hearty German food. In one of them we ordered the classic dish of *eisbein und sauerkraut*, pigs' knuckles and sauerkraut. It proved to be delicious (and also very substantial), and we liked it very much indeed. We also enjoyed the light, flowery German wine, and the heavy, thumping German beer-hall music.

Back at the hotel, just before retiring, we could hear not a sound. All was silence, and of the kind rarely encountered in the twentieth century—absolute and complete. Within minutes, we were both sound asleep. In what seemed like just a few more minutes, I awakened (as did my husband) to hear a loud, clattering noise outside in the first rays of dawn. We jumped out of bed and found to our amusement and dismay, that the farmers had picked that particular dawn to harvest their crop. Sleep was obviously impossible, so we rang for breakfast. By 6:30 A.M., we were in the car and driving toward Paris. The next night, however (just to reassure you), we stayed overnight at a remodeled château in France, inquired before taking the room as to whether any crops were to be harvested, and slept quite late the following morning.

Eisbein und Sauerkraut

(PIGS' KNUCKLES AND SAUERKRAUT, GERMAN STYLE)

4 pigs' knuckles
2 pounds sauerkraut
1 tablespoon caraway seeds
4 cloves
2 onions

3 cups dry white wine or beef broth
8 small potatoes, peeled
4 knockwurst (thick frankfurters)

Pour boiling water over the pigs' knuckles, scrub with a brush, and scrape with a knife. Wash under cold water and dry.

In a Dutch oven or heavy saucepan, make layers of the sauerkraut, sprinkled with caraway seeds, and the pigs' knuckles. Stick the cloves into the onions, and add with the wine or broth. If liquid doesn't cover the ingredients, add more of either, or water. Cover, bring to a boil, and cook over low heat 3 hours, or until knuckles are almost tender. Add the potatoes and knockwurst. Recover and cook 30 minutes longer.

Serves 4–6.

Canadian Bacon and Lima Bean Casserole

16 slices Canadian bacon
3 tomatoes, sliced
1½ cups chopped onions
4 tablespoons chopped
  parsley
½ teaspoon basil

1½ teaspoons salt
½ teaspoon freshly
  ground black pepper
3 packages frozen Lima
  beans, thawed
½ cup tomato juice

Arrange half the bacon slices on the bottom of a casserole. Cover with some tomato slices sprinkled with some onions, parsley, basil, salt, and pepper. Spread half the beans over it; repeat the layers, reserving some tomatoes for a top layer. Add the tomato juice. Cover the casserole; bake in a 325° oven 45 minutes or until the beans are tender. Remove cover and bake 10 minutes longer. *Serves 6–8.*

Oxtail Stew

2 oxtails
¼ cup flour
2 teaspoons salt
½ teaspoon freshly
  ground black pepper
2 tablespoons vegetable oil
1 cup chopped onions
1 cup diced carrots
1 cup diced turnips

½ cup diced ham
2 cups beef broth
1 clove garlic, minced
1 bay leaf
⅛ teaspoon thyme
3 cups peeled cubed
  potatoes
1 package frozen green
  peas, thawed

Have the oxtails cut into 2-inch pieces. Pour boiling water over them, then drain and dry. Toss the pieces in a mixture of the flour, salt, and pepper. Heat the oil in a Dutch oven or heavy saucepan; brown the onions and oxtails in it. Add the carrots, turnips, and ham; cook until browned. Add the broth, garlic, bay leaf, and thyme. Cover and cook over low heat 2½ hours. Add the potatoes and peas; recover and cook 15 minutes longer. Taste for seasoning. *Serves 6–8.*

Ragoût de Queue de Boeuf

(OXTAIL STEW, FRENCH STYLE)

2 oxtails
¾ cup flour
2 teaspoons salt
½ teaspoon freshly
   ground black pepper
½ teaspoon thyme
4 tablespoons olive oil
2 cups boiling water
3 cups dry red wine
2 cloves
12 small white onions

1 clove garlic, minced
2 sprigs parsley ⎫
2 stalks celery   ⎪ tied
1 bay leaf   ⎬ together
1 leek   ⎭
3 carrots, cut in eights
   lengthwise
4 potatoes, peeled and
   diced
1 cup sliced mushrooms

Have the oxtails cut into 2-inch pieces.

Pour boiling water over the oxtail pieces; drain and dry. Roll in a mixture of the flour, salt, pepper, and thyme. Heat the oil in a Dutch oven and brown the oxtails on all sides. Pour off the fat. Add the boiling water and wine. Stick the cloves into one of the onions. Add to the casserole with all the onions, the garlic, and the parsley, celery, bay leaf and leek. Cover tightly and bake in a 300° oven 2½ hours. Add the carrots, potatoes, and mushrooms. Recover and bake 1 hour longer. Skim the fat and taste for seasoning. *Serves 6–8.*

276

Queue de Boeuf à la Monegasque

(BRAISED OXTAILS, MONACO STYLE)

2 oxtails	1½ pounds tomatoes,
1 carrot	peeled and chopped or
3 sprigs parsley	1 29-ounce can, drained
3 teaspoons salt	½ teaspoon freshly
2 tablespoons butter	ground black pepper
¾ cup chopped onions	⅛ teaspoon nutmeg
¾ cup diced celery	2 cups potato balls
¼ pound ham, cut	¼ cup sliced almonds
julienne	2 tablespoons seedless
¾ cup dry white wine	raisins

Have the oxtails cut up into 2-inch pieces. Wash well, place in a saucepan, cover with water; add the carrot, parsley, and half the salt. Bring to a boil and cook over medium heat 1½ hours. Drain well.

Melt the butter in a saucepan; sauté the onions, celery, and ham 5 minutes. Add the oxtails; cook 10 minutes. Mix in the wine; cook until evaporated. Add the tomatoes, pepper, nutmeg, and remaining salt. Cover and cook over low heat 50 minutes. Add the potatoes; cook 15 minutes. Mix in the nuts and raisins; cook 5 minutes longer. *Serves 6–8.*

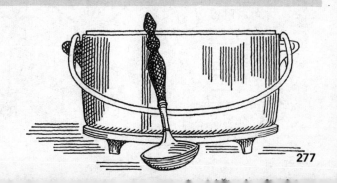

Venison Ragoût

3 pounds venison
2 cups dry red wine
¼ cup flour
2 teaspoons salt
¼ teaspoon freshly
   ground black pepper
3 tablespoons vegetable oil
1 cup chopped onions
2 cloves garlic, minced

½ teaspoon thyme
½ cup water
1 tablespoon tomato
   paste
1 pound green beans, cut
   into 2-inch pieces
3 cups cubed potatoes
1 cup sour cream

Cut the venison into 1½-inch cubes and marinate it in the wine for 4 hours. Drain and dry the meat. Reserve the wine.

Toss the venison in a mixture of the flour, salt, and pepper. Heat the oil in a casserole; brown the meat in it. Add the onions and garlic; cook 10 minutes, stirring frequently. Add the thyme, water, tomato paste, and reserved wine. Bring to a boil, cover, and cook over low heat 2¼ hours. Watch carefully, and add a little boiling water if necessary. Add the green beans and potatoes; cook 20 minutes longer. Just before serving, stir the sour cream into the gravy. Heat, but do not let boil.

Serves 6–8.

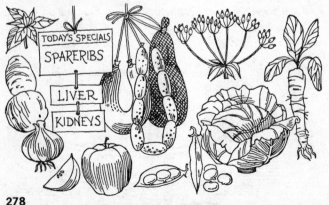

279